MORE OF HOLLYWOOD'S UNSOLVED MYSTERIES

Other Books by John Austin

Hollywood's Unsolved Mysteries
The World I Lived In: The George Jessel Story
Sex Is Big Business
Surrogate
How to Syndicate to Newspapers

MORE OF HOLLYWOOD'S UNSOLVED MYSTERIES

John Austin

SHAPOLSKY PUBLISHERS, INC.
NEW YORK

A Shapolsky Book

Copyright © 1991 by John Austin

For any additional information, contact:
Shapolsky Publishers, Inc.
136 West 22nd Street
New York, NY 10011
(212) 633-2022

10 9 8 7 6 5 4 3 2 1

ISBN 0-944007-73-2

Design and Typography by Owl Graphics, New York

Manufactured in the United States of America

———————————————

"Every unpunished murder takes away something from the security of every man's life . . ."

– Daniel Webster

"At the risk of losing something of a reputation as a prophet, the writer will predict that some day one of the scandal scented mysteries of filmdom will be cleared up. Motion picture circles have suffered alike from scandal and rumors of scandal. Deaths from violence or by mysterious means have been hinted at but never proved."

– C.F. Adelsperger,
Long Beach (California)
News, 1932

Author's Note and Acknowledgments

The deaths recounted herein, and the lack of motive, or the absence of any discernible rhyme or reason for those deaths, form the basis for *More of Hollywood's Unsolved Mysteries*.

In some cases, dialogue between characters has been "invented" by the author, but in such fashion as to fit the scene being written and dialogue which could have transpired between the parties: police, protagonists, antagonists and others involved.

Other dialogue has come from news accounts of the day about the murders, suicides or whatever, and from the author's memory and notes "covering" the death scenes as an accredited press representative in several of the cases. Dialogue has also been reconstructed from accounts of others who were present at some of the scenes. In any book of this nature it is necessary to use this method.

The author wishes to acknowledge the staff at Shapolsky Publishers, and Ian Shapolsky, for their guidance, help and enthusiasm in bringing this project, and the previous volume, to fruition.

In addition, many thanks go to Marvin Paige's Motion Picture and TV Research Service for locating most of the very important pictures that illustrate this book. No other research service could provide such exclusive illustrations "of the past" as those which appear in several chapters herein, and in the previous volume.

Acknowledgment also goes to SPC (Software Publishing Corp.) and Professional Write 2.2.

– John Austin
Killarney, Ireland
1991

★★★

Oligarchy: n. pl. *-chies: -ical:* a form of government in which the power is vested in a few persons, or in a dominant class or clique. Government by the few. A state or organization so ruled. The person or persons so ruling.

— Random House Dictionary

★★★

What New Facts Have Come to Light Since Volume 1 of Hollywood's Unsolved Mysteries? ◆ *What Are the General Public's Feelings and Suspicions About Marilyn Monroe's Death?* ◆ *Do They Doubt the Official Investigation Report?* ◆ *Who Does the FBI Believe Responsible for the Murder of Marilyn Monroe?* ◆*Who Engineered Marilyn's Murder?* ◆ *Who Was the Mistress Being "Shared" by John F. Kennedy and a Mafia Figure?* ◆ *Was the Former Bootlegger, Joseph P. Kennedy, Involved in Marilyn's Death?* ◆ *Why the Kennedys Could Not Replace J. Edgar Hoover with the Former Police Chief of Los Angeles, William H. Parker* ◆ *What Did Hoover's Files Contain About John F. Kennedy?* ◆ *Who Retrieved Marilyn From the Santa Monica Hospital?* ◆ *Who Was It Who Administered What an Ambulance Attendant Claims Was a "Fatal Injection"?* ◆ *Which Member of the Los Angeles Police Department "Changed" the Chronology of Events of That Night?* ◆ *Who Attended the "Sex Parties" with Bobby and Jack Kennedy?* ◆ *Was the Secret Service Aware of the Parties?* ◆ *Who Was the Nazi Agent JFK Dated During World War II?* ◆ *Did Chief Parker Retrieve Marilyn's Diary from the Coroner's Office?* ◆ *Why Did the "Official" Report Differ from That of Sergeant Clemmons of the Events of That Night?* ◆ *Why Did the Autopsy Surgeon Remark That He Found No Needle Marks on Marilyn's Body Even Though She Had Received an Injection the Day Before Her Death?* ◆ *Will the Truth Ever Come Out?*

Why Did the Butler Call the Studio When He Found the Body of Paul Bern Instead of the Police? ◆ *Why Were the Police Not Notified for Two Hours?* ◆ *What Scenario Did L.B. Mayer, Irving Thalberg and Howard Strickling Put "In Place" Before the Police Were Called?* ◆ *Was The So-Called Suicide Note a "Forgery"?* ◆ *Who Was Paul Levy, aka Paul Bern?* ◆ *Was He Leading a Double Life?* ◆ *Why Did He Break Off His Friendship with Soon-to-Be Mob Figure Meyer Lansky?* ◆ *Why Did Bern Leave New York for Hollywood?* ◆ *What Was So Prophetic About the Article Herbert Cruickshank Wrote About Bern?* ◆ *Why Was Hollywood Astounded When Jean Harlow and Paul Bern Became Engaged?* ◆ *Did L.B. Mayer "Arrange" the Union?* ◆ *What Happened to Jean Harlow on Her Wedding Night Which Led to Her Death Five Years Later?* ◆ *How Did*

Buron Fitts and Sheriff "Gene" Biscailuz "Cover Up" Thelma's Murder? ✦ *Why?* ✦ *To Protect Joe Schenck?* ✦ *What Was the Final, but Unbelieved, Verdict?*

Why Was Carol Wayne Bankrupt and Filed Bankruptcy Following 101 Appearances on the Tonight Show *with Johnny Carson?* ✦ *Why Was She Hooked on Cocaine and Alcohol?* ✦ *Who Was the Mysterious Figure Who Accompanied Her to Manzanillo on That Fatal Vacation?* ✦ *Who Was the Other Actress He Was Visiting When She Jumped Out of Her Apartment Window in West Hollywood?* ✦ *Why Did Carol Wayne's Companion Not Bother to Look For Her When She Disappeared from the Front of the Playa de Santiago Hotel?* ✦ *Why Did He Not File a Missing Persons Report with the Police?* ✦ *Why Did He Check Them Both Out of the Playa de Santiago Hotel?* ✦ *And Why Did He Take Wayne's Luggage to the Airport Telling Employees She Would Pick It Up the Next Day?* ✦ *What Questions Do the Manzanillo Police Want to Ask Her Companion Even Now, Over Five Years After Carol Wayne's Death?* ✦ *Why Did Her Companion Not Even Bother to Call the Manzanillo Authorities Following the Discovery of Her Body?*

Why Did the Glamorous, 31-Year-Old Star Take Her Life? ✦ *Was It Because of the Unrequited Love of the Snobbish and Loathed Rex Harrison?* ✦ *On Her Death, Why Did Harrison Lie About Having Had an Affair with Carole Landis on Two Continents?* ✦ *Why Was Carole Landis Doomed from the Start?* ✦ *How Did She Begin Her Career in San Francisco as a Hula Dancer at the Age of 15?* ✦ *Was She a Teen-Aged Call Girl as the "Bitches of Bel Air" Were to Accuse Her of at the Height of Her Success?* ✦ *If Not, Why Were the Accusations Made?* ✦ *Was She Darryl F. Zanuck's Mistress at One Time, as "The Bitches" Claimed?* ✦ *Why Did Carole Landis Not Deny the Rumors and the Accusations Being Spread Around the Industry About Her?* ✦ *Was Carole Landis Pregnant with Harrison's Baby When She Died?*

CONTENTS

Not Call for Help on the Telephone a Few Inches Away? ✦ *How Did Nick Adams Get into Movies?* ✦ *He Had No Background, Was Short, and Not Good-Looking* ✦ *Was It "True Grit"?* ✦ *What Was the Story of "The Silver Tassle" in His Biographies?* ✦ *How Did Jack Palance Influence Nick Adams's Career?* ✦ *Why Could the Police Find No Trace of Paraldehyde in Adams's House, Nor Any Empty Container?* ✦ *How Did Adams Ingest It When There Was No Means of Ingestion Visible?* ✦ *Did Someone Force Nick to Drink It and Then Hide the Evidence or Otherwise Dispose of It?* ✦ *What Happened to Nick's Diaries and Journals Which He Kept Religiously All His Life?* ✦ *Was There Something Incriminating to Someone on Them?* ✦ *What Happened to Nick's Tape Recorder? His Memorabilia? Why Was It Later Seen in His Attorney's House?* ✦ *Why Was That Same Attorney Gunned Down in a Possible Contract Murder Eight Years Later?* ✦ *And His "Live-In" Companion?*

What Are the Other Unsolved Mysteries Yet to Come? ✦ *Who Was Suspected in the Murder of Actress Karyn Kupcinet?* ✦ *Whose Career Did It Bring to a Screeching Halt?* ✦ *Was It Because of Suspicion in Her Murder?* ✦ *What About the Murder of the High-Powered Cuban Executive and His Wife?* ✦ *Was It Their Two Sons Who Killed Them?* ✦ *Why Did Disney Blacklist Hollywood Writers and Ban the Associated Press from a Warren Beatty Interview?* ✦ *Will There Be Yet Another Book of* Hollywood's Unsolved Mysteries?

Just Who Was Johnny Roselli? ✦ *In How Many of Hollywood's Unsolved Mysteries Was "Don Giovanni" Involved?* ✦ *How Did He Get into the Motion Picture Industry?* ✦ *Why Did the U.S. Government Enlist the Aid of Roselli and His Mentor Sam Giancana over Cuba?*

Carole Landis in a scene from Hal Roach's "One Million Years B.C." (1940) in which she starred with Victor Mature and Lon Chaney, Jr. A remake of the same film in the 1960s created another star: Raquel Welch! *(John Austin Collection)*

Don Murray and Marilyn Monroe on location during the shooting of "Bus Stop."
(John Austin Collection)

PROLOGUE

"Cover–Ups" – A Hollywood
Way of Life . . .

As expected, we received many threats following the publication of Volume One of *Hollywood's Unsolved Mysteries*. All of the calls, except one, were anonymous, as they usually are. Callers of this nature generally do not have courage of their convictions. The gist of most of the calls was ". . . forget about ever 'making it' in the industry again. You've had it!"

We never dignify such threats with a reply, as it was obvious most of the callers had been put up to it. Obviously, they had not read the book. If they had, "they" would have learned that "we" have "retired" from covering the film industry, and no longer live in Los Angeles. We couldn't care less about the day-to-day operations of "the business." The closest we come to the industry these days is an occasional reading of *The Hollywood Reporter* and *Weekly Variety*.

We also received threats concerning Marilyn Monroe and the accusations leveled against the Brothers Kennedy, President John F. and Robert, about their affairs with Marilyn. On the plus side, many astute questions were asked by the listeners of the 150 talk shows on which we appeared to publicize Volume One. A very good question listeners asked was:

"Is there really a free press in Hollywood?"

The answer, of course, is a resounding "No-o-o way!"

☆ ☆ ☆

1

Many of the unsolved mysteries herein took place when Los Angeles and the surrounding communities had very corrupt police forces. The LAPD was supposedly "cleaned up" in the 1950s, when William H. Parker took control. By then the policies of the studios were already set. Bribes and favors were rampant from the 1920s through the 1940s, and although the scandals waned, the dictatorial polices of the oligarchy remained intact. However, with regard to the murder of Marilyn Monroe, Parker transgressed his own order-enforcing "rules" in the hope of becoming director of the FBI during the Kennedy administration. We will go further into the Monroe murder in these pages.

In the cases of Thelma Todd, Jean Harlow's husband Paul Bern and, indirectly, Harlow herself, there were blatant cover-ups, false death certificates and "missing witnesses." This applies as well to movie pioneer Thomas Ince and Carol Landis's death to protect a British actor and 20th Century-Fox. In some cases, of course, there were no cover-ups; just no solution to the murders. These include "The Black Dahlia," aka Elizabeth Short, and the still-unsolved murder of Karyn Kupcinet. Someone recently asked us: "Is that one 'really' unsolved?" These two and more, however, are the subject of yet another volume, along with "tough guy" Steve Cochran, Barbara (Mrs. Mickey) Rooney and the Yugoslav connection, and Albert Dekker's bizarre death.

The real reason for John Belushi's drug-related death can also be considered another of *Hollywood's Unsolved Mysteries*. So are the murders of Jose and Kitty Menendez, which were scheduled to come to trial in late 1990. New evidence being developed may even free the two sons, Erik and Lyle, charged, as of this writing, with the murders. There is still a lot yet to be written about the unsolved murder of William Desmond Taylor. While two authors within the past five years claim to have "solved" his murder, it still raises doubts.

Nevertheless, under all circumstances, "the industry has to be protected!" The general consensus is that major scandals could have an effect on the entire filmland community.

This was particularly true in the Twenties and Thirties when many of the unsolved mysteries recounted herein took place. The United States was in the midst of the worst depression in its history, brought about by the greed of stock manipulators of the era. The moguls, in concert, felt that any scandal involving Hollywood stars could effect the box office – something they could not afford.

The Fatty Arbuckle affair of 1921 is a case in point. Even though the rotund comedian was acquitted, after a third trial, the fact that he was questioned about the rape and death of starlet Virginia Rappe lost him forever the public's admiration as a screen favorite. Despite the acquittal, his career was over.

Following this experience, the industry vowed never to let another scandal stand in the way of box office grosses. Withdrawing the Arbuckle comedies, which were already making the rounds of the nation, cost the producers and theaters millions of dollars, not to mention the Arbuckle films "in the can" and awaiting release.

Fans who, a few weeks before the scandal broke, had been convulsed by Arbuckle's antics on the screen, now tossed rotten eggs whenever Fatty's image appeared. Considered classics, the comedies were never again to be seen on the screens of the world. His contract, which would have paid Arbuckle $3 million, a mega-fortune in those days, was canceled. At the age of 46 he died from a heart attack.

It was then that the "The Arbuckle Syndrome" came into effect: cover-up, through whatever means possible, of any future scandal that could hurt the oligarchy and the box office. Sometimes it has succeeded; other times the truth has prevailed – many years after the fact, in some cases. But for many of Hollywood's mysteries, the truth has managed to leak out, partially or in full.

Unfortunately, however, not in *most* of these cases.

Enjoy!

A studio portrait of Marilyn while under contract to 20th Century-Fox.
(John Austin Collection)

Fade In...

A studio portrait at MGM of Harlow in the early 1930s. *(John Austin Collection)*

1... In Hollywood – It Is Su-PRESS-ed

"They [Hollywood's founding moguls] preached of the good, noble and beautiful, and they themselves fostered in their lives and works the evil, the ignoble, the ugly. . ."
– Ezra Goodman
The 50 Year Decline &
Fall of Hollywood, 1961

"There is not a reporter in Hollywood who could not rock the country by sitting down at his typewriter and recalling merely a portion of the things he knows. In a business reeking with incompetence and corruption, the excitement of the lads at having an uncensored (Hollywood studio) press is understandable! . . ."
– Douglas Churchill
Editor & Publisher
August 10, 1935

*H*ollywood. The name invokes a thousand fantasies. Dreams of the good life. Stardom. Fame. Fortune. Little does anyone understand the physical and emotional price that must be paid to fullfill these fantasies. That magic vision of mass acceptance and the good life cost many their lives: Marilyn Monroe, Tom Ince, Carol Landis, Jean Harlow, Nick Adams . . . the list continues endlessly, and for many, their deaths remain a mystery.

In order for the reader to understand how the unsolved mysteries of Hollywood related in this book (and in the first volume) could have occurred, an important facet of Hollywood must be related.

For many decades, dating back to the Arbuckle scandal of 1921–22 (recounted in the prologue), many members of the Hollywood press corps have engaged in critical battles with those who rule the movie industry. During the Twenties and Thirties, reporters covering the industry were often the victims of vicious, well-calculated cover-ups. News was altered to suit the circumstance. Journalists were to believe what the Hollywood oligarchy told them, whether it was the truth or not.

Hollywood's media manipulation continues to this day. It is carried out by so-called power brokers – egotistical agents, like Michael Ovitz (founder of the CMA Agency), who control the distribution of information.

Over the years Ovitz has developed a stranglehold on most of the major talent in Hollywood. Ovitz, who sits like a "Little Dictator" at his semi-circular desk in his I.M. Pei–designed Wilshire Boulevard monument to himself, instinctually decides the fate of those in pursuit of stardom. He is one of the most feared – and loathed – men in the industry.

Aided and abetted by the film studios, Ovitz, and power mongers like him, control what is said about Hollywood and who says it. It is local lore that if you cross one of these power brokers, you can forget about career advancement in Hollywood.

☆ ☆ ☆

The determination of the film industry to control news originating within or about itself came out into the open in the early 1930s.* Editors of newspapers and fan magazines alike were told that NO STORIES WERE TO APPEAR WITHOUT THE WRITTEN PERMISSION OF THE STUDIO PUBLICITY DEPARTMENT INVOLVED. The Hays Office, as this censorship bureau was known throughout the industry, even insisted that it stamp the back of every "still" photograph used by the studios for publicity purposes. If any photograph was published without having "APPROVED FOR PUBLICATION" rubber-stamped on the back, the magazine could be

---

* The industry's arbitrary censorship policy publicly surfaced again in March, 1990, when 20th Century Fox banned renowned critics Gene Siskel and Roger Ebert from advance screenings of their films because of their remarks about the Fox film *Nuns on the Run*. Censorship tactics cropped up again in June of that year, when Disney/Touchstone "controlled" the media on *Dick Tracy* (see epilogue).

boycotted by the industry for both advertisement and story material. One such imprint, from RKO-Radio Pictures, reads:

"Permission is hereby granted to newspapers, magazines and other periodicals to reproduce this photograph. This is an exclusive photograph, therefore it may not be syndicated, rented or loaned, nor used for advertising purposes."

Imprints from other studios were far more stringent, with some even containing the words, **"Written Permission Must Be Obtained From Miracle Pictures Before This Photograph Can Be Reproduced."**

This control "problem" reached the point that newsmen with the reputation of not adhering to studio "journalism rules" were barred from many studios. Others writers were threatened, and there were even a few minor skirmishes during the very difficult days of the 1930s when money ruled Hollywood, and Hollywood was the eighth wonder of the world. Many of the unsolved mysteries herein took place during this period.

The Hollywood "crackdown" was started by William Patterson, an executive of Paramount Theatres in New York. In concert with George Trendle, a Paramount partner, they succeeded in having syndicated columnist Sidney Skolsky of *The New York News* banned from running articles in *The Detroit Free Press*. They also dictated that unless Skolsky's column was "pulled," there would be no more "industry advertising" in the Detroit tabloid. They indicated that Alfred Lasker, president of Lord & Thomas, then the country's largest ad agency, would be asked to "cooperate" in "pulling" all L&T advertising. That meant a considerable amount for the paper, and since the dollar always rules in business, Skolsky's column was pulled.

In Boston, St. Louis and other major cities throughout the country, newspapers bowed to the pressure and ran nothing of a detrimental nature to Hollywood, specifically Skolsky's nationally syndicated column.

The irony of it all is that the column in question was so innocuous that condemning its contents defied common sense. If the actions taken by the studios had not had such a far reaching effect, the material in the column would never have been given a second thought. But the powers at Paramount decreed that the following statements by Skolsky destroyed screen illusions:

✦ "Although appearing as an aviator, James Cagney is afraid to look off a tall building."

✦ "A pane of glass protected the baby in *Sequoia* from the snake."

✦ "In spite of studio publicity declaring Jean Harlow sang and danced in *Reckless*, doubles were used."

✦ "Scenes in *Les Misérables* between Charles Laughton and Frederic March were filmed a month apart, although they were supposedly looking at each other!"

✦ "A night shot in *The Glass Key* was made at noon and the door seen in the background was that of Marlene Dietrich's dressing room."

✦ "Paramount (is) having trouble adapting the stories of Dashiell Hammett."

✦ "*Public Hero No. 1* was made quickly and at a very small cost to cash in on the 'G-Man' cycle and the popularity of the FBI."

★ ★ ★

With this type of censorship it can be seen how easy it was for the founding fathers of the industry and the oligarchy to sweep the causes, reasons, motives and/or what have you of notorious Hollywood deaths under the rug.

Douglas Churchill in the 1930s wrote a scathing article about the problems of the Hollywood press for the newspaper publishing trade magazine, *Editor and Publisher*, "While the charges against Skolsky were unimportant, they [are] significant in one respect: they indicate the true frenzy to which the industry would be aroused should an attempt be made to report more serious dereliction [by any Hollywood stars or the industry]."

Most newsmen reading the article, of which (mimoegraphed) copies were widely distributed in Hollywood, knew what Churchill was hinting at: murders, mayhem, maliciousness. And up to the time of that article, there had been several strange, Hollywood-related murders and suicides which had been "under-reported" by all members of the Hollywood press "corps(e)."

No charges were ever levelled at the ACCURACY of Skolsky's reports. But the move was viewed by the film industry as a "master stroke" by Patterson. It was a way to keep the press in line and permit only WHAT THE STUDIOS WANTED TO REPORT.

William Pine, Paramount's chief of publicity and head of West Coast advertising (he was later "rewarded" with a producer's post) made certain that the "Skolsky Matter" was well publicized by having it prominently printed in trade journals including *The Hollywood Reporter*, *Daily Variety* and *The Motion Picture Herald*, the latter a Quigley Publication which was widely read among distributors and exhibitors. These three trade papers featured stories which ensured that the Hollywood press corps was well aware of the "quasi-censorship" being imposed upon it.

In many ways, whether overground, underground, via telephone or at lunches at the Brown Derby, the industry, spearheaded by The Hays Office, put out the word that it would brook no interference. While the Skolsky matter was in progress, Pine told members of the press * that if their newspapers and magazines persisted in printing revealing material regarded by "his organization" – Paramount – as contrary to the studio's interest, then advertising would not only be shut off to their publications, but that the correspondent involved would have his accreditation "pulled." It was out-and-out economic blackmail, and total censorship.

Another method the industry "uses" which more or less assures a subjective press is the time-worn practice of wining and dining the press following screenings of "borderline" films. These parties for the press are given with the sole intention (and generally successful) of softening reviews on bad pictures, or inspiring extraordinary ones on good films.

Another favorite move is to bring writers and reviewers face to face with producers, stars and directors for "a chat" during the party following the screening(s). It is only natural for a journalist to temper his remarks in discussing a bad film with its makers, especially after a few drinks and a Chasen's-catered dinner.

If the reviewer or writer treated the picture with candor in print

---

* Including the author's father who represented *The London Daily Express*, The Fairfax Group of Australia, and several British "fan" magazines as Hollywood correspondent.

Bing Crosby and Marion Davies in a scene from the 1974 MGM special "That's Entertainment" from one of Crosby's earlier films in which he appeared with Davies. (*John Austin Collection*)

If the reviewer or writer treated the picture with candor in print (if it was a bomb), very often his words spoken at such a party were regurgitated to him. The obvious mistake was then, and still is, attending the parties – or perhaps a better term would be "inquisition." But, then again, didn't most film journalists get into the industry for the glamour?

✷✷✷

Reporters today are considered to be in "good standing" on the "lots" only when they act as unpaid press agents for the studios.

There is no tolerence toward negative press, hence the reason for so many "unsolved mysteries!" The press kow-tows to the industry when it comes to sweeping scandals under the rug. The scandals printed in the national tabloids, by contrast, are generally tips from inside informants picking up substantial "finders' fees" from the tabloids for the information. Many times those tips come from members of the Hollywood press corps, afraid to use the material themselves because of the threat of losing their accreditation.

✷✷✷

This lengthy preamble has been necessary in order for the reader to understand how Hollywood operates. It also serves as an illustration as to how easy it is for the oligarchy to use its powers of (economic) "persuasion" to keep the dirt under the rugs of the Beverly Hills mansions in which it (usually) originates.

It was in this fashion that Universal Pictures managed to keep the homosexuality of Rock Hudson under wraps for three decades. In fact, when the defunct *Confidential* magazine advised the studio that it was going to publish a story of Hudson "cruising the gay bars," the studio gave the magazine the story of George Nader's homosexuality instead. It destroyed Nader's promising U.S. career, but Hudson's was saved. When Hudson died, George Nader inherited the bulk of his estate. Nader, the victim of one of the more vicious, underhanded double dealings in Hollywood, did go on to make several films in Italy and Spain.

Nevertheless, the total destruction of a man's career is just one more example of how vicious members of the oligarchy can be when it comes to protecting one of its favored box office powerhouses who could put one more Rolls-Royce, along with a Ferrari, in the garage.

Rock Hudson at the time he was "saved from homosexual stigma" at the expense of actor George Nader. *Confidential* magazine was going to claim that Hudson liked to cruise "gay bars." The studio gave them a story on George Nader's homosexuality to save Hudson's career. (*Marvin Paige's Mot. Pict. & TV Research Svc.*)

George Nader, the "Sacrificial Lamb" for Rock Hudson's career. (*Marvin Paige's Mot. Pict. & TV Research Svc.*)

★★★

"Hollywood" has always been envisioned by many millions of people the world over as the epitome of glamour, money, sex, beautiful women, and (many) affluent gays – but not necessarily in that order. Hollywood has also been the backdrop for some of the most mysterious deaths, suicides and other forms of mayhem in the annals of police files.

Few of those deaths, supposed suicides or otherwise, have been solved to the complete satisfaction of the Los Angeles Police Department. In many cases during the '20s, '30s, '40s and into the early '50s, those same police departments did the bidding of the oligarchy. The "honorariums" had to be earned when the LAPD was known to be corrupt or at the very least, "co-operative."

★★★

It is our observation, after covering the Hollywood scene for more than thirty years (as our father did before us), that none of the cases herein, or in our previous volume, will ever have the "case closed" stamp printed on the files.

Most of the following cases, and others, are still "open" although the chance of solving any one of them are remote indeed, particularly as most of the crime scenes had been "sanitized" and "rigged" prior to the arrival of the police.

✦ THOMAS H. INCE: One of the early pioneers of the industry, and a known genius of the (early) cinematic art. When he was shot, who was William Randolph Hearst aiming at: Ince or Charlie Chaplin? Why was the real cause of Ince's death "pulled" from *The Los Angeles Times* after one late night edition?

✦ CAROLE LANDIS: Why did she commit suicide when her career was on the wane? Was it over the "dishonorable" intentions of the married British cad and roue, Rex Harrison? Or over the rumors spread by the bitches of Bel Air about Carole's early days?

◆ LUPE VELEZ: Would the shame of being an unmarried mother cause this tempestuous, beautiful and famous Mexican-born film star, who was a devout Catholic, to commit suicide?

◆ PAUL BERN: Even though it "appeared" to be a suicide, we have pieced together evidence that the death of Jean Harlow's husband was engineered by mobster Abner "Longie" Zwillman. The Chicago gangster was Harlow's lover for several years. Why did MGM mogul Louis B. Mayer attempt to remove the supposed suicide note left behind by Bern?

☆ ☆ ☆

For some of these mysteries we believe we have found the solutions. We believe you will agree that most of our conclusions make sense in light of the foregoing, and from what follows in these pages.

Over the years there have been many, many strange aspects to the deaths of Hollywood legends. The case files are filled with star deaths from "accidental homicides," suicides with no apparent motive(s) as well as tales of disappearing evidence and sycophants who saw or heard nothing. There are legends of district attorneys, and others, who have accepted "honorariums" or guarantees of large "campaign contributions" for a run at whatever office to which they might (later) aspire.

Through hype, support, expert public relations, free celebrity endorsements, and cash, the oligarchy has been responsible for electing three Presidents of the United States and at least three governors of California, to say nothing of many congressmen and senators. Behind the scenes, it has been responsible for the appointment of innumerable judges to the right benches. These include Fitts who was "on the take" for years, starting with the William Desmond Taylor case of 1922.

Is it, then, any wonder that the oligarchy has had the "muscle," the power and the wherewithal to keep many of the "mysteries" recounted herein "unsolved" – if that was what they wanted? You be the judge *and* the jury!

Los Angeles Police Captain Bert Wallis (rumored to be a relative of Warner Bros. producer, Hal Wallis) looking at Thelma's body behind the wheel of her car in the garage. To illustrate how the press was immediately misled by Wallis, he claimed her death was due to heart disease, and without the benefit of a Coroner's opinion! *(John Austin Collection)*

Nick Adams (upper right) in a scene from "Fury at Showdown." *(John Austin Collection)*

Elvis performing very early in his career at the Las Vegas Hilton. It was at the Hilton that it appeared that Elvis's "manager," Andreas van Kuijk, aka "Colonel" Tom Parker, made better deals for himself than he did for Elvis. This included a year-round suite and a "gambling fund."
(*Marvin Paige's Motion Picture Research Service*)

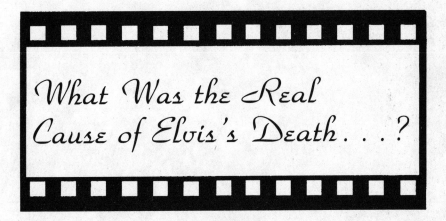

What Was the Real
Cause of Elvis's Death....?

A studio portrait of Elvis while at Paramount Pictures. *(Marvin Paige's Mot. Pict. & TV Research Svc.)*

2... Elvis: The Mystery Lingers and Deepens

"You've got to accept the challenge of death.
Otherwise you'll live in fear of it . . . "
— Elvis Aron Presley

*I*t has been over 13 years since the death of Elvis Presley in the bathroom of his Memphis, Tennessee mansion, Graceland.

With continuing sales of his records and other licensed assets, trustees have admitted that Elvis's estate has increased many times over *since* his death.

Why? What is the legend surrounding the continuing popularity of Elvis Presley?

What was the real cause of Elvis Aron Presley's death?

Within an hour of Elvis's demise, an autopsy was conducted. At its conclusion Dr. Jery Francisco, the county coroner, had determined that the cause was a cardiac arrhythmia, a coronary disease – natural causes – a phrase generally reserved for someone in their 70s, not a man of 42. But, following the autopsy, everyone asked: "What had happened to the prescribed drugs Elvis had been taking?"

When questioned about the drugs, Francisco stated, "The only drugs detected were those prescribed by Mr. Presley's personal physician for hypertension and blockage of the colon."

A strange statement for a coroner to make.

How could all the drugs Elvis was known to have been taking even the night before his death not show up?

★★★

On his last night on earth, only hours before his death, Elvis and his twenty-year-old fiancee, Ginger Alden, had gone to the dentist at midnight. The reason for treatment at that strange hour was to avoid being mobbed by fans. Admirers from all parts of the country – in fact from throughout the world – were always on a vigil outside the gates of Graceland, waiting for a glimpse of their idol.

Ginger Alden had her teeth x-rayed; Elvis had a cavity filled and his teeth cleaned. By this time in his life, Elvis was a 250-pound caricature of himself. Nevertheless, to his intensely loyal fans and admirers he would always be Elvis, The King.

According to Alden's account of Elvis's last night as a mortal, when the two returned to Graceland (the 22-room mansion Elvis purchased when the money started to roll in), Alden and Presley discussed plans for their upcoming wedding, and decided to make the announcement at Christmas.

Then they went in to see Lisa Marie, Elvis's nine-year-old daughter born to his first wife, Priscilla, who had divorced Elvis in 1973. Lisa Marie was at Graceland on a visit. By this time it was 5 a.m. Next, Elvis decided he wanted to play racquetball. He and Ginger woke up two visiting cousins, and the four of them trooped outside and played on the lighted court until 7 a.m.

Obviously, because he had taken some "uppers," Elvis was still not sleepy. He dressed in a pair of blue pyjamas and told Ginger he was going into the bathroom to read.

Alden retired to her room adjoining that of Presley and went to sleep. She did not awaken until 2 p.m. Once she was alert, Alden checked in Elvis's bedroom, and noticed the bed had not been slept in. She went to the bathroom door and called his name.

In an interview with the Memphis *Commercial Appeal*, she described what happened next:

> "He didn't answer so I opened his bath-
> room door and that's when I saw him in
> there. I thought at first he might have hit
> his head because he had fallen . . . and his
> face was buried in the carpet. I slapped him
> a few times and it was like he breathed once
> when I turned his head. I lifted one eyelid
> and it was just blood red. But I couldn't
> move him."

Alden said she then ran out and called Elvis's bodyguards, who obviously weren't guarding the body, and apparently had not even checked on their charge since he had answered the front door and signed for a delivery at 9:30 a.m.

The two men beat on Elvis's chest and tried mouth-to-mouth resuscitation, but it was too late; he had been left too long before being discovered.

The King of Rock and Roll was dead at the age of 42.

☆ ☆ ☆

Elvis Aron Presley was a phenomenon without equal in the entertainment world. Ever since his first electrifying appearance on the famed *Ed Sullivan Show* in 1956, Elvis was acclaimed as a musical deity. His lusty blend of sensual charm and rock 'n roll created a musical style which has been copied ever since.

Following his death, John Rockwell, music critic for *The New York Times*, summarized the impact Elvis Presley had on the world:

> "For most people, Elvis Presley WAS rock'n roll. And they were right. Bill Haley may have made the first massive rock hit, and people such as Chuck Berry and Little Richard may have an equally important creative impact on this raucous new American art form. But it was Elvis who defined the style and gave it an indelible image."

During his lifetime Presley's record sales totalled more than 500 million discs. Presley's records to date have sold more than a BILLION copies in all forms. Elvis is second only to the The Beatles in total sales.

But his fans say there was more to Elvis than his music. There was sex appeal.

When he first appeared on the *Ed Sullivan Show* on CBS Television, he was photographed only from the waist up. The Standards and Practices Division of CBS had seen a rehearsal of Presley's spot and decided that America, and particularly the network, would not be allowed to see his wildly gyrating hips that mesmerized his young female followers wherever he appeared.

To all of his fans, and to many of his detractors in the music press, Elvis had it all! With his black hair cascading over his forehead and his dark, brooding eyes, he was considered ruggedly handsome. Elvis Presley won the hearts and ears of a generation as he swivel-hipped his way across the concert stages of the United States to the pounding rhythms of such classics tunes as "Jailhouse Rock" and "All Shook Up!"

As one early critic admitted:

> "Elvis Presley has a sex appeal that guar-antees his future success. Unlike other rock'n rollers of his era, Elvis possesses, to our mind, real musical talent which should elevate him to the top of the rock'n roll heap!"

And so it did!

★ ★ ★

Elvis Aron Presley was born to dirt poor farmers in Tupelo, Mississippi on January 8, 1935, one of twins. The other was named Jesse Garon Presley. Unfortunately, Jesse died soon after birth. This irony affected Elvis all his life.

When Elvis was 14, the Presley family moved to a subsidized housing project in Memphis. Gladys Presley told interviewers that she and her husband, Vernon, had dreamed of making the move to Memphis. "We thought it would be more fun for Elvis," she declared.

In his poverty-ridden upbringing, the one joy in Elvis Aron's life was music. His parents taught him to sing, and the three Presleys sang and entertained the congregations at rural revival meetings and local churches.

For the Presleys it was hard going in 1949-50. Neither Vernon nor Gladys had received much more than a token education at the ramshackle schools in and around Tupelo, and they had none of the necessary job skills for urban, post-war America.

"His mother and I walked the streets looking for work," recalled Vernon. "Often it was snowing. Eventually, I got work with a tool company."

His parents kept their unhappiness from

Elvis. He was too busy settling into his new
life at L. O. Humes High School. Said his
teacher, Susie Johnson: "He melted easily
into his new life. Though we used to give
him a bad time because of his English. It
was atrocious . . . and still is," she remarked after listening to a Presley interview on a local radio station after he had
achieved stardom.

George Klein, a fellow student of Elvis's
recalled, "I first noticed Elvis when we
were singing in class one day. He sang
'Cold, Cold Icy Fingers,' and there was
something about the way he sang that
stayed with me for weeks and weeks."

Each day Presley took his guitar to school, which he had bought
at a local pawn shop from seven dollars he scrounged together, and
kept the instrument in his locker. He would then play it incessantly
during his lunch break. "When he found people listening to him, he
began to grow those sideboards."

When questioned about this a few years later, Elvis replied, "I
wanted to appear older to the other boys. I thought if I grew
sideboards and a moustache it would help. Well . . . I couldn't
manage the moustache so I had to settle for the sideboards.

"Frankly, I'm sick of them now, but the fans won't let me change."

As soon as he was old enough, Elvis helped the family with odd
jobs to pay the bills. While attending high school, he worked as a
movie usher at the Loew's State Theatre at a salary of $25 a week.
Most of Elvis's pals took similar jobs to earn "date money," but there
was no "date" for Elvis. His weekly earnings went into the family
fund.

Unlike other entertainers who had come up the hard way, Elvis
never imagined he would one day be up on the silver screen. "I never
dreamed no such-a-thought," he told a journalist. "People from my
station in life seldom make it that far. Guess I was an exception."

"We hated to take his money," said Gladys Presley years later.
"But we needed it. And when Elvis realized he could make more for
the family by driving a truck, he quit the theatre job straight away.
He was always thinking of us."

But this is where fate rewarded Elvis Aron Presley. It was while

Elvis and Priscilla Presley at their reception following their marriage in Las Vegas. *(John Austin Collection)*

driving his delivery truck that Elvis spotted the sign that was to change his life – and *that of the music world – forever.*

Following graduation from Humes, Elvis obtained a job as a truck driver for $35 per week. It was while driving around Memphis in 1953 that Presley often passed the Sun Recording Company. A sign in the window read: "Recordings: $1.00."

On one of his trips past Sun he vowed to stop in during a lunchtime and record a song for his mother's birthday. He did, and that was the beginning of it all.

Elvis thought at the end of the session that was the end of it, but Sun Recording's owner, Sam Phillips, was impressed with his voice.

Several days later Phillips remembered ". . . the boy with the mellow voice" and called Elvis to ask him if he could return to the studio to record the song, "Without You. "

> The ballad was a failure. Phillips was dis-
> appointed, but fate again stepped in and
> gave Elvis a boot upstairs.

After being told to "Forget it," Elvis, on his own, started to sing with a rock and roll beat. Phillips and everyone else in the studio, who heard this new music, stood transfixed. They had never heard or seen anyone like this dynamic young man with a guitar pound out a song with such fervor.

Under Phillips's direction Sun Recording taped Elvis singing "That's All Right, Mama" and "I Don't Care If The Sun Don't Shine." Then Phillips had the disc played on a local radio station.

The record sold 7,000 copies that first week in Memphis! Word of this hot, young star filtered through the South to a country slicker known as "Colonel" Thomas A. Parker. He agreed to manage Elvis Aron Presley and his career at fifty cents on the dollar (or so it was rumored), plus lucrative "side deals."

☆ ☆ ☆

"Colonel" Tom Parker (the name he chose for himself) was a rather interesting individual. As a young man, he arrived in the United States by very strange means. Parker's clandestine background was the most compelling reason why Elvis Presley never played a single overseas concert, despite the millions of dollars that were frequently offered for international appearances.

Did Elvis ever suspect that "Colonel" Tom Parker of Huntington, West Virginia, wasn't who or what he claimed?

Gladys always viewed with suspicion the fact that Parker's "title" was honorary, not earned in service but granted by a crony, probably for a cash "consideration."

What would Gladys, Vernon and Elvis Presley have thought if they had lived to learn that "Colonel" Tom Parker, besides not being a real colonel, was not even a bonafide mint julep and straw hat plantation colonel? Parker was actually Andreas Van Kuijk, an illegal immigrant from Holland fleeing from a slight problem with the Netherlands *Polizie.* Through self-promotion and dogged attention to detail, Parker rose above whatever and whomever he left behind in the land of tulips, to become one of the most powerful, and least understood, managers in show business.

Because he allegedly entered the United States as an illegal alien, Parker could not afford to travel outside the U.S. for fear of being discovered. This was why Parker never allowed Presley to perform outside the States. He always had to be with "my boy" whenever Elvis worked. Promoters often wondered why Elvis never made appearances, for example, in England, Germany, or Australia, countries in which many had begged for a chance to promote an Elvis concert. Parker was afraid he would not be allowed to re-enter the country because of "moral turpitude," a catch-all phrase used by the INS. But Parker did manage to guide Elvis to the very pinnacle of stardom and fame internationally with concerts in the U.S., movies, television, and recordings.

By the time "Parker" entered the twilight world of carnivals in the backwaters of the South, where they flourished for lack of any other colorful *divertissement,* he was a master at carny flimflams, a purveyor of "snake oil" (usually castor oil with color), Hadacol tonic and "foot-long" hot dogs. These sausages were, in reality, regular weiners cut in half with each end sticking out of a genuine foot-long bun.

When the "mark" complained, the Colonel would point to a real foot-longer lying in the dirt, claiming the customer dropped it.

In the late thirties he worked an act called "Tom Parker's Dancing Turkeys." It consisted of a sawdust-covered table, about two dozen live turkeys, and an ancient, scratchy recording of "Turkey in the Straw."

At the flip of a switch the music would come on and the birds begin to gyrate. The Colonel, as he was known by then, had a hot plate under the saw dust, and a thermostat which he turned up and down in perfect time to the music.

In the forties he turned to country music, managing singers like Eddy Arnold, Gene Austin, and Hank Snow. He produced a record for Senator Dudley LeBlanc, the last of the old time southern pitchmen, called "Hadacol Boogie," after the "tonic" the senator and Parker were flimflamming as a cure-all of everything from gout to hemorrhoids.

"I'm still not sure who came out best," laughed the Senator from his headquarters in the Louisiana State House. "I found out later he was making as much as I was." The Senator admitted to making $20,000,000 on Hadacol over the years.

Then the Colonel found Elvis.

☆ ☆ ☆

Elvis found drugs to keep him going after Parker had propelled him to the top of the show business heap.

In an interview he did for radio and print a year or two following Elvis's death, his former bodyguard, Sonny West, opened up about his charge.

"Elvis the performer was at odds with Elvis the man he preferred to be," said West. "When he gave a good show and he felt he had a good audience, he was sky high. He had confidence, but I think Elvis the legend helped destroy Elvis the person. The image got so big that it reduced Elvis the person to a smaller level, making it harder for him to cope with the image."

According to West, it was in the early '70s that Presley's dissipation really began in earnest. "Most of us had taken diet pills with him, which at the time gave us a false sense of security, made you feel you could do anything. Elvis told us he started taking Benzedrine and Dexedrine while in the army."

After the uppers came the sleeping pills to "counteract" the other pills being prescribed for him by a Memphis doctor, Dr. George Nichopolous.

Presley, West said, even started experimenting with pain pills such as codeine to counteract the high of diet pills. "He also bought a PDR (*Physicians Desk Reference*) and started studying it," West revealed. "He would tell doctors what he would like to have, and some doctors would give it to him, especially Nichopoulos."

Many people told us they felt Parker did little to stop Presley's drug use as a means of keeping Elvis in line to work constantly and to keep the money flowing into the Presley coffers, and also into the Colonel's "Gambling Fund!"

After spending 16 years with Presley, West noted that Elvis did not need pills to enhance himself. "He did it out of boredom. He had that charisma, but the pills helped him escape from (the) realities of not being able to do too much in between his stage performances.

"Elvis loved to perform. He would be sky high; then back to his bedroom. He would lock himself in there until the next day when we left for the next city," said West, describing Elvis on the road.

At Graceland, his bedroom became Presley's retreat for weeks at a time, ". . . and when everything was closed to the public, that's when Elvis would go out."

Around 1970, Presley started losing interest in everything around him. "From 1972 on it was downhill, and it was bad," West related. Shows had to be cancelled, he couldn't get completely awake, and then he'd have to cancel parts of tours."

A satellite-beamed TV show in January, 1973, which had a projected audience of close to a billion people throughout the world, put Presley back into shape. He had trimmed his weight from 240 pounds to 170 pounds. "That show was beautiful," said West. "Elvis looked fantastic! He met that challenge, but then he started going downhill again."

During his years with Priscilla, West said "Elvis looked great." But after their separation and divorce it created a void in him. Something abruptly was taken out of his life.

He felt remorse.

Yet, West firmly believed that Presley was not the marrying kind. "Part of him wanted to be freed," he stated, "but he also seemed to want to be with Priscilla and their daughter."

Sonny West and Elvis were a few years apart in age, but for 16 years the two men were as close as brothers.

In July 1976, the relationship that began when West first met Presley 18 years earlier, was shattered. A hasty firing by Vernon Presley left West hurt and bitter. But when we interviewed West three years later, he held no bitterness or rancor toward Elvis.

⭐ ⭐ ⭐

According to Elvis's stepbrother, Billy Stanley, Elvis began taking prescription drugs as a way to get himself out of a funk and into a performance. This confirms what Sonny West told us.

Elvis used the drugs when he made movies he didn't like or recorded songs that he felt weren't worth recording, but did at Parker's insistence.

It was after Priscilla left in 1972 that Elvis turned more to the prescription drugs which would, in a few years, create a "polypharmacy" condition within his system.

The drugs were meant to be a temporary solution to temporary problems, according to Stanley, whose mother Dee married Vernon Presley following Gladys's death. But pills had a permanent effect on The King.

Elvis told Stanley at four o'clock one morning that Dr. Nick's sedatives weren't working. "Go wake him up. I need something more." *

"Elvis, it's four in the morning," Stanley told him.

"Wake him. That's what he's here for. That's why I pay him."

Such was the state of Elvis Presley's dependence on drugs, and by this time it included cocaine. By 1975, two years before his death, Presley's health had declined drastically.

⭐ ⭐ ⭐

Because he realized the eyes of the world would be on him during and following the autopsy on the remains of Elvis Aron Presley, Dr. Francisco sought the advice of Los Angeles County Coroner, Thomas Noguchi. He followed Noguchi's dictum in a high profile case: he appointed a panel of distinguished pathologists to assist him with the autopsy. This would assure the public that the autopsy on Elvis Presley was properly performed.

Unfortunately, the findings of that autopsy, instead of quelling public suspicion, aroused a heated controversy which is still going on today – almost 13 years following The King's death!

---

* Elvis was referring, of course, to Dr. George "Nick" Nichopoulos, Elvis's personal physician who was later to come under a great deal of fire for being so free and easy with his prescription pad. According to Stanley's recollection, when "Dr. Nick" went on tour with Elvis he carried a large suitcase full of "prescription" drugs.

After Francisco made the announcement that the only drugs "detected" in Presley's system were those prescribed by Nichopolous for hypertension and a colon problem, the audience was incredulous.

What had happened to the Percodan, Quaalude, Dilaudid and the other pills that made up Elvis's "nine pack" of drugs which he always carried with him?

Elvis, according to Stanley's account, had been given a "nine pack" the night before he died and he received a second pack about nine the following morning, approximately 18 hours before he was found by Ginger Alden on his bathroom floor.

How could all those drugs not show up in an autopsy?

ABC-TV did a news special questioning the Francisco report.

It brought up statements made by another of the Presley entourage that Elvis had "loaned" "Dr. Nick" the money to buy a house, and also said that a Los Angeles dentist would give Elvis any drug he wanted.

ABC also pointed out that there had been no police investigation into his death, which is usually the case when a sudden, unexplained death is reported.

ABC also reported that Elvis's internal organs had been removed and discarded. The network "demanded" that Elvis's body be exhumed and a more thorough investigation begun.

> Rumors of a drug overdose were already circulating around the country, and were rampant in and around Memphis. Francisco dismissed all of them with the statement that ". . . there was no indication of any kind of drug abuse(!) except the two for hypertension and a "colon problem."

Why?

That statement by Francisco turned out to be the understatement of that, or any other, year.

It turned out many months following the Presley autopsy that Elvis had died with an almost unheard of variety of drugs in his system.

Among them were (1) an antihistamine often used to control hayfever and allergies; (2) codeine, a derivative of opium used to relieve pain; (3) Demerol, a narcotic used as a sedative; (4) several tranquilizers, including Valium; and (5) a hypnotic sedative.

. . . But the biggest shock of all was to come later.

A very early Elvis Presley film. Female co-star unidentified. *(John Austin Collection)*

In total, there were eight different drugs in Presley's blood, but all were "harmless" prescription drugs. There was no trace of illegal drugs such as heroin, cocaine or hashish as is normally found in overdose cases. Furthermore, not one of the prescription drugs was at a toxic level.

But Elvis Presley's heart was 50 percent bigger than normal, causing heart problems and his subsequent death.

Nevertheless, because all those drugs were found, it shifted the attention away from Francisco to Dr. George (Dr. Nick) Nichopoulos. Presley's fans were demanding to know whether their idol had been "hooked" on drugs by an unscrupulous physician.

Because of the uproar, an official investigation of Nichopoulos was begun, and the facts that investigation uncovered were startling; they dismayed Presley's idolators everywhere.

The figures were staggering; incredible to laymen and doctors alike. In the seven months before Elvis died, Nichopoulos had prescribed 5,300 odd stimulants, depressants and painkillers for Presley to take.

With this new evidence staring him in the face, Dr. Francisco was forced to call another press conference almost two years after Elvis had died.

At this time he told the press, "I am not involved and never have been involved in a cover-up."

And then he made good use of the panel he has assembled at the suggestion of Noguchi. He said that three pathologists and one toxologist from the University of Tennessee, as well as two other toxicologists from other areas, had agreed: "There is no evidence the medication present in the body of Elvis Presley caused or made any significant contribution to his death!"

★ ★ ★

By this time the American public was very confused over the conflicting stories. From urban slums to Beverly Hills drug overdoses have become so common since the early 1970s, and yet suspicion lingered about Presley's death.

That question, to a great extent, was answered on ABC-TV's *20/20* program in September 1979. The news programs televised a story on the investigation of Nichopoulos. A highly respected pathologist, Dr. Cyril Wecht, vividly explained that prescription drugs at nontoxic levels still can kill.

Elvis Presley, he said, ". . . was a walking pharmacy." According to Dr. Wecht, his death was caused by a condition pathologists call "polypharmacy." In this condition, it is not the individual drugs that kill, but their reaction with each other to form a fatal combination.

"The combined effects of eight different drugs in Presley's body at the time of death was to depress first the brain and then the heart and lungs," explained Wecht.

However, he believed Presley's death was accidental "with the patient not realizing what the effect would be."

Obviously, Elvis's prized reading material, *The Physicians Desk Reference*, did not point this out. As the old saying goes, "A little knowledge is a dangerous thing," but lack of all necessary information might have caused Elvis to create his own coffin within his body by not realizing the danger of interaction of one drug with another.

But surely Nichopoulos knew about it. Shouldn't he have told Presley?

Or did he and Presley ignore the warning?

At a hearing before the State Board of Medical Examiners in 1980, Nichopoulos convinced the Board that Presley was a "psychological" addict who had been treated in hospitals twice for detox purposes from Demerol and other drugs.

Then he went on to give insight into Presley's life "on the road." Nichopoulos admitted that he always went along carrying not one, as Stanley had said, but three suitcases filled with drugs for Presley and his retinue.

The week before a concert was scheduled, Nichopoulos would prescribe a "protocol," a program of strong doses of amphetamines, depressants and painkillers. Presley, who was to start a tour the day after his death, had died during one of those "protocols," involving the staggering total of 680 pills and 20 cubic centimeters of liquid downers, uppers and painkillers.

Dr. Nichopoulos also presented persuasive evidence — at least to a jury of his peers — that he had sought to control Presely's drug habits, but admitted that he could not prevent his patient from gobbling drugs from the time he woke up in the morning until he fell asleep at night.

The Board of Medical Examiners declared Nichopoulos innocent.

But, one might ask, where was Colonel Parker? Did he not know that "his boy" was "gobbling" all these drugs and that they would eventually kill him?

Throughout his career Elvis Presley never at any stage hinted that his relationship with Parker was anything other than congenial and lucrative. On Presley's death, however, a different story began to emerge which leaves Presley's "sudden" death even more mysterious.

★ ★ ★

Many questions were raised in probate court that didn't seem to receive satisfactory answers from those in charge of the King's "fortune."

Was it even a fortune? Because of Parker's slipshod (on purpose...?) management practices, and in spite of the fact that Elvis Presley was reckoned to have earned over $1 billion during his career, *his estate was rumored to be worth a "paltry" $1 to $4 million.*

Elvis left all his money to Lisa Marie, who will inherit the entire principal when she is thirty years old. The court battle over his estate started in 1980, when Lisa was twelve years old. The executors of the will were her mother, Priscilla, and, of all people, the carny — Andreas van Kuijk, alias "Colonel" Tom Parker — as well as Vernon Presley.

Attorney Blanchard E. Tual was appointed by the Memphis Probate Court to protect Lisa Marie's interests. As Tual started his investigation into Presley's business affairs, he began to ask a lot of embarrassing questions about the dubious "Colonel."

According to Tual, Parker had seldom acted in the best interests of his client and also displayed — accidentally on purpose, one might ask? — an amazing lack of business acumen. For example, he had never registered Elvis with the British Performing Society (where his music and records sold in the millions), nor did he register Presley with Broadcast Music, Inc. or ASCAP. As a result, Presley lost out on an additional fortune — which would still be paying out a great deal of money from the performing rights of songs which he had composed — songs such as "Love Me Tender" and "Don't Be Cruel."

Tual was appointed to protect Lisa Marie after the executors of the will had asked the probate court to hand over half the estate's annual income to Parker. They claimed, but correctly so, that was the "commission" Parker had extracted while Presley was alive. Why they made this request has never been uncovered.

Tual filed a report in December 1980 which said that Parker's "commissions" on Presley's earnings had been "excessive" even by the standards of the traditional steep cuts taken in the music industry by managers and promotors who leech off talent.

As an example, Tual cited a deal Parker had struck with RCA in 1973 *which did not favor Presley*. He "negotiated" a flat royalty rate of fifty cents per record *regardless of price - half of that given to other star performers*.

Parker also arranged for RCA to buy Presley's master tapes at the absurdly low price of $5 million. *

A merchandising deal, also cut by Parker, split the income 40 percent in Parker's favor and only 15 percent in Presley's.

Another deal that Tual cited as not being in Presley's best interests was when Parker signed for the singer to appear in Las Vegas in 1972. It came out that Elvis's low performance fee – compared to other superstars – was compensation for free food and drink for Parker as well as a suite of rooms year round. It was also revealed that Parker had gambled an incredible $1 million in one year at the hotel.

> [At this stage, one might ask, where were his father, Vernon, and all the syco-phants on Elvis's payroll? Surely they knew the type of "side deals" Parker was making for himself. Didn't Elvis care; or was he too zonked out?]

Record royalties were split 50-50 and it was later discovered that Parker did not ask for the audit clause. Tual had to surmise that the former carny con man did not know how to maximize the money which was pouring in, and that far too large a sum went into taxes which could have been minimized by a better financial brain, something Parker never sought out.

> It was also said in court that Parker had "received expensive gifts" from record companies when making deals.

In August of 1981, a little less than a year after he was appointed conservator of Lisa Marie's inheritance, Tual presented his case to the Memphis court. He proved that Lisa Marie's interests would be neglected if Parker were allowed to take 50 percent from the estate's earnings, and also that Parker should be forced to repay the estate

---

* When you consider that these were priceless, timeless and represented over 700 songs which had been on the charts.

earnings which he had built up since Presley's death. "A considerable amount," Tual told the court.

It was also revealed that for the first 11 years of their association Parker received 25 percent of Presley's earnings.

But in 1967, ten years before he died, he and Elvis "agreed" on a 50 – 50 split. There was no written agreement to prove it. It was also revealed that in the 21 years since they had worked together, they had never once had dinner together. At Presley's funeral Parker showed up in a gaudy Hawaiian shirt and a baseball cap.

The probate judge had no choice but to rule that Parker's compensation was excessive, and ordered the executors to stop dealing with him and to start litigation within forty-five days to recover money owed to them. RCA, in lieu of a contractual clause to the contrary, refused to allow the estate to audit their books for the period 1973 to Elvis's death in 1977. They claimed that Parker, acting on behalf of his client, "agreed with their accounting!"

It also came out during the hearings that Parker had other side agreements with RCA – quite separate from Presley – but which obviously emanated from Parker's "association" with Presley and paid him over $400,000.

To add to the already burgeoning scandal, it was revealed that the estate was owed $500,000 by a Parker-owned company, Boxcar Enterprises; $6.7 million from RCA Records; nearly $3 million from Britain's Chappel Music; $1.25 million from film rights and percentages and $1.35 million from TV residual payments from his special broadcasts.

The IRS, who got into the act, ascertained that Parker had not given Presley a fair amount of revenue from his many and varied sources of income.

> It also ascertained that Parker could not prove that he had paid his client ANY income from royalties at all for the last four years of his life – the years of Elvis's heaviest drug use.

Did Parker realize, or was he told, that Elvis would be worth more dead than alive with his ongoing record sales and accruing royalties and therefore did not care about Elvis's drug use?

☆ ☆ ☆

Such financial gain for the estate, once Parker was paid off, has certainly been the case. Graceland has been a tourist bonanza with thousands of people admitted to the grounds every month at varying fees; Elvis memorabilia is a major industry in and around Memphis.

The additonal sale of Elvis records, tapes, video cassettes of his movies and now CD's have increased the Presley estate tenfold since his death, thanks to the astute management of Priscilla Presley. In order to preserve the estate of Elvis for their daughter, Lisa Marie, she became involved in managing Elvis's estate.

☆ ☆ ☆

There are still many questions about the unsolved mystery of Elvis Presley's death at the age of 42:

◆ Why did none of his so-called bodyguards bother to check on Elvis before Ginger Alden said she went into his bedroom?

◆ Why do so many people around the country keep insisting they "see" Elvis Presley? Is it because diehard fans still refuse to believe The King Is Dead?

◆ Why – and how – did Parker keep such a tight rein on Elvis throughout his career? Why did he hold Elvis back from singing (and recording) some of the songs he wanted to instead of those Parker selected for him?

◆ Why did Parker not step in and prevent Elvis's excessive drug use? He must have been aware of it.

◆ Why did Nichopoulos not warn Presley, or counsel him on the "polypharmacy" possibility or probability? As a physician, Nichopoulos must have been aware of the potential of this occurring. The question, as far as research shows, was never raised at the Board hearing.

The most compelling research on the mysteries and contradictions surrounding Elvis's "death" was done by Gail Brewer-Giorgio in her new book *The Elvis Files: Was His Death Faked?* (Shapolsky Publishers, 1990). Brewer-Giorgio's earlier book, *Is Elvis Alive?*, sold more than one million copies and rose to the top of the National Bestseller List, demonstrating the strong interest people still have in the unsolved mystery of Elvis's "death."

The Elvis Files raises some interesting points about his "death" that are worth noting:

◆ Why is much of the official documentation missing from government files, such as:
  – All photos taken at the death scene
  – All the notes made in the medical examiner's investigation
  – All the toxicology reports allegedly prepared

◆ Why is Elvis's weight listed on the coroner's report as only 170 pounds when he really weighed 250?

◆ What was the nature of Elvis's secret role as an undercover agent for the DEA under then-President Richard Nixon?

◆ Why was Elvis fearful of certain organized crime figures?

◆ Why has no one ever filed a claim for his multimillion-dollar life insurance policy?

◆ Why have expert graphologists been able to conclusively verify that Elvis forged his own death certificate?

These questions at this late date, and perhaps others, will never be answered.

★ ★ ★

The Elvis legend that was born that day at the Sun Recording Studios will never happen again.

But the legend of Elvis Presley will always remain – and so will the questions about his unnecessary death which could have been prevented if those around him had paid more attention to his well-being.

Elvis Presley still exists today in the memories of his millions of fans worldwide.

Elvis is not driving a taxi in New York, playing the role of a "beach bum" in Hawaii, fishing in Ireland, or tramping the woods of the Northwest.

Unfortunately.

☆ ☆ ☆

Elvis Presley –The King of Rock 'N Roll – is probably dead. Well over a decade later his death can be considered one of the greatest of all Unsolved Mysteries.

Elvis Presley arriving home from his stint as a draftee in the U.S. Army. (*Marvin Paige's Mot. Pict & TV Research Svc.*)

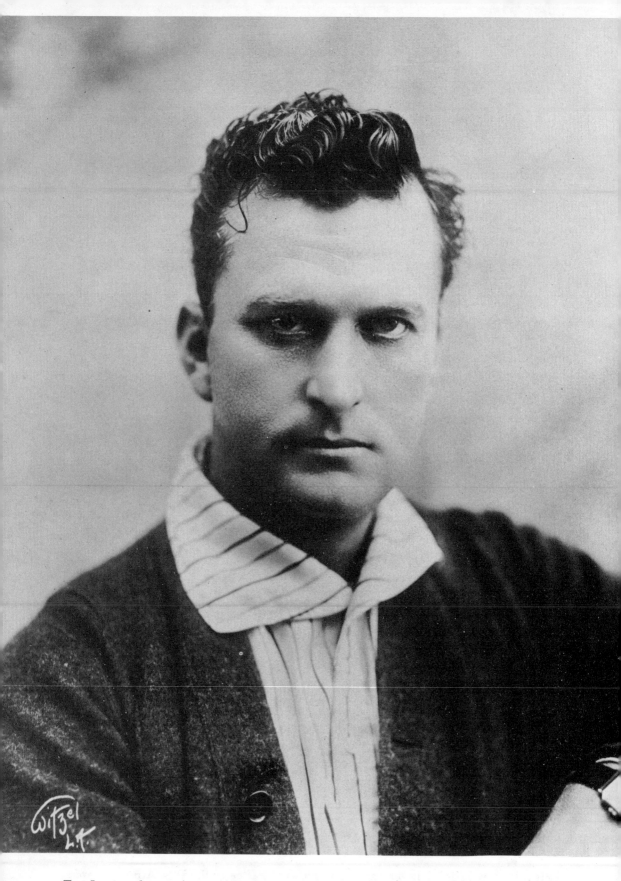

Tom Ince on the set of one of his films, year unknown. *(John Austin Collection)*

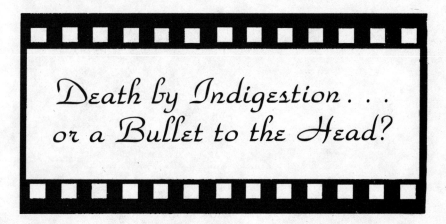

Death by Indigestion . . .
or a Bullet to the Head?

Marion Davies in a studio portrait. (*Marvin Paige's Mot. Pict. & TV Research Svc.*)

3... Thomas Harper Ince—Death by Indigestion or a Bullet?

"All you have to do to make William Randolph Hearst turn white as a ghost is mention Tom Ince's name. There's plenty wrong there, but Hearst is too big to touch ..."

— David Wark Griffith
Pioneer Producer/
Director

*T*HIS WAS THE YEAR, 1924, days of the roaring twenties in America. The time of prohibition, of bootleggers, of peace and plenty, of early films and film stars: Charlie Chaplin, Douglas Fairbanks, Mary Pickford, William S. Hart, Harold Lloyd, Mary Miles Minter, Buster Keaton, Ramon Navarro, Rudolph Valentino, Pola Negri and other famous idols of the silent screen.

☆ ☆ ☆

IT WAS THE GOLDEN DAYS of the moguls, producers and directors just gaining a toehold in Tinsel Town, Never Never Land, Oz, Hollywood Boulevard – the Yellow Brick Road to Riches: D.W. Griffith, Thomas Ince, Cecil B. DeMille, Samuel Goldwyn, Jesse Lasky, Louis B. Mayer, Jack Warner, Samuel Goldwyn, Joseph Schenck, Adolph Zukor.

✩ ✩ ✩

IT WAS THE HALCYON DAYS of William Randolph Hearst – the greatest newspaper baron ever spawned in America, possibly the world. His newspapers not only reported on world events – Hearst attempted to create them. Sometimes he succeeded, thus creating circulation-building headlines for the Hearst newspapers and International News Service.

✩ ✩ ✩

Only one "bulldog" edition of *The Los Angeles Times* bore the headline:

PRODUCER SHOT ON HEARST YACHT

By contrast, Hearst's *Los Angeles Examiner* carried a little different banner lead the next morning:

SPECIAL CAR RUSHES STRICKEN INCE HOME FROM RANCH!

The editors (and publisher) of *The Los Angeles Times* "killed" the yacht story in all further editions. Over the years, employees of the venerable newspaper searched the archives for that edition. Even though the *Times* regularly published an early (midnight) edition, all other issues for the week of November 16, 1924 were accounted for but not that edition for November 17, the day of the headline.

This was an example of the far-reaching power of William Randolph Hearst during that era. Even though the *Times* was a Hearst competitor, and in itself generated a great deal of power in the community, it agreed to kill the story because of the lack of evidence and corroboration. At least that is the story as told by the "old timers" on the paper.

When the word came down from the publisher's suite to "kill the Ince story," we were once told by an old time staffer assigned to the "Arts" pages, ". . . everyone guessed something was going on somewhere in Never-Never land, and that a massive, gigantic cover-up was starting to form." Many said word was telephoned from the San Diego area by a Hearst secretary to various editors of Hearst's *Los Angeles Examiner* and to the publisher's suite of the *Times*.

In the 1920s, William Randolph Hearst was America's most

powerful (and feared) man. In his heyday, he was so feared that not even rival tabloids or broadsheets would risk open warfare with "W.R." It just was not worth the gamble.

☆ ☆ ☆

Hearst's alleged fortune of $400,000,000 from silver mines was so colossal in those days that he could buy anyone or anything he wanted. Word spread throughout the city rooms of the nation's newspapers, into editors' offices and publishers' suites that many newsmen, some editors and even some publishers had been forever barred from further employment in the profession. They had "displeased W.R."

Hearst's extramarital relationship with actress Marion Davies was already notorious but at no time were their names linked publicly in the nation's press, particularly in Los Angeles and Hollywood. There was no *National Enquirer* or *Star* in those days to expose the foibles of man.

Even several heretofore "fearless" yellow sheets, the tabloids of their day, and usually engaged in dog-eat-dog circulation wars, decided to pass on that coupling.

In the 1920s, William Randolph Hearst had such a strong impact on corporate America that no one hoping for power and acceptance dared to make him cross.

☆ ☆ ☆

Besides being a newspaper tycoon, William Randolph Hearst was a giant among film financiers.

The beacon of American publishers had entered the movie industry in 1911, via the newsreels. At first it was a hobby, but when newsreels became a popular feature at the local theatres, the profits began to roll in.

That amateur film interest then turned into a zealous professional one, as a means of furthering the film career of Marion Davies. The power of the Hearst press, the Hearst magazines (most still in existence today), the Hearst radio stations and the Hearst syndicated columns assured the tycoon an obeisance from the sycophants of the burgeoning movie colony.

Hearst leapt into feature films when he purchased several thousand shares of Metro-Goldwyn-Mayer, which released the Hearst Movietone News (later Fox Movietone). Using his stock as clout, he

From L to R: Douglas Fairbanks, Mary Pickford, Chaplin and early movie pioneer D.W. Griffith. *(John Austin Collection)*

A New Year's party at San Simeon. L to R: Irene Dunne (who passed away in 1990), Hearst, Bette Davis, Louella Parsons (never far from her meal ticket) and an unknown starlet. *(Marvin Paige's Motion Picture & TV Research Service)*

D.W. Griffith, one of the earliest film pioneers and a friend of Thomas Ince. He said several years following Tom Ince's death that if the producer's name was ever mentioned around William Randolph Hearst, he turned white as a ghost and whoever mentioned it would be banned from San Simeon, the Santa Monica house, or the yacht for life, and probably his or her career would be on the line as well. *(John Austin Collection)*

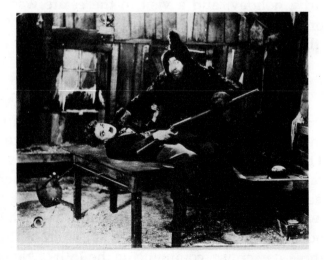

Charlie Chaplin in "The Gold Rush," one of his most famous comedies. *(John Austin Collection)*

organized Cosmopolitan Pictures to produce films exclusively with Davies. He first made several deals with MGM, then with Warner Brothers-First National for distribution. Hearst told intimates that nothing was going to stop him from making Marion Davies one of the world's best-known film stars.

Hearst never took into account the fact that Davies had no depth of acting ability.

☆ ☆ ☆

For someone with a modicum of ability, Davies had come very far. Her beach house on Pacific Coast Highway in Santa Monica, built for her by Hearst, was a block long, three stories high and had three marble swimming pools. The Pacific Ocean was 150 yards away, across the sandy beach. The green and white mansion became the meeting place for Hollywood's elite. It was here she gained artistic respectability.

Accepting Davies as an acting talent came with a bigger bonus . . . an entree into Hearst's personal circle. Friends and admirers of Davies were known to occasionally receive an invitation to Hearst's vast domain at San Simeon (now a California State Park). This lavish estate was filled with millions of dollars worth of imported furnishings, tapestries and paintings. The garage housed 35 cars. There were numerous guest houses, each with many rooms, as Hearst would not allow nonmarried couples to share the same bedroom – not even himself and Marion. Regardless, San Simeon was an extraordinary way to spend a holiday, and a visit to the estate was a must-have invitation for the 1920s elite.

Over all this splendor Marion Davies reigned as star and mistress.

☆ ☆ ☆

Invitations to galas thrown by Hearst were coveted items, as the millionaire media mogul was known for his wild, star-studded parties that ignored the era's prohibition of alcohol. These extravaganzas took place in a variety of locales: some at San Simeon, others at Marion Davies' beach house or on Hearst's prestigious yacht, the Oneida. Often they were fun festivals of wild abandon, but when the cream of Hollywood's elite circle received an invitation from the newspaper baron for a three-day cruise, commencing the 15th of November, 1924, Hearst had other motives.

The invitation stated that the trip was to celebrate the 43rd birthday of Thomas Harper Ince, one of the true pioneers of Hollywood film making, the innovator of the "they went that-a-way" westerns.

Fifteen socialites were scheduled to be on board the Oneida for the festivities, including Ince and his wife, Nell; Ince's business manager, George H. Thomas, and his mistress; Charlie Chaplin; Margaret Livingston; British writer Elinor Glynn *; actress Eileen Pringle; Seena Owen; Julanna Johnson; Dr. Daniel Carson Goodman, production head of Heart's Cosmopolitan Pictures (named after his successful magazine of the same name); Hearst's chief secretary, Joseph Willicombe; *Los Angeles Herald* publisher Frank Barham and his wife. Also included were Marion Davies, her sisters, Ethel and Reine, and her niece, Pepi.

☆ ☆ ☆

In all pretense it seemed like a glorious weekend of pleasure, but Hearst was a calculating man who had more in mind than just the indulgence of a few favored friends. In fact, he had two ulterior motives in mind when he planned this voyage.

First, Hearst was trying to lure noted producer Tom Ince into working with Cosmopolitan Pictures. His goal was to create a movie empire to match that of the already entrenched moguls, and Ince, who had a noteworthy reputation, was part of this plan.

Although Ince was renowned for his westerns, the which-way-did-he-go shoot-em-ups were beginning to lose popularity among the masses. Romantic love stories had now come into vogue. This suited 27-year-old Davies' very limited acting ability, as her strength lay in fluttering her eyelids. Ince, on the other hand, had yet to find his niche in the changing movie market, so he was interested in the ideas the omnipotent Hearst had to offer.

The logical move was for Hearst to take over the Ince Studios in Culver City (where *Gone With The Wind* would eventually be filmed), a proposition over which he and Ince had already begun negotiations. This was the reason Ince's business manager, George Thomas, and Hearst's production chief, Dr. Goodman, were invited aboard the Oneida. Hearst had hoped to wrap up the deal before the yacht returned to San Pedro harbor Monday evening.

There was a second and more compelling reason for Hearst to have invited Ince, as well as Charlie Chaplin. Hearst wanted to ascertain

---

* Glynn studiously avoided mentioning this weekend cruise in her own autobiography several years later.

which of the two men were sleeping with his mistress, Marion. He had heard rumors that, while he was off on his various business trips, she had been trysting with Charlie Chaplin, and possibly Ince.

Hearst had gotten this information from a squad of gumshoes he employed to keep him informed of Davies' dalliances during his many absences on business.

Heretofore, Chaplin had a penchant for deflowering vestal virgins. A virgin Davies was not. It was out of character for Chaplin to "make" Marion Davies, especially as he was about to marry Lita Grey. But an impending marriage never stopped Chaplin before, and the silent screen star was intrigued by Davies' stutter.

William Randolph Hearst was uncommonly jealous of other men's attentions to Marion Davies. When he received reports that Davies was intimately involved with one of the great studs of early Hollywood, Charlie Chaplin, he was fuming.

Chaplin was invited to attend the party on the yacht so that Hearst could observe his deportment around Davies during the long weekend. Charlie, his friends said later, had some qualms about going along on the cruise, but decided to throw caution to the winds even though he might incur Hearst's wrath if he so much as spoke to Davies.

On this voyage, Hearst was to find out the truth, and with tragic results which ended up as one of the greatest cover-ups in Hollywood history.

☆ ☆ ☆

In the early morning hours of Saturday, November 15, 1924, Hearst and Thomas Ince went horseback riding on the bridal trail that ran through Beverly Hills and down the middle of Sunset Boulevard. No one knows exactly what the two men talked about during that post-dawn ride. Whether they spoke of their possible business merger, whether they had an argument, or just talked about the events of the day has never been revealed. The only thing that has been established was that Ince told Hearst that he had to attend the preview of his latest film, *The Mirage*, that evening, after which he would take the last train to San Diego in order to board the yacht early Sunday morning to celebrate his birthday in fine style.

It had the potential for a glorious weekend! The weather was balmy and spirits were high on that fateful Saturday. Marion Davies was collected on the set of a film called *Zander the Great* by two other yaching guests: Charlie Chaplin and a Hearst writer, Louella Parsons. They were all chauffeured to the San Pedro Marina by Chaplin's personal servant, Kono.

This was Louella O. Parsons' first visit to Los Angeles, but the city of Angels was to become her home after the start of her infamous career. "Lolly," as she was known to her friends, along with Hedda Hopper, was one of the piranhas of Hollywood gossip from late 1924 until her retirement fifty years later.

Louella Parsons always denied that she had been on the cruise that weekend. Unfortunately, those denials never rang true because several people saw her leave the studio that Saturday morning with Chaplin, Davies and Kono in the comedian's huge Packard touring car.

Nevertheless, Parsons was given the job as motion picture editor of Hearst Newspapers and International News Service just after that fated weekend. It was a prestigious and lucrative position. "Lolly's" income reached a peak of $16,000 during the late thirties, a far cry from the $50-a-week salary she received for writing a daily column for Hearst's *New York American*.

The power that "Lolly" Parson wielded from that weekend forward was unbridled. It was hell for the stars who married without calling "Lolly" first, or who became pregnant without telling her how they consummated the act. Heaven forbid if a starlet had a baby between her deadlines! Such a snubbing would forever banish them from the pages of the Hearst Newspapers – unless she was passing along negative information.

As part of the cover-up for that weekend, and to kill any idea that Parsons had been on the yachting guest list, Hearst ordered Willicombe, his secretary, to instruct editors to dateline all Parsons' columns for that week "New York," in an attempt to disprove that she had been on board.

From that decisive day forward, Louella O. Parsons, with an unswerving career goal to become the most powerful motion picture writer and columnist in Hollywood, saw her dream come true by being in the right place at the right time.

Parsons' unswerving loyalty to "W.R." for giving her an opportunity remained intact. She, single-handedly among the Hollywood press corps, lauded the "talent" of Marion Davies . . . and she took the secret of the cruise to her grave.

★ ★ ★

William Randolph Hearst's 280-foot-yacht, the Oneida, set sail from Los Angeles, bound for San Diego with his star-spangled passenger list on board. As the yacht steamed out of San Pedro harbor, Hearst and his hostess-cum-mistress, Marion Davies, entertained their guests with live jazz music and the finest vintage champagne.

In the days of prohibition, the act of serving alcohol constitued a felony.

As he had told Hearst earlier that morning, Thomas Ince did not board with the other guests in San Pedro. Instead he boarded the yacht Sunday morning in San Diego. His wife remained in Los Angeles, claiming she didn't feel well. When Ince joined the contingent of merrymakers he appeared to be in perfect health.

What happened from the moment he boarded until his sudden death a few days later continues to be one of the most bizarre murder mysteries in the annals of Hollywood scandals.

☆ ☆ ☆

From bits and pieces of conversations put together over the years, a possible scenario for tragedy unfolded on that Sunday night.

☆ ☆ ☆

Late afternoon during the Sunday celebrations, Hearst noticed that Davies and Chaplin were not in Le Grande Salon of the yacht where the guests had been summoned by the publisher for cocktails prior to dinner. He went on a search for them, fearing the worst.

As passed down by eyewitness Kono, who was always hovering near Chaplin in case his master needed him, Hearst spotted Chaplin and Davies leaning against the rail, Chaplin's massive manhood about to navigate the love canal of Marion Davies, obviously with her consent. Hearst swore at the pair as he ran along the upper deck shouting at the two stars. The shouting attracted other guests, including Ince, who ran downstairs and attempted to shield the pair from Hearst's view. Enraged, Hearst yelled down from above that he would kill both of them. He then ran for his pearl-handled revolver.

Hearst had always prided himself on his marksmanship, some-

Charlie Chaplin in Hollywood, circa 1920's. *(John Austin Collection)*

Chaplin as The Tramp. *(John Austin Collection)*

Marion Davies strolling at MGM Studios with famed playwright George Bernard Shaw. *(Marvin Paige's Motion Picture & TV Research Services)*

Marion Davies in a studio portrait. *(John Austin Collection)*

Chaplin upon receiving his Honorary Oscar in 1971, amidst great controversey over his left wing leanings. One columnist wrote of the episode: I'm old enough to remember how he sat out WWII, helping neither his adopted country, this one, which had made him rich, nor his native one, England, which was fighting for its life. Too old, I suppose, to have been drafted or enlist, he didn't follow Joe E. Brown's example and do camp shows and benefits, nor did he do anything else, including pay his taxes." Because of the ambivalence toward him by practically everyone but the oligarchy, he had to make his entrance through the underground garage. *(John Austin Collection)*

times knocking off a sea gull with a hip shot from his favorite pistol.

From the upper deck, Ince and Chaplin looked alike, especially in the dim light on the lower deck, and with their backs to Hearst. In the ensuing confusion, Ince, not Chaplin, dropped with a bullet to the head from the hand of marksman William Randoph Hearst. In her famous stutter, Davies was heard to yell "mmm . . . ur . . . ddd . . . e . . . rrr!"

Unknown to Hearst, the Japanese servant witnessed the entire confrontation, including the shot which would be fatal to Tom Ince, not Charlie Chaplin, as intended. Kono retired to the servant's quarters, not wishing to be seen by Hearst or by anyone else. He was frightened for his own life, given the wrath of "W. R." at that particular moment.

This story was passed down to Kono's relatives over the years, and to other Japanese domestics in Beverly Hills with whom he associated. *

☆ ☆ ☆

Once they boarded the yacht in San Pedro and joined the other guests, the yacht sailed straight into the controversy which has not waned to this day. What happened to Thomas Harper Ince on the cruise? W.R. had his secretary, Willicombe, put out a story to the Hearst editors which was an absurd piece of garbage:

> "Ince, with his wife, Nell, and his two
> young sons, had been visiting the Hearst
> Ranch in upstate California for several days
> prior to the acute attack of indigestion.
> When the illness came upon him suddenly,
> Ince was stricken unconscious. He was
> then removed to a private railroad car with
> two doctors and two nurses, and sent home
> to Beverly Hills to recuperate."

Unfortunately for Hearst, witnesses had seen Thomas Ince board the Oneida at San Diego. But even more regrettable for Hearst, and responsible for allowing the truth to leak out over the years, Charlie

---

* During the 1920s and 1930s, Japanese domestics were favored by the film colony and the Los Angeles elite because of their subservience and discretion. This changed following Pearl Harbor when all Japanese living on the Pacific Coast were interned.

Chaplin's secretary, an obsequious little Japanese man who answered to Kono, saw something he shouldn't have seen. He later related his experiences to other domestics over the years, with the story in turn being related to the employers of the domestics, including the author's family.

☆ ☆ ☆

In the aftermath of Tom Ince's death, a series of strange events gave every appearance of "foul play" on the yacht; many observers, because of the demeanor of the crew and tight-lipped guests, deduced it involved Hearst himself.

The Oneida's captain had the entire crew sworn to secrecy in fear of losing their jobs. Hearst slipped away to New York in his private railroad car which he had ordered to San Diego but left Davies behind because she was in the middle of filming a new Cosmopolitan production. The note he left her is said to have contained the words: "I think it best to go east since the situation in California is so unsatisfactory." Hearst, it was said, had an aversion to funerals.

The oath of secrecy also added fuel to the fire that something definitely untoward happened on the cruise. Why did all the guests refuse to talk to the press or anyone else as to what happened that fateful weekend? Motion picture people of that era were usually very quick to talk to the press. One of the guests, the novelist, screen writer and social entrepreneur, Elinor Glyn, was very outspoken about other Hollywood scandals in her biography. She failed (as mentioned in an earlier footnote) to say anything about this one even though she was a guest on the cruise.

Similarly, Charlie Chaplin appeared to have a total lapse of memory in his autobiography, *Chaplin*, many years later. Chaplin claims he was not present on the cruise in his 500-page tome. Instead, he wrote, he visited Tom Ince on his sickbed TWO WEEKS BEFORE HIS DEATH from a heart attack he suffered while on that cruise. Strange, but "two weeks before his death" Tom Ince was shooting a film in Culver City and appeared to be perfectly healthy when he walked on board the Oneida at San Diego that fateful Sunday morning. It is amazing how widespread amnesia is in Hollywood when it comes to these affairs. The "power" of William Randolph Hearst reached out even from the grave to silence those who could tarnish the old goat's memory.

☆ ☆ ☆

Rumors were rife in and around San Diego where the Oneida had docked to bring Ince ashore and into a waiting ambulance. The story put out by Willicombe preceded the disembarkation of Ince from the yacht. Bystanders, police and others were told that Ince was ". . . suffering from a bad attack of indigestion and 'heart problems'."

In Hollywood few knew anything about the Hearst yachting trip. Little by little information leaked out, aided and abetted by Kono and his friends all anxious to hear what had happened.

But in San Diego, the rumors flew so fast that the District Attorney, Chester Kemply, was forced into calling an investigation.

At the hearing, the principals were strangely absent and had not been subpoenaed and Hearst could not be reached by anyone. However, Kemply did not call Seena Owen, Marion Davies, or Elinor Glyn, known for certain to have been on board. Dr. Daniel Carson Goodman, the Hearst employee, did appear and his was the only "official" story of what was supposed to have transpired that Sunday on the Hearst yacht. The story told by Goodman, as released by the D.A., was "On Saturday, November 15 . . . I boarded the yacht belonging to International Film Corporation (another Hearst company) with a party on board to San Diego. Mr. Ince was to have been one of the party. He was unable to leave Saturday, stating that he had to attend a preview of his latest film but would join us in San Diego on Sunday morning. *

"When Mr. Ince joined us on Sunday morning, he complained of nothing but being tired. I discussed during the day details of his agreement just made with International Film Corporation to produce pictures in combination with each other. Mr. Ince seemed well," continued Goodman, ". . . he ate a hearty dinner, retired early.

"Next morning he and I arose early before any of the other guests to return to Los Angeles. Ince had complained during the night he had an attack of indigestion, and still felt bad. On the way to the train station he complained of a pain in his heart, but at Del Mar [30 miles north of San Diego] a heart attack came upon him and we got off."

At no time during Goodman's "dissertation" did Kemply or his aides ever question him about the veracity of his account, or of Ince being seen removed from the yacht into an ambulance. A writer could not have concocted a better scenario to fit the facts as Hearst wanted

---

* Never once during his testimony did Goodman mention Hearst's name, nor was he ever questioned about Hearst by Kemply. The obvious inference drawn from this by the spectators was that Hearst "had gotten to" Kemply.

them put out.

Following a brief respite for lunch, Goodman continued: "I thought it best to take him off the train, insist upon him resting in a hotel. I immediately telephoned Mrs. Ince that her husband was not feeling well. I then called in a local physician and remained myself until the afternoon when I continued on to Los Angeles.

"Mr. Ince told me that he had similar attacks before, but that they had not amounted to anything. He gave no evidence of having had any liquor of any kind. My knowledge as a physician enabled me to diagnose the case as one of acute indigestion." Goodman never mentioned "lead poisoning" as a possible diagnosis!

But a "Dr. Truman Parker," a supposed Del Mar physician who had been summoned by Dr. Goodman, told the District Attorney a quite different version that added considerable mystery to the case and gave rise to a great deal of speculation as to what actually had transpired on board and at the hotel.

"Dr. Parker" and Dr. Goodman had obviously got their signals mixed. "Parker" diagnosed Ince as having a "mild heart attack," recommended rest and called in a nurse, and said he would return later. But before Parker could return, Nell Ince had arrived from Los Angeles and left a note for "Parker" and the nurse he had summoned that their "services were no longer required!"

Ince, according to Goodman's story to Kemply, was taken from the hotel by ambulance to a private railroad car attached to a Los Angeles train. The family was told in Del Mar that his condition "was not serious." During all this, Nell Ince must have known something other than "indigestion" was ailing her husband. She remained strangely silent following a meeting with Dr. Goodman in Del Mar.

In the early hours of Wednesday morning, November 19, 1924, Thomas Harper Ince died at his Benedict Canyon home. His death was attributed to "heart failure!" His three sons, William, 15, Thomas H., Jr., 11, and Dick, 9, and Nell Ince were with him when he passed away.

☆ ☆ ☆

Because of her silence and total reticence to discuss the case, Nell Ince received a large monetary settlement from Hearst for her silence and cooperation in "agreeing" to the "official" Hearst story of her husband's death. Tom Ince did not die a

wealthy man and Nell Ince had three sons
to raise. She left California almost immediately.

☆ ☆ ☆

Tom Ince's death came as a terrible shock to the then closely knit
oligarchy. Production at the Ince Studios came to a halt until things
could be sorted out. Four films were shooting, all under the aegis of
Ince. The funeral was private, and Ince was cremated almost
immediately.

This, in itself, added more to the speculation because Mrs. Ince
refused to allow an autopsy and ordered the immediate cremation.
Then there was a new and even stranger turn to the mystery.

Kemply, who had first declared that he intended to call every
person on board the yacht that fatal Sunday to give their version of
what happened, did not call any of them following Goodman's
"testimony"!

Suddenly, after that first session, he called off any further inquiry
into the "sudden illness" of Thomas Ince on board the yacht and his
subsequent death.

Kemply said he was "satisfied" that Ince died of a heart attack
following "acute indigestion." At a press conference he called to
announce his stand, he told the press that "I called this investigation
because of many rumors brought to my office regarding the case, and
have considered them until today in order to definitely dispose of
them.

"There will be no further investigation of stories of drinking
aboard the yacht, or anything else which has been rumored to have
transpired. If there are to be any further hearings, even involving the
illegal liquor believed to have been on board, then the hearings will
have to be heard in Los Angeles where the liquor was undoubtedly
obtained.

"People interested in Mr. Ince's sudden death have continued to
come to me with persistent reports and in *order to satisfy* them I did
conduct an investigation. But after questioning the doctor privately
who allegedly attended Mr. Ince in Del Mar, I am satisfied the death
of Tom Ince was from natural causes."

The long arm of William Randolph Hearst had reached out once
again, probably through Dr. Daniel Carson Goodman.

Following the press conference, C.F. Adelsperger, an editorial
writer for what is now the *Long Beach* (California) *Press-Telegram*, but

then the *Long Beach News*, wrote:

> "If there is any foundation for suspect-
> ing that Thomas Ince's death was from
> other than natural causes, and there is
> good reason to believe there is, then an in-
> vestigation should be made in justice to the
> public as well as to those concerned in the
> case".

As far as anyone could ascertain, not one reporter covering
Hollywood attended Kemply's press conference. *

☆ ☆ ☆

There was yet another strange angle added to the mystery in a
statement made by Nell Ince (through a spokesperson, obviously
"provided" by Hearst) immediately following her husband's death.

She said she had been invited to accompany her husband on the
yacht on the Saturday night, but that she and Ince had attended a
preview of *The Mirage* that evening, and she was not feeling very well.
They then agreed her husband should go by train to San Diego and
join the yacht there while she rested at home.

Very few answers to very serious questions have ever been
answered over the years. There should have been a charge of murder
or, at the very least, manslaughter, brought against the shooter of
Tom Ince. In this case, according to Kono, William Randolph Hearst,
although there is no corroboration or proof. But the facts do seem to
confirm that it was highly probable even though Kono's description
was passed down through two generations.

Many other questions also will never be answered.

◆ If Nell Ince was well enough to attend the preview of
   Ince's film in an outlying suburb, why did she suddenly
   become too ill to attend the party for her husband?

◆ Why did Louella Parsons deny until her death that she
   was on board the yacht that weekend? This, in spite of

---

* A few years following Hearst's death, an investigative reporter tried to locate "Dr.
Thomas Parker" of Del Mar. No trace of him could be found in the area between 1922 and
the three years following Ince's death, either from telephone directories or other sources.
Likewise, no "Dr. TRUMAN Parker," as he has been referred to in other accounts.

the fact a witness saw her leave the studio with Chaplin and Marion Davies and with Kono at the wheel.

◆ Was it also not odd that Ince, if Nell was really ill, would go off alone and leave her and the children behind on his birthday?

◆ Why could no trace of "Dr. Thomas Parker" be found in Del Mar, the doctor Dr. Goodman claimed he had called in to assist Tom Ince?

◆ Were differences brewing between the Inces over "other women," including Marion Davies?

◆ How did Hearst and Goodman keep "Dr. Thomas Parker" quiet about the bullet wounds?

◆ Or could "Dr. Parker" have come from Central Casting, summoned to Del Mar by Dr. Goodman who was head of Cosmopolitan Productions? As such, he was in a strong position to ask for such favors from an actor.

◆ Could it be that Tom Ince was already dead or dying when he was being carried off the yacht in San Diego and that the Del Mar visit was to allow Goodman time to summon a phony "Dr. Parker?" And also time to obtain Nell Ince's acquiescence to the cover-up to protect W.R. Hearst?

These questions and the statements of Dr. Goodman at the so-called "inquest" called by Kemply also made the statement issued by Willicombe that Ince and his family had been "visiting the ranch" so much garbage. It was obvious that at the time he issued the statement, a "cover-up" had not been completely thought out by those involved.

Even though no members of the Hollywood press corps attended Kemply's "investigation" into Ince's death, several statements were made by other members of the press who were present.

"It was understood," wrote one, "that District Attorney Kemply's investigation was to establish what had actually occurred at the party directly preceding the director's death."

The 'probe' halted before any members of the party had ever been questioned.

It appears that others also had their doubts at the time but never followed through.

★ ★ ★

The Hearst-Davies diarchy rode out the scandal unscathed because of the old man's power in keeping a muzzle on not only his own newspapers, but those of his rivals as well. Such was the unbridled power of William Randolph Hearst.

But as David Wark Griffith remarked in later years when asked about the Ince death, he replied: "All you have to do to make Hearst turn white as a ghost is mention Ince's name. There's plenty wrong there, but Hearst is just too big to touch!" It was also well known and passed around the film colony that any mention of Tom Ince's name within Hearst's hearing would kill any future invitations to the Santa Monica Beachhouse, the yacht, or San Simeon.

★ ★ ★

A perverse footnote concerning Ince became known to the film colony when Nell placed their Benedict Canyon home on the market following Ince's death. This was an enormous Spanish style mansion built by Ince and completed only six months before his death.

Dias Doradas – Golden Days – in Benedict Canyon, which Ince had designed himself, was a showplace where the "Golden People" – as he called them – delighted in spending carefree weekends.

"The Golden People," however, completely ignored, or did not know about one feature: a secret gallery above the guest rooms provided with concealed peepholes over the beds. These provided Tom Ince with a bird's eye view of some of the most expensive asses in Hollywood grinding their way home into some of the most sought after vaginas in Tinsel Town.

Some of Hollywood's most celebrated couples had thus repaid their host's bounty by a gracious demonstration of their boudoir calisthenics. Only Tom Ince had the key to the concealed passageway.

The large trust fund Hearst set up for Nell Ince was eventually wiped out by the depression. This gesture alone, if it had been revealed, would have pointed to Hearst's guilt for Ince's death.

After this disaster, Nell Ince ended her days driving a taxi to support herself, aided by her sons. The $550,000 she received for *Dias Doradas* from producer Carl Laemmle was also wiped out by the stock market crash. Nevertheless, the legend of Tom Ince's mysterious death will always remain one of Hollywood's Unsolved Mysteries, one that has been puzzled over for decades.

We believe we have come up with the answer, the true cause and method of Tom Ince's mysterious death, not by "indigestion," but by the "ingestion" of a bullet to the back of the head!

From L to R: Louella O. Parsons, Hearst, and Marion Davies at a costume party at Simeon. The identity of Parson's doormat is unknown. Parsons became the most powerful columnist in Hollywood for being in the right place at the right time: the cruise on the Hearst yacht, *The Oneida,* the weekend that Ince was shot. For whatever reason, Parsons always denied that she was on the cruise although several people saw her arriving in San Pedro— with Charlie Chaplin, Kono (the latter's servant), and Marion Davies, who was picked up on the set of "Zander the Great," and driven to San Pedro in Chaplin's touring car—and board the yacht. *(Marvin Paige's Motion Picture & TV Research Service)*

Thelma in a scene from her most famous comedy, "Duck Soup," with Groucho Marx. The film is still shown on late night television. *(John Austin Collection)*

"*A Neat and Tidy Solution Was Required . . .*"

Thelma in repose at a funeral home prior to the services. *(Marvin Paige's Mot. Pict & TV Research Svc.)*

Thelma and DeCicco in a happier moment on a night out at Hollywood's favorite watering hole, The Trocadero. Favorite, because it was owned by W.R. "Billy" Wilkerson who also owned *The Hollywood Reporter*. You went to "The Troc" or your name and/or activities were seldom mentioned in the paper. *(John Austin Collection)*

4... The Strange and Unsolved Death of Thelma Todd

*"The real and underlying causes of death of many
well known Hollywood figures, past and present, will
never be known because of cover ups by an oligarchical
community, police and citizens alike, protecting its
own and the millions of dollars in revenue such
causes of death, if they were really known by
the public, could be harmed...."*

— Hollywood Citizen News
October 1936

*I*t was 4:00 a.m. on Sunday morning, the 15th of December, 1935. The scene was a lonely stretch of the Pacific Coast Highway. According to the Farmer's Almanac and news stories of that Sunday, a stiff wind was blowing off the Pacific Ocean, rattling the glass windows of *Thelma Todd's Cafe and Roadside Rest* across the road. The breakers whipped on to the beach, leaving behind a white foam which shimmered in the light of the full moon in the chilly predawn hours.

A chauffeur driven Packard limousine pulled up outside the high, arch-shaped entrance to the famous beach retreat. The long, two-story building, with a three-story tower at a slight angle at the south end, abutted the corner of the highway and Positano Road. Alongside the tower was a 270-step cement stairway to the road above, which figured prominently in the death of the Ice Cream Blonde.

☆ ☆ ☆

Thelma Todd, then 29 years old and one of the screen's most famous stars of the day, stepped out of the Packard on to the pavement. She was wearing an expensive full length mink coat over a metallic blue sequined evening gown and matching cape, new blue silk slippers, and $20,000 in jewelry – $400,000 in today's market.

As Thelma got out of the limo, the cold, biting wind from the Pacific hit her. According to her driver, Ernest Peters, who always drove her to evening engagements, she drew the mink further around her shoulders and turned to him. "You don't have to walk me to the door tonight, Ernest," she stated. "And by the way, I must owe you a lot of money. Please send me a bill."

With that she walked toward the tower. Peters remained long enough to see his employer enter the mosaic tiled entrance way and disappear inside. He then made a U-turn on the deserted coast highway (then known as the Roosevelt Highway) and headed for his garage in Santa Monica.

That was the last time Thelma Todd was ever seen alive.

☆ ☆ ☆

Thelma Todd began her career as a beauty contest winner with the title "Miss Massachusetts." She was proud of this achievement but modest enough to realize that it inspired no interest in acting for her.

Thelma Todd was born in Lawrence in 1906. Her father was an important local figure, a merchant and perennial alderman. At 15, Thelma went to work in the local F.W. Woolworth, but when crowds of people, mostly young men, jammed the store merely to look at her natural beauty and hourglass figure, the manager had to fire her – regardless of the business she was bringing in to the establishment.

The Lawrence Elks Club proclaimed her "Miss Lawrence" and sponsored her in the statewide competition. She won the contest and was crowned Miss Massachusetts. Thelma was quite proud. This was the start of her show business career.

For extra spending money during her high school years, she modelled in a local theater. She also impressed the manager of a community theater troupe, so much so that he sent her picture to Jesse Lasky, the man in charge of talent for Paramount Pictures.

Lasky liked what he saw and offered Thelma a tryout.

Her studio "bios" described her as a former school teacher, but despite being elected spokesman for the freshman class at Hood Normal, a teacher's college, Thelma dropped out after one year to accept Jesse Lasky's offer to attend the Paramount Pictures training school in Astoria, Long Island.

She graduated with the class of 1926, a class which included the future husband of Mary Pickford, Charles "Buddy" Rogers. Paramount gave her a role in *The Fascinating Youth*. The studio nabobs liked the way Thelma looked in fine clothes and her forceful, intelligent looks. She appeared in thirteen silent films, easily making the transition to sound in 1927. Her voice was vibrant, cultured and she strove to improve it with voice lessons.

Her personal motto was, "While we're here, we should laugh, be gay and have fun!" And this is how she came across on screen.

Thelma Todd lived up to her philosophy and became a top Hollywood star, performing in 92 films in a nine-year period either as the star, co-star or as a featured player.

✫ ✫ ✫

Thelma's mellifluous voice was a strength, but her acting forte was her sense of humor. Thelma Todd had the rare ability to be elegant and funny at the same time.

Despite this innate ability, Thelma was still cast as the serious, sensuous ingenue on many occasions. The first was when she was contracted by director Roland West in 1930. He appreciated her more for her beauty than her sense of humor, and changed her screen name to Allison Lloyd, ". . . so that no taint of comedy would cling to her skirts." West then starred Thelma as a jaded, manipulative, pleasure-seeking debutante opposite Chester Morris in the film *Corsair*.

Before the film was finished, West and Todd had begun a tempestuous affair which was to continue sporadically until her death some five years later.

Shortly after completing *Corsair*, comedy czar Hal Roach contracted Thelma Todd to again become a comedic princess. He thought the idea of Thelma performing under a pseudonym was so silly that he half-seriously threatened to change her name to "Susie Dinkleberry . . . so that no taint of drama would cling to her skirts!"

Roach knew that the Depression era audiences wanted to laugh their troubles away, and nobody was funnier than Thelma Todd. She tickled America's funny bone in such slapstick classics as the Marx

Brothers' *Horsefeathers* and *Monkey Business*.

Demonstrating her versatility, she acted in other dramas, but this time she used her own name. It appeared up on cinema marquees next to the monikers of such classic superstars as Humphrey Bogart, Randolph Scott and Gary Cooper. Thelma Todd's serious films were received as well as her comedies, and she was a Hollywood sensation.

During the height of her career Thelma met part-time talent agent Pasquale "Pat" De Cicco. Irreverently known behind his back as "De Sicko," he used his title and connections as a front to pimp and procure women for Louis B. Mayer and other MGM executives. *

In July 1932, much to everyone's astonishment, Thelma eloped to Arizona with De Cicco. Marriage kept neither Thelma nor Pat monogamous. Thelma, who enjoyed life in the fast lane, continued her affair with Ronald West as well as conducting liaisons with Ronald Colman and band leader Abe Lyman, among others.

De Cicco used Thelma's name and reputation to his own benefit. Thanks to the help of *The Hollywood Reporter* and other fan magazines, he attracted many aspiring starlets to his talent agency. He told young actresses that he could make them stars, the way he claimed to have done for Thelma, and after making brazen promises he had his way with them on the large office couch.

The luxurious celebrity lifestyle appealed to Thelma. She liked big houses, fancy clothes, the elegant nightlife where liquor flowed like water, and fast cars. As soon as newer, speedier automobiles were released onto the market, Thelma would acquire them. Subsequently she was cited for speeding and/or driving under the influence on countless occasions.

Early in 1933 she ran into a palm tree near Nichols Canyon on Hollywood Boulevard and suffered three broken ribs, a broken collarbone and internal injuries.

From these injuries Thelma contracted peritonitis and hovered on the brink of death. The heavens were in her favor, and she eventually rallied to health. The Hal Roach Studios, to whom she was now under contract, forbade her to drive. Thelma began taking her maid, Mae Whitehead, along to drive for her, and contracted Ernest Peters as her party chauffeur.

Again in the pink of health, with a grueling acting schedule laid out before her, and a libido that demanded variety, Thelma grew tired

---

* Mayer was a loathsome (and loathed) creature. Many times he remarked to friends, actors and actresses, that "All women are whores!"

of her contractual marriage to De Cicco. They divorced in March 1934.

Her affair with Roland West continued. West claimed he wanted to break off the deteriorating relationship with Thelma for some time, but he never did, and eventually turned it into a venture to suit his own interests, and one that would inevitably take Thelma Todd's life.

☆ ☆ ☆

West was to figure prominently in Thelma's murder investigation. He was believed by many within the oligarchy to have been guilty. This opinion was held particularly by Hal Roach.

Thelma was the producer's most valuable star and her death cost his company millions, not to mention causing another scandal which the oligarchy could ill afford.

☆ ☆ ☆

The romance between Todd and West led to a business partnership. Two years before her death, West, then aged 49, his ex-wife, the actress Jewel Carmen and Thelma had gone into partnership to open *Thelma Todd's Cafe and Roadside Rest*.

As is usual with such stars, Thelma had no cash invested in the cafe; she just allowed her name to be used. For this she was a 50 percent partner. Her name was the catalyst for drawing Hollywood's elite and the wealthy "downtown" Hancock Park crowd to the coast hideaway.

West maintained a small house on Positano Road, but always slept in quarters above the cafe, quarters that were divided from Thelma's apartments by sliding doors which were always kept locked. Entrance to the living quarters was reached by a stairway from the tower entrance, and through a heavy door to which both Todd and West had keys.

☆ ☆ ☆

The evening of Saturday, December 14, 1935, was a special occasion for Thelma. The star was at the height of her career, and this evening she was the guest of honor at the Trocadero, one of

Hollywood's most celebrated nightspots. It was owned by W.R. "Billy" Wilkerson, who was the publisher and sole owner of *The Hollywood Reporter*. If Hollywood's finest did not frequent "the Troc," it would be very difficult to find their names in the pages of *The Hollywood Reporter*, its gossip column or casting pages.

The party was being given in her honor by the British comedian Stanley Lupino, his wife and daughter. A few years before, Thelma had co-starred with Lupino in a film they made in London. Lupino, visiting Tinseltown for the first time, wanted to entertain Thelma as she had entertained him in London at the conclusion of shooting.

At the party were actor Fred Keating, Grace and Gertrude Durkin and a half dozen others. Earlier in the day, Ida Lupino, Stanley's daughter, had talked to Pat De Cicco, Thelma's ex-husband. She told him about the party. DeCicco, according to Lupino in a statement to the police, said he would like to come and that he and Thelma were still good friends. Lupino said she replied, "Good. It's dress. And at 8:30."

☆ ☆ ☆

Thelma spent that afternoon prior to the Lupino party having a tooth filled and shopping at her favorite department store, Bullock's Wilshire. She purchased new blue evening slippers to match the gown she planned to wear.

When Peters arrived in the Packard to chauffeur Thelma to her party, he found her dressed to the nines. Her hair was meticulously waved, and her jewelry was much in evidence around her neck and on her wrist. After all, she was considered one of the best dressed women in Hollywood, and with the fan magazine photographers hovering around the entrance to "the Troc," she wanted to be sure she was "presentable" for the pages of the popular "fanzines" of the day.

Before she entered the car, Ronald West told her, probably in a fit of jealousy (or envy), "I'll be locking the restaurant at two o'clock . . . better be back by then."

"I'll be back five minutes after," her chauffeur recalled her reply. She told Peters to return and pick her up at 1:15 a.m. because she had an appointment at the cafe at 1:55. Peters assumed she meant she wanted to return before West locked the doors.

The party, which was meant to be a gay and happy affair, began with a very embarrassing incident. Because De Cicco said he would attend as "he and Thelma were still good friends," Ida Lupino, the ex officio hostess for her parents, reserved a seat next to Thelma's in the private dining room.

That chair remained empty throughout dinner. DeCicco was seen dancing in the main dining room with actress Margaret Lindsay, one of his clients. When Lupino reminded him that he had accepted her invitation to join the party, De Cicco supposedly told her, "It was all a joke! I never intended to come!"

Ida, at a loss, told Thelma, "I know he was serious when he spoke to me. I know it!"

Ida was furious at the snub – and the embarrassment.

Thelma reassured her that she didn't mind; that she expected it from her ex-husband whose pride (and income) had been hurt when she divorced him.

It obviously did not upset Thelma because everyone who attended the party reported that she was her usual hilarious self. Lupino later testified that Thelma had told her she was having " . . . a dynamite affair with a man from San Francisco. She said it was the most wonderful love affair she'd ever had and she hoped I could meet him very soon." Around 1:45 a.m., the time she told Peters that she must be home, Thelma excused herself from the party and went to the ladies room.

An attendant told a reporter from *The Los Angeles Examiner*, "When she came in, she was happy, smiling, like always. She made a phone call and was very secretive about it. She kept it real confidential."

The police later asked the attendant if she thought Thelma had been calling Pat De Cicco in another part of the club. "I couldn't guess who she was talking to, but after the call, she was upset. I asked her if I could get her anything. She said she was fine, but I could see she wasn't." On Thelma's return to the party, those present noticed her mood change. Theater owner Sid Grauman, also a guest, asked if he could help. "Yes," she replied, ". . . would you call Roland at the cafe and tell him I'm on my way!"

Even though Grauman made the call, Thelma remained at the party until 3:30 a.m. Her mood did not improve. Even the doorman and hat check girls at the Troc said Thelma seemed "disturbed."

Ernest Peters noticed it too. He testified that Thelma hardly said a word to him on the way home. However, some of the press quoted Peters as saying Thelma told him to "Drive faster, Ernest. I'm afraid of being kidnapped or killed." This was probably for headlines to sell papers. In truth, it was only when she arrived at the cafe that she spoke, asking Peters to send her a bill for services.

★ ★ ★

About 30 hours after Thelma walked into the mosaic archway of the cafe, she was found dead in her 1933 Lincoln Touring car.

It was a cold, but sunny, Monday morning. Thelma's housekeeper, Mae Whitehead, intended to follow her usual custom of pulling Thelma's car out of the garage of Carmen Jewel's house, Castillo del Mar, on Positano Drive and move the Lincoln to the front of the cafe for Thelma's use.

Whitehead could not believe what she found! Thelma Todd was slumped over the steering wheel of the Lincoln. The garage doors were closed, but not locked. The ignition switch, Whitehead noticed, was on. Thelma was wearing the same clothes she had on when she left for the Trocadero, the same diamond necklace, the same valuable rings on her fingers. But there was blood on her dress, her coat, and on her head and face.

At the age of 29, at the height of what promised to be a brilliant career on the screen, Thelma Todd had died. She was one of the few silent film stars whose voice suited the new sound medium of the "talkies."

Whitehead ran to her own car and drove down the hill to the cafe where she got hold of Charles Smith, the 70-year-old cafe treasurer and veteran assistant director who had served Roland West for decades.

Smith buzzed West on the intercom, who was upstairs in his apartment and apparently still asleep. Dressing quickly, West appeared in minutes, ashen-faced at the news Smith had imparted. He leaped into Mae Whitehead's Ford. In her excitement on her way back to the garage, she missed a turnoff and had to turn the car around in the narrow lane on the side of the hill.

At the garage, West rushed inside and put a hand to Todd's face. He pulled his hand back, and wiped off the blood which had adhered. He showed little sign of emotion about the death of his meal ticket.

West told Mae to get Rudolf Schaefer, his cafe manager and brother-in-law, who was living in Castillo del Mar with his sister, Carmen. By this time it was 11:15. All three agreed the police should be called as soon as possible and trooped back to the cafe. They left the garage door unlocked.

The police arrived forty-five minutes later.

At the death scene, Captain Bert Wallis, alleged to be a relative of famed producer Hal Wallis, noted there were no signs of violence. He did not notice the look of absolute astonishment on the faces of Mae Whitehead and Roland West. Somebody had moved Thelma's body.

When first seen, it was wedged between the seat and the wheel. When Wallis arrived, the corpse had fallen to the left. Roland West turned white and shook quite violently; Mae Whitehead almost fainted. Wallis put it down to shock.

There was still more than two gallons of gas in the tank, and the ignition key was "on," but the battery was dead. Thelma's beaded purse was beside her with a key to the outside door of her apartment. The key to the inside door was nowhere to be found.

Thus began one of the most bizarre chapters in Los Angeles crime history. Thelma Todd's death made headlines across the country, and the news spread throughout the world.

The local papers used her death as front page fodder for weeks. Speculation, innuendo, rumors and charges littered the headlines. The comedienne's death became Hollywood's most sensational demise to that time.

A "neat and and tidy solution" was "requested" by the oligarchy, the Hays Office and the L.A. County Sheriff. They wanted a verdict and they wanted it fast. The compelling reason was the fact that in downtown Los Angeles famed Warner Brothers choreographer Busby Berkeley was going on trial on three counts of manslaughter on the very day Thelma's body was discovered. Driving while under the influence of alchohol, Berkeley had struck another car on Roosevelt Highway, killing three people. The accident occurred just a few hundred yards north of Thelma Todd's cafe. The cinema oligarchy could not stand another high profile scandal on top of the Berkeley trial.

☆ ☆ ☆

The star's death was, therefore, the most intentionally inept probe of a suspected murder in the history of Los Angeles. Strewn about everywhere were contradictory clues.* These included conveniently "discovered" false "sightings" of Thelma all during Sunday, leads that were never followed up, suspects who were never questioned, and others who were spirited out of town by unknown "benefactors."

In fact, the investigation could have created the idea in the minds of screenplay authors Howard Koch and the Epstein brothers for that immortal line of Claude Rains in *Casablanca:* "Round up the usual suspects!"

☆ ☆ ☆

Even though the coroner determined that Thelma had been dead "around 30 hours" when her body was found, many witnesses came forward claiming to have seen and/or talked to the star all during Sunday.

Two men in a cigar store in downtown Los Angeles claimed to have recognized Thelma when she ran in and asked them to dial a telephone number for her.

Carmen Jewel, in another astounding statement under oath, swore that she had seen Thelma ". . . and a dark, swarthy man" driving down Sunset Boulevard at 11:15 a.m. Sunday morning. However, Jewel very adroitly escaped cross-examination. She fainted and was excused. By the next day, though, she had recovered sufficiently to grant Louella Parsons an "exclusive" interview confirming Roland West's testimony that he and Todd were "just friends!"

Even more astonishing, another charter member of the oligarchy, Mrs. Wallace Ford, wife of the noted actor, insisted that Thelma had telephoned to confirm an invitation to the Ford's cocktail party that afternoon – Sunday.

In a split from tradition, one grand juror told a reporter from *The Los Angeles Examiner,* "Several witnesses have not told all they

---

* In 1935, Mayor Frank Shaw ruled Los Angeles like a private piggy bank. Police corruption was so widespread that when Shaw was recalled in 1937, dozens of police officials "retired" to Mexico. In 1935, the year of Todd's death, anyone with money to spread around, such as the oligarchy, could have gotten to the Los Angeles Police Department. An LAPD Dectective Chief, Thad Brown, was told to "back off" on any arrests in the Todd case. On Brown's death, his files were seized.

know. It wasn't long before many of us began to suspect a very clever cover-up."

Added grand jury foreman George Rochester, "Some of those who appear most mute, most dumb, apparently are deliberately concealing facts. *Potent Hollywood interests have attempted to block our probe from the beginning.* I hope the witnesses understand the law of perjury."

Prosecutors were aware that all was not kosher in the hearing room. Said Deputy D.A. George Johnson, in an interview cited: "Falsehoods have been told by certain witnesses inside the grand jury hearing room. Someone is covering something up. Someone, we think, knows how Thelma Todd died. None of the facts, as we have heard them, bear out the physical evidence."

A reporter asked Rochester, "Has pressure from some influential source been brought to bear in an attempt to cover up the investigation, bring it to an end?"

"We are not stopping," he replied, noncommittally.

But the witnesses stuck to their stories. In the end, the grand jury did stop. It had no choice, no evidence for an indictment. *

District Attorney Buron J. Fitts, in concert with Sheriff Eugene Biscailuz, who had taken over the case under a little-known law that allowed the Los Angeles County Sheriff to intervene in a case occurring within its boundaries, had done their job well.

Biscailuz elected to invoke that little-known law at the urging of Joseph Schenck, co-founder of 20th Century Fox and a close friend and benefactor of Roland West. As sheriff and a deeply rooted Los Angeleno from an old California family, Biscailuz had a deep interest "in the industry." He often visited film sets with Darryl Zanuck and Joe Schenck. He made Louis B. Mayer an "Honorary Deputy Sheriff." Biscailuz also knew Roland West intimately as a 33rd Degree Mason and lodge brother. For the icing on the oligarchy's cake, insofar as a cover-up was concerned, Biscailuz was a very close, personal friend of the deputy district attorney preparing the Todd case for the grand jury.

Because of clever maneuvering behind the scenes by everyone involved from Fitts to Schenck to Biscailuz to the cops on the case, the verdict came down:

"Accidental Death from Carbon Monoxide Poisoning."

---

* District Attorney Buron J. Fitts, who was still receiving payoffs from the William Desmond Taylor "cover-up," did the bidding again for someone in the oligarchy, a major player, to shield the real culprit of Thelma's Todd's death.

The panel could have returned an indictment if there had been no cover-up by any of those involved, but money talks. They asked for, and got, "a neat and tidy solution" to Thelma Todd's death.

Yes, Hollywood is a company town!

☆ ☆ ☆

Several years before he died, we were told by one of the most powerful attorneys in the industry that Joe Schenck intervened with his friend "Gene" Biscailuz and Buron J. Fitts over the verdict in Thelma Todd's death.

From information that has been collected over the years it has been deduced that the following is the chain of events which led to Thelma's death:

It will be recalled that when Thelma left for the party at the Trocadero, West admonished her that he would be "locking the restaurant at two o'clock . . . better be back by then."

It would have been in character for Thelma to tell West that she would ". . . come and go as she pleased," as she did. When Todd asked Sid Grauman to call West around 2:30 a.m. to tell him she was on her way, in a jealous fit, West could have gone into Thelma's apartment and locked her out. He wanted to teach Thelma a lesson as he had done, according to their friends, several times before. This would have been in character for West.

Thelma only had a key to the OUTSIDE door to her apartment and would have to get West to open the inside door. So when Thelma was dropped off by Ernest Peters at 4 a.m., she requested not to be escorted upstairs because she was afraid there would be a scene, as there had been many times before under similar circumstances.

Thelma probably shouted at West through the door, demanding he let her in. Then they had another argument. West, in a jealous rage, could have told Thelma he didn't want her going to so many parties. Todd, still a bit drunk, screamed that she'd go to any "damn party I choose."

She probably told West that she had been invited to one later that day (Sunday) at the Ford's, and that she would be going.

It was then that Thelma, not knowing what else to do, trudged up the 270 steps to the garage to sleep in her car or to drive to her mother's house in Hollywood. (Her mother later claimed that her daughter had a weak heart and ". . . couldn't possibly have climbed all thoses stairs without fainting!")

West obviously followed Thelma. It is the only scenario which fits all the facts.

When he reached the garage, Thelma was already in her car and the engine had been started. The garage doors were open. West, noting the situation, closed the door but did not lock it. He obviously knew nothing about the almost immediate effects of carbon monoxide poisoning, or he wanted her death to look like a suicide. He then returned to the cafe and went to bed.

When Thelma didn't show up on Sunday – and West (probably) knew she wouldn't – it is probable that he returned to the garage and found her dead. Not knowing what to do, he probably telephoned Joe Schenck for advice.

All that Sunday, when people called for Thelma, they were told by West that he did not know where she was; perhaps she was with her mother in Hollywood. It would have been typical of West, if he hadn't really known where she was, to be calling everyone Thelma knew trying to locate her.

☆ ☆ ☆

Upon examination of Thelma's body, which had been well-preserved during the cold night, the medical examiner pronounced that the probable time of death was thirty hours prior to the inspection. The police were undoubtedly aware of West's culpability in Thelma Todd's death.

It was also suggested that Charles "Lucky" Luciano, who had been pressuring Thelma to let him open a gambling casino on the third floor of the cafe, was somehow involved in her death. This was ruled out by the LAPD and the sheriff's department, as a gangland hit would have been far more decisive than death by carbon monoxide, and there was the possibility that it would not do the job.

From many, many years of experience in how these things work in Baghdad-By-The-Sea, we are certain that a handful of Hollywood insiders, in concert with a very corrupt district attorney and a "cooperative sheriff," maintained a conspiracy of silence over Thelma Todd's death for many years after.

The architect of that silence?

Joseph P. Schenck, the multimillionaire co-founder of 20th Century Fox (with Darryl F. Zanuck).

Joe Schenck had a great concern for the oligarchy of which he was one of the charter members. Most probably, he wanted to keep his lifelong friend (West) away from a prison sentence for Thelma Todd's death.

The reason?

According to accounts of Joe Schenck's trial for tax evasion and fraud in 1941 (which included charges of a great deal of unreported income by Schenck over a period of several years), there was one outlandish "business deduction" taken by Schenck and/or his "creative accountants," as well as a stock sale fraud.

Joe Schenck controlled Baja California's lucrative gambling business, including the race track at Agua Caliente, a favorite weekend hangout for the Hollywood crowd. But a new president of Mexico had recently outlawed gaming because of the temptation to Mexico's dirt poor population to indulge what little money they did have on gambling activities.

Joseph Schenck eventually spread enough pesos around Mexico City and Baja to come to "an agreement with the new government." Meanwhile, in his old friend Roland West he had found a way to recoup his "bribery losses."

As West testified at Schenck's trial, Schenck "sold" him approximately $400,000 in racetrack stock for $50,000.

Then Schenck took a tax "loss" of more than $350,000, though he never actually transferred the shares to West.

The deal was structured so that Schenck had his company, Fox, "loan" West the $50,000. West gave Schenck a check, and then Schenck reimbursed West under the table in cash. He would then pay off the Fox "loan" with the cash.

According to testimony at Schenck's trial in federal court, West paid the second installment and was secretly reimbursed on December 17, 1935, the day after Todd's body was found in his garage.

☆ ☆ ☆

No one was ever indicted or accused of Thelma Todd's death – at least openly. Any attempt to dig into the case by journalists in the intervening years was met by stony silence for as long as Schenck and his cronies were alive.

Thelma's producer, Hal Roach, the one who probably best knew the circumstances surrounding her death denied *any knowledge of a connection between Roland West and Joseph P. Schenck – even though that relationship is a matter of public record from the trial of Schenck for tax fraud.*

Biscailuz, with a little help from his friends in the industry –
money and hype – kept getting re-elected from 1936 until he retired
in 1958. He chose his successor, Peter Pitchess, who in turn anointed
with holy sheriff's water his successor, Sherman Block. Oh, the
incestuous relationships of the oligarchy and Civil Service!

☆ ☆ ☆

Despite the verdict of an accidental death, no one ever bothered
to clarify all of the contradicting information:

✦ Despite the statement of a police captain on the investigation that the soles of Thelma's new evening slippers
were "scuffed" to commensurate with a climb up 270
cement steps, the press reported that the slippers
showed no signs of wear.

✦ Did Carmen Jewel really "see" Thelma driving on Sunset Boulevard that Sunday morning with a "swarthy"
man? It must be remembered that Carmen had more to
gain by keeping West OUT of jail because of their
impending divorce and alimony.

✦ It could also have been Carmen Jewel, imitating Thelma,
who really called Mrs. Wallace Ford that Sunday to
r.s.v.p. Carmen Jewel was an actress and could easily
have passed for Thelma on the "scratchy" and unreliable
telephones of the era.

✦ How could Thelma Todd have been seen at a cigar store
Sunday morning if she was dead? It would have been
an easy matter for the district attorney's office to "con-
vince" the store owner to "testify" that Thelma asked
him to make a telephone call for her that Sunday
morning. The cigar store was not far from the DA's office
and was frequented by employees of City Hall for the
occasional wager.

✦ It is highly doubtful that Luciano would order a "hit"
on Thelma Todd. The "take" from a gambling casino in

the cafe would have been infinitesimal compared to the shakedowns "the Mob" was extracting from the industry in other, more subtle ways.

☆ ☆ ☆

The official verdict of the coroner's report came as close as it could to calling Thelma Todd's death murder. But in the final analysis those behind the scenes had engineered the verdict they wanted, "The Neat and Tidy Solution!"

"Thelma Todd, the decedent, died by asphyxiation, perhaps intentionally. The cause of death: carbon monoxide poisoning."

The finding further stated:

"The Decedent, *finding herself locked out of her apartment*, climbed the 270 steps of the outside stair case from the cafe to the garage where Decedent garaged her automobile. Decedent huddled in the front seat of the vehicle and started the engine and was asphyxiated by the carbon monoxide fumes."

This was the verdict that the doyens of the industry, behind the scenes, had demanded – and whatever payoffs were necessary to accomplish it were made.

The attitude was, "Let's face it, boys. Thelma Todd is dead and nothing is going to bring her back. There are plenty of dames out there to replace her."

The official, tidy result of the "investigation" of Thelma Todd's death, accidental or otherwise, and no matter how ludicrous to those who had studied the facts, put an end to the speculation about murder.

It got the "Thelma Todd Problem" off the front pages and with a minimum of fuss. Bank accounts "down town" became a little fatter, and some new cars rolled out of several show rooms. The case was closed.

We repeat the statement of Ezra Goodman from his book of many years ago, *The 50 Year Decline and Fall of Hollywood*. It is very apropos to the Thelma Todd murder:

> They [Hollywood's Founding Moguls]
> preached of the good, noble and beautiful,
> and they themselves fostered in their lives
> and works the evil, the ignoble, the ugly. . .

☆ ☆ ☆

One final twist to the unsolved mystery of Thelma Todd's death is that West, obviously wishing to cleanse his soul of his sordid past, "confessed" to accidentally killing Thelma to his old friend, actor Chester Morris, when on his death bed in a Santa Monica hospital. The actor, who starred in West's most famous film, *Corsair*, confided this to several other people, one of whom told us several years ago when we were digging into the case.

☆ ☆ ☆

Roland West died in 1951, almost ten years to the day before Joe Schenck's death in Beverly Hills. Roland West, director of the brilliant silent films such as *The Bat Whispers* and *The Monsters*, was punished for his actions by the oligarchy by never being allowed to direct or produce another picture. That was his sentence for taking the life of Thelma Todd, one of the brightest stars of the screen in one of the most famous of all of Hollywood's Unsolved Mysteries.

Roland West, the director and partner in the cafe, and Thelma's sometime lover, discussing her death with R.H. W. Schafer, the manager and accountant of Thelma Todd's Roadside Rest. They are waiting to testify at the corner's inquest, rigged before it even got started. *(John Austin Collection)*

Carol Wayne, "The Matinee Lady" of Johnny Carson's *Tonight Show*. Carol made over 100 appearances with Carson, and in several films in which she had a bit part. Her death, to the Mexican police, is believed to have been murder and they would like to question Carol's companion on the trip, Edward Durston, the same man who was with Diane Linkletter when she leaped to her death from a sixth floor window several years before Wayne's death. (*Marvin Paige's Motion Picture & TV Research Service*)

"We Lost a Very Valuable
Show Business Asset . . ."

Carol Wayne (R) with actress Donna Penterotto on the NBC *Comedy Theater.* **There are very few pictures of Wayne's professional appearances available. She did a** *Playboy* **layout one year before her death.** *(Marvin Paige's Motion Picture & TV Research Service)*

5... Carol Wayne: "The Matinee Lady" and Her Mysterious Death

"Carol Wayne's death is unsolved, certainly. But I don't think it was a drowning. A drowning, yes, of course, but there's more to it than that..."

– William LaCoque
U.S. Consular Official
Manzanillo, Mexico,
June 1990

*B*uxom blonde actress Carol Wayne was bankrupt and hooked on cocaine and booze when she jetted off to Mexico in January 1985, to get away from her woes and attempt to "dry out."

Accompanying Wayne was a Los Angeles used car salesman, a mysterious figure named Edward Durston. It was Durston who was with another aspiring actress the night of October 4, 1969, when she either jumped or fell from a sixth floor apartment window near the Sunset Strip.

The mysterious circumstances surrounding Carol Wayne's shocking death at the end of that "Get-Away-From-It-All, I'll-Have-A-Last-Fling" vacation, pointed out the probability of murder to Mexican officials investigating the death.

The fully clothed but horribly bloated body of Carol Wayne was found floating in sun drenched Santiago Bay at Manzanillo on January 13, 1985. Fisherman Abel de Dios was casting a net from his wooden fishing boat about 300 yards out in the bay when he spotted the body floating no more than twenty feet away. When the body was brought ashore in a police launch and identified as that of Carol Wayne by employees of the Las Hadas resort, Edward Durston, with whom she had checked in earlier in the week, could not be located. A few hours later it was discovered he had left for Los Angeles two days before Wayne's body was discovered. Strangely, he deposited her luggage at the airport, saying she would "pick it up in the morning!"

★ ★ ★

When *The Tonight Show* starring Johnny Carson was a 90-minute affair five nights a week, one of the more popular sketches was *"The Tea Time Movie"* with the lecherous Art Fern (Carson) and his assistant, *"The Matinee Lady."* The lady with the bounteous chest and a drop dead figure was Carol Wayne.

When 30 minutes of the most successful show on late night television was eliminated (at Carson's request), the skit had to go.

With its demise Carol Wayne lost a lucrative income as the foil of Johnny Carson.

Some say that many times she was more than just a foil to Carson. In fact, people on and off the show noticed that Carol and Johnny hit it off so well onstage that it was only logical they'd get together offstage.

In a 1984 *Playboy* layout and interview Carol explained, "There was always bad timing." She, like Carson, had been married and divorced three times.

"We were never not together when we were apart," she said. Translated, that meant, "We were never between spouses at the same time." Maybe it was the best timing.

In that same interview one year before she was found dead in Manzanillo, Wayne got both mystical and misty about Johnny Carson. "He loves me," she said at the time. "I love him. It's an understanding, a given. He still sees me every day in his dreams. When he shuts his eyes, what does he see? Me!"

Carson, himself, never voiced his feelings toward Carol Wayne – at least not publicly – at any time.

What Carol Wayne really meant was never made clear; perhaps it was her fantasy, part of the Carol Wayne act that enhanced all her public appearances and interviews – which were delivered in her unusual, squeaky, dumb blonde voice. It was that voice which made her the master of the double entendre. If Carol Wayne asked somebody if they would like a cup of coffee, it sounded as if she was asking them to go to bed with her. Carol Wayne's forte was her ability to make innocent statements seem suggestive.

She was one of a kind and Hollywood lost a good one when she was drowned – either accidentally or on purpose in the bay at Manzanillo.

☆ ☆ ☆

Carol Wayne became a very familiar face to late night television addicts through more than 100 appearances on *The Tonight Show* – a record, apart from Carson and the other regulars – for any performer.

Said Pat McCormick, a long time writer for Carson and *The Tonight Show*, "I met Carol when she first came on the show at the request of Johnny and became his sidekick on *"The Tea Time Movie"* skit.

"Johnny did tons of shows with Carol, and Johnny Carson would not work with anyone who is not a professional. When he enjoys working with somebody, the whole country enjoys them. Johnny had a good time with Carol," said McCormick ambiguously when he was once asked about her relationship with Carson.

Carol Wayne was a favorite with all the legends of show business. Somehow in a town where sexy and overly built starlets are a dime a dozen, or a hundred dollars a a night, Carol Wayne managed to become everyone's first choice.

Thanks to a figure that could turn even the head of Hugh Hefner – and did – she decided to bare all for *Playboy* in February 1984.

By then she had been divorced three times, on the verge of bankruptcy and, some say, dependent on drugs and alcohol to get her through the days and long nights with no work of a regular nature.

The bubbly, happy Carol Wayne of *"The Tea Time Movie"* was a far cry from the emotional wreck she had become since losing the regular appearances she enjoyed with Carson. The *Playboy* interview reveals her vulnerability.

☆ ☆ ☆

Friends and acquaintances say her heavy cocaine habit had grown even heavier until her departure for Manzanillo and the exclusive and very expensive Las Hadas Resort. Her alcohol intake also increased daily.

With the cocaine chewing up her bank account, she was forced to declare bankruptcy on December 13, 1984, just three weeks before she went on that fateful vacation which was to claim her life. On the bankruptcy petition she listed her income at the time as "$000.00."

Insiders told us at the time of her death that Richard Pryor had offered her a part in his next movie. But the offer was contingent upon Carol checking into a booze and drug rehabilitation center. It was said that Pryor would also guarantee the cost.

Instead, Carol Wayne tried to take an easier way out: she attempted to dry out in Mexico. On January 4, 1985 she and Edward Durston flew to Manzanillo and checked into the Las Hadas complex.

☆ ☆ ☆

Insofar as her squeaky voice was concerned, Carol told us prior to an appearance on *The Tonight Show*, that her whole family had the same voice.

"My sister, Nina, with this voice – is a telephone operator; in fact, almost a supervisor. If you ask for help at the telephone company, you might get my sister on the other end."

Nina, who was 12 months and 12 days younger than the 42-year-old Carol (her age when found dead), was also in show business, appearing in the very forgettable *Camp Runamuck* TV series. The two sisters were raised as virtual twins by their parents – particularly their ambitious mother – and sentenced to a life as performers, due to her ardor for their success.

During a polio scare many years before her death, Mrs. Wayne thought no polio germs could live in an ice rink. "Such logic," laughed Carol, resulted in years of ice skating lessons. "Our grandmother made all of our clothes. We were never in fashion. We were Chinese one year, Pilgrims another, Japanese the following year. We did shadow skating, and because we were tall and had long legs and stupid ponytails, we were offered a professional contract when we were 15 and 16. Yes," she sighed, ". . . neither of us finished high school. Yes," she repeated, ". . . zip education!"

For three years the "nerd" Wayne sisters – Carol's expression for them – did their 42-city tour with the Ice Capades – that is, until Carol's big accident.

Exhibiting a five-inch scar on her knee, Carol explained, "Sometimes, people would unconsciously, or perhaps on purpose, throw pennies that would stick on the ice and make you fall down. It was," she laughed, ". . . a very unforgiving sport. When your blades hit something that wasn't meant to be, you crashed . . . " Like Carol did.

Carol later returned to the Ice Capades to finish the tour, but it was the end of the Wayne Sisters skating career. "When you train for something so young and become good at it as we did, you never know if that's what you were meant to do in the scheme of things of life, or if it was just because it was someone else's idea. We missed a childhood of growing up, dating, junior and senior proms and all those goodies," she observed solemnly.

Following the ice skating caper, the girls found jobs in Las Vegas with the Folies-Bergere. "We were two pretty girls with no education. There was nothing else to do, "she lamented. Although there were probably very few polio germs backstage at the Tropicana, their mother was not necessarily pleased. "Girls," she complained, ". . . could you ask them for a couple more feathers?"

☆ ☆ ☆

On their days off from the Tropicana, Nina and Carol would always head for Los Angeles, a six-hour drive. "Nina and I would always go to L.A. when we got off, so to speak," she explained with another "Wayneism" or double entendre.

"One time I went to a party and a man said to me, 'We're looking for a girl just like you.' I thought, 'Sure they are.' He told me to meet him at Desilu Studios in the morning. And I did, just for a lark. They gave me a screen test and I got the part. And I got all my parts ever since then," she laughed, looking down at her ample chest.

☆ ☆ ☆

It was while she was working in Las Vegas that Carol Wayne met husband Number 1. Less than a year after the wedding, they split. She remarked at the time of her divorce that ". . . skating taught me to be limber, but that marriage really taught me how to be flexible". A typical, cryptic "Waynese" remark.

Carol married for the second time in Hollywood. On this occasion the lucky man was rock artist and photographer Bary Feinstein. When they met, Feinstein was married to Mary Travers of Peter, Paul and Mary. Following their wedding, Carol always referred to the trio following the wedding as Peter, Paul and Scary.

It was with Feinstein that Carol Wayne had her one and only child, a son, Alex. Carol found herself dividing her time between Alex and the music world her husband inhabited as an album designer and concert photographer.

It all went bust after seven years. "The Frey boots, the Levi's – I couldn't stand the whole New York cowboy thing anymore."

It was then that Feinstein became, in Carol's words, "my second to last ex-husband."

Carol Wayne's third and last marriage ended in divorce in 1980. Her husband was Burt Sugarman, * producer of the long-running *The Midnight Special*.

It was following her divorce from Sugarman that Carol Wayne started on the long, slow ride to her death in Manzanillo. Oh, she worked several bit parts in movies – among them the forgettable *Savannah Smiles* which, when last heard from, was playing 30,000 feet in the air on Pakistani Airlines or Air Burma 747s.

Carol then spent most of her time being corrupted by her 14-year-old son, Alex. In 1984 Alex was attending Beverly Hills High School where, she remarked, "The kids all know how to spell Omega but not cat. They all know the year of your Rolls Royce but not that two dimes and a nickel make a quarter."

Carol also, at the urging of Alex's "corrupting influence," took up smoking, but not the type of cigarette manufactured in Durham, North Carolina.

At irregular intervals, Carol Wayne used to pull out a clove cigarette, the aroma of which was strong enough to get them banned from practically every restaurant in Los Angeles. Alex told her the cigarettes would give her ". . . a big head rush."

Little did she realize, but Carol Wayne was on the way to finding even better "head rushes" that would lead to her final destruction – a cocaine and alcohol habit.

☆ ☆ ☆

While they were at the Las Hadas, hotel employees told us that Carol and Durston appeared to be having fun, dancing and drinking. Drinking was the reason Carol Wayne was at the resort – to overcome the habit. Durston was a bad influence. "She certainly didn't seem suicidal at all – just the opposite. She was full of life," said the hotel guest relations director, Hans Rothliesberger.

On January 10, the day they were due to leave, the couple missed

---

* Sugarman married Entertainment Tonight co-anchor Mary Hart in 1989. He is still a low profile producer of TV and feature films.

their 7 p.m. flight. They did not have enough money, or credit cards, with which to check back into the Las Hadas. Besides, their room had already been assigned to another guest and the hotel was full. According to Rothliesberger, the staff found them a room at a cheaper hotel on the bay, the Playa de Santiago.

When they arrived at the hotel at 8:30 p.m., Carol refused to get out of the taxi. She and Durston got into a furious argument, according to hotel manager Gabriel Torres.

"She screamed at Durston, 'Why have you brought me to a dump like this?'" Torres recalled several days following the discovery of her body.

"It's only for one night," Durston explained to her.

"Finally, she told the bellboy to take their luggage up to the room. But she still refused to join Mr. Durston, so he followed the bell-boy, leaving Miss Wayne behind in the street," vividly recalled the hotel manager.

"A few minutes later Mr. Durston and the bellboy came back downstairs – and found that the 'blonde lady' had disappeared."

The police later learned that Carol Wayne had walked toward the beach. Durston went into the hotel bar, but left soon afterward. He returned, according to the hotel staff, at 2:30 a.m., and again the next morning, asking if Carol had shown up. Durston, who was told she had not, had checked into another hotel. Durston flew back to Los Angeles that afternoon, taking his and Carol Wayne's bags to the airport. He told the airline she would ". . . pick them up in the morning." A rather strange statement when he said he had not seen her and had been asking the hotel employees if she had returned.

- ◆ Why did Durston show such a lack of concern about Carol Wayne's whereabouts? And why did he check into another hotel when his baggage was at the Playa de Santiago?

- ◆ Why did Durston not search for Carol on the beach after he was told she had walked in that direction? Instead, why did he go into the hotel bar as though nothing had happened, and then leave?

- ◆ What was he doing from 9 p.m. until he returned to the Playa at 2:30 a.m.?

- ◆ Why did he check out of the hotel without her, and,

more importantly, why did he not make inquiries at the airport to see if Carol had left on earlier flight? Or, why did Durston, at the very least, not file a missing persons report with the local police?

No missing persons report was ever filed nor any of these questions answered. Once Durston was out of Mexican jurisdiction he could not be questioned by the local police. But why the latter never asked the Los Angeles Police Department to question Durston was never explained.

Following discovery of Carol Wayne's body, District Attorney Jorge Hernandez of Manzanillo said, "There are many questions. The case certainly will not be closed until they are answered satisfactorily."

Manzanillo Police Chief Rafael Blanco stated: "I cannot rule out murder. There are too many things to be suspicious of at this stage of the investigation."

The two important questions Chief Blanco would liked to have asked Durston are obvious:

> "Why did he leave Manzanillo so suddenly? He left for Los Angeles while he knew Miss Wayne was still missing. I find that very strange."

> "I also find it very strange that he did not contact us since Miss Wayne's body was found. We did not hear from him at all and he must have heard about her death in Los Angeles."

Further questions were asked by District Attorney Hernandez:

> "We know that Mr. Durston and Miss Wayne quarreled and that they had some money problems at Las Hadas. It is very expensive and they didn't have enough money to check back in after they missed their flight, and the hotel was full besides.

> "But I – we – do not know what they

quarreled about, nor does anyone else who saw them.

"And another question that remains un-answered is, why did Mr. Durston take Miss Wayne's luggage to the airport before he left?

"It would be more logical for him to leave it at the hotel in case she returned. There were a lot of, er, shall I say, personal items a lady needs for everyday use in the luggage we picked up at the airport."

Hernandez again stressed that Carol Wayne's body was fully clothed when it was discovered in the bay. "This arouses my suspicions, immediate suspicions, about the nature of the death.

"Even if she was upset and unhappy, I do not think it likely," continued Hernandez, "that she would kill herself by drowning. In my experience, it's a method that's rarely used, even by the most deranged or unbalanced person."

★ ★ ★

In an autopsy it was estimated that Carol Wayne had been dead about 36 to 48 hours when she was discovered. The authorities could not understand how she drowned.

Initial tests found no traces of alcohol or drugs in her blood, and the waters of Santiago Bay are gentle. Near the beach the bay is so shallow that Carol Wayne would have had to wade out 250 to 300 feet just to reach water four feet deep.

There were, said deputy district attorney Arturo Leal, two outcroppings of rocks on the beach but he ruled out an accidental fall because there were no signs of cuts or bruises anywhere on Carol Wayne's body.

◆ How did Carol Wayne drown in such shallow water? As the district attorney stated earlier, seldom does any-one commit suicide by drowning unless they are unbal-anced or deranged and Carol Wayne certainly did not fit that category.

◆ Because no drugs or alcohol were found in her blood,

perhaps Carol Wayne had accomplished the purpose of the getaway from it all vacation – she had "dried out" from alcohol and had ingested no drugs for at least a week.

A representative of the American Consulate, William LaCoque, investigated Carol Wayne's death for the family.

"My investigation was to reveal that she had been a heavy user of drugs. It also revealed that she and Durston had a hot and heavy argument at the Playa de Santiago Hotel and she had taken off from that location and was never seen again.

"She didn't like the accomodations, I guess, even though she did not see the room reserved for them. She was mad at everything.

"I did some checking and found out that her boyfriend had also checked out of the hotel and did not spend the night there. He checked himself into another, smaller hotel while she was still missing. He returned the following evening – the day he left – to *check them both out of the Hotel Playa!*

"He took her luggage to the airport with him and told the airline clerks 'she will pick it up in the morning.'

"With that," said LaCoque, ". . . Durston took off for Los Angeles. I understand he never even bothered to file a missing persons report with the local police. This would have been the correct thing to do."

On reopening their files in 1990, the official conclusion of the Manzanillo police was that it was an "Accidental Death" for want of any other evidence to the contrary.

◆ The police state that Carol Wayne's body showed no sign of physical violence.

◆ There was no evidence that it was a homicide although the situation was "unusual."

◆ Could Carol Wayne have had her head held under water until her lungs were full and she drowned?

◆ The Manzanillo Police studiously avoided that question in their report.

◆ The best theory the police could come up with is that,

after leaving the Hotel Playa, she went walking along some slippery rocks and accidentally fell into the water.

How could Carol Wayne, who could not swim and never liked to be near water, drown in a calm, shallow bay? This was a tragically ironic demise, especially considering the clichéd joke she inspired around *The Tonight Show*, "With that chest, this lady will never drown!"

Unfortunately, she did.

However, in the police summation, the possible cause of Carol Wayne's death – slipping off some rocks and into the bay – they (conveniently) overlooked the fact that there were no bruises or other marks of a fall on Carol's body when it was discovered.

If she had "slipped or fallen" off those rocks, surely there would have been some bruises somewhere on her body as she went down?

Said Manzanillo Police investigator Arturo Reyes early in 1990, "The investigation into Carol Wayne's death is still open, and we regularly review the case.

> "Unfortunately, the man we would most like to question, Mr. Durson, will probably never return to Manzanillo so that we may ask him several questions to help clear up the case."

Another Hollywood-connected Unsolved Mystery?
Definitely.

The American Consulate official who investigated the case thoroughly agrees:

> "Unsolved, certainly. But I don't think it was a drowning. A drowning yes, of course, but there's more to it than that!"

> The official would not elaborate on that statement.

Pat McCormick, who wrote most of her lines as "The Matinee Lady" on *The Tonight Show*, lamented:

"Carol Wayne stood out as an original.
I think we lost one. We lost a very valuable
[show business] asset."

That may be the case but, in any event, Carol Wayne's death will be just another of Hollywood's Unsolved Mysteries of which no solution – no definitive and positive solution at the very least – will ever be found.

☆ ☆ ☆

Just who is Edward Durston and what is his background? This is a question asked many times in the past few years by the friends of Carol Wayne and the Manzanillo police.

☆ ☆ ☆

In October 1969, 20-year-old Diane Linkletter, daughter of famed TV host and advertising pitchman Art Linkletter – *Kids Say the Darndest Things!* – leaped, fell, or somehow slipped to her death from a sixth floor window of her apartment. Reports state there was LSD in her system.

"It wasn't suicide," said her father at a Sunday press conference following his aspiring-actress daughter's death. "She was not herself. She was murdered by the people who manufacture and distribute LSD."

Diane Linkletter was found on the sidewalk in front of the Shoreham Towers apartments in West Hollywood at 9 a.m. Saturday morning, October 4, 1969. The police said, ". . . a young man who was with her grabbed for her as she lunged through a casement window."

That young man was Edward Durston. Diane Linkletter, 20, an aspiring actress/model died at County-USC Medical Center following a stop at Hollywood Receiving Hospital. The doctors there said she was too badly hurt and needed more help than they could give her.

Durston said he was "too late" to help her. Edward Durston was, apparently, also too late to help Carol Wayne 16 years later in Manzanillo, Mexico.

He told sheriff's lieutenant Norm Hamilton, since retired, that Diane had called him Friday night at his apartment. Durston lived a block away from Shoreham Towers on Horn Ave., just off the Sunset

Strip. He told Lt. Hamilton, "She was very upset."

After talking to Durston, then a used car salesman who hung around on the fringes of show business, Hamilton said he was convinced that Diane Linkletter had been ". . . in a despondent, emotional state" and that she was ". . . concerned with her identity, her career." She also complained that she ". . . could not be her own person."

Durston also told sheriff's deputies that she had made cookies after he arrived at her apartment – about 3 a.m. – and that they had sat up the rest of the night "talking."

Durston later related that at 9 a.m. Diane went into her kitchen and did not return. Minutes later she was found below her kitchen window.

A discrepancy. Earlier, police had told the press that Durston ". . . made a grab for her, grabbed the belt of her dress just as she went out the window."

Lt. Hamilton pointed out that Diane Linkletter had to stand on an object – what, he didn't say – in order to reach the sill, and plunge 65 feet to the sidewalk below.

Durston, on further questioning, described Diane Linkletter as ". . . despondent and very emotional." He added that she was very concerned about her condition.

At the conclusion of his investigation, Hamilton stated, "We believe we have heard a true story from the witness and we also believe we have a good idea of her condition before the incident."

Nothing – at least publicly – had been heard about Edward Durston until Carol Wayne's body was found floating in the bay at Manzanillo.

Carole with Dennis O'Keefe in a scene from "Topper Returns" for Hal Roach and United Artists. *(Marvin Paige's Motion Picture & TV Research Service)*

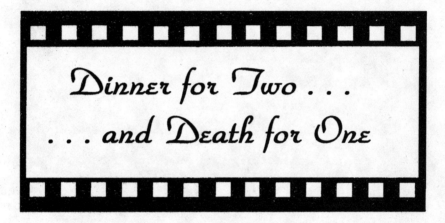

Dinner for Two . . .
. . . and Death for One

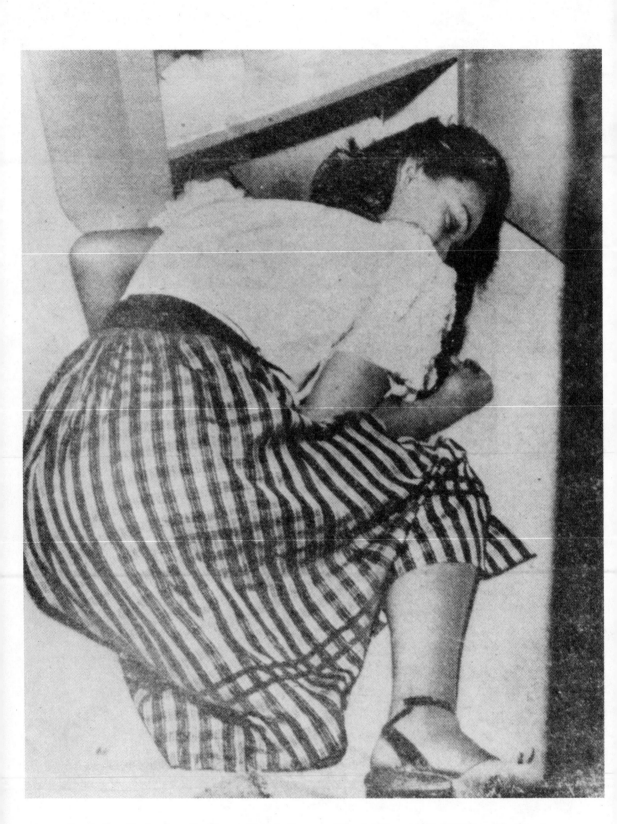

Carole Landis dead on the floor of her bathroom. Her clothing contradicts Rex Harrison's "recollection" in his autobiography when he claimed that he discovered her body ". . . clad in a housecoat." *(Marvin Paige's Mot. Pict. & TV Research Svc.)*

6... The Tragic Death of Carole Landis

"You fight so hard and then what have you got to face?
You begin to worry about being washed up. You get
bitter and disillusioned. You fear the future because
there's only one way to go and that's down..."

– Carole Landis
April 1948

The death by "natural causes," so to speak, of Sir Rex Harrison at the age of 82 in June 1990 recalled for us the time we covered, as the correspondent for a London newspaper, the not so natural death of the beautiful 31-year-old film star, Carole Landis. Even though he was to deny it later, Harrison was deeply involved with Carole, in fact up to the very night of her death.

It was a sad drive to Carole's home on Capri Drive in Pacific Palisades that sunny late Monday afternoon of July 5, 1948.

Sad, because Carole Landis was the same vivacious blonde we had known so well in London and Algiers during World War II while we were attached to SHAEF in Special Services for the Air Force. We had several lunches and dinners together in the wartime capital at the Duke Street (U.S.) Officer's Club on the days or evenings that Carole and her troupe of Kay Francis, Mitzi Mayfair and Martha Raye were not performing at some base of the 8th Air Force, or an Army encampment "somewhere in England," as the old saying went.

Carole was in England in a show sponsored by the USO and was later to write about her experiences in England, North Africa and the

South Pacific called Four Jills in a Jeep. This was later filmed under the same title with the original "Four Jills" plus Betty Grable and Alice Faye at 20th Century Fox.

☆ ☆ ☆

On the afternoon of Sunday, July 4, 1948 the 31-year-old Landis gave a swimming party for a number of close friends at her Capri Drive home just a block or two from the fashionable Riviera Country Club. Carole was, her guests were to say later, in high spirits, swimming, laughing, and entertaining as if she did not have a care in the world. If only they had known!

◆ Just the opposite was true as those same friends were to find out in the days and weeks to follow.

After the last of her guests had left at around six p.m. on the bright, sunny afternoon, Carole Landis went up to her large and well furnished bedroom to change. She had a dinner date that evening with Harrison in her home – one of many cozy dinners they had shared together in the Capri Drive house over the past months while Harrison was busy filming *The Foxes of Harrow* for Darryl F. Zanuck at 20th Century Fox, just a short drive from Pacific Palisades.

Landis donned a white silk blouse, flaring black and white checked skirt, golden sandals, but no stockings. *

It was to be a dinner alone for Harrison and Carole, for Sunday was Fannie Mae Bolden's day off, Carole's live-in maid for the past several weeks.

It was also to be the last dinner on earth for Carole Landis and, it was said later, Rex Harrison had a lot to do with her demise at such an early age.

☆ ☆ ☆

She was pretty. She was blonde and they said later that she was doomed from the start. Her real name was Frances Lillian Mary Ridste of Polish stock from Wisconsin. Her father had abandoned the family

---

* To illustrate the callousness of Rex Harrison, many years after her death in his autobiography, *Rex*, he described a completely different outfit. He wrote: "I saw Carole lying on the floor in a housecoat!" This, despite the fact that the three local newspapers ran pictures of Carole as she lay on the bathroom floor which distinctly showed the black and white skirt, blouse and sandals.

when she was a youngster, and her mother moved her brood to San Diego, California, and later to San Bernardino, 60 miles west of Los Angeles on the old Route 66.

She later changed her name to Carole Landis after her favorite star, Carole Lombard. The Landis, it was said, was her mother's maiden name.

Carole had to learn the hard way, unfortunately, that happiness does not necessarily accompany stardom – a lesson which has been learned by so many Hollywood stars – both male and female.

While attending San Bernardino High School, she realized that in order to pursue her lifelong ambition of becoming an actress, she would have to start somewhere else other than San Bernardino – and not necessarily in Hollywood. She had to have some experience before attempting to crash the studio gates. Local beauty contests were a start.

She quit school and with what money she had saved from odd jobs, headed for San Francisco. Her start was at the Royal Hawaiian Cafe as a hula dancer – a job she bluffed her way into, lying about her age, 15. But the confidence she experienced there was enough to get her started. Eventually, she joined the big band of Carl Ravazza at the Rio Del Mar Country Club south of San Francisco as a singer.

But Carole Landis never lost sight of Hollywood as her goal. After saving $100 – a goodly sum in those days of seven cent bread and milk at five cents a quart – she knocked on filmland's door. It opened, but very slowly.

On January 24, 1934, at the age of 16, Carole met and married actor/ writer Irving Wheeler, then 19. Finally, whether through Wheeler or not is unknown, she got a break. Busby Berkeley was casting dancers for a Warner Bros. film, *Varsity Show*, and she was picked by Berkeley, who knew her husband, as an extra in the film.

When the female star refused to dance solo, Carole got the assignment. It was also rumored – then and later – that off-stage Carole Landis, in spite of being married, was bestowing her favors upon Berkeley. Wheeler later sued the famed choreographer for alienation of affections, a very common law suit in those days until it was outlawed.

Wheeler asked for $250,000 but lost the case and Carole won her divorce and a contract at $50 per week from Warner Bros.

She was featured in *Blondes at Work* with Glenda Farrell, and in *Hollywood Hotel*. Many more pictures were to follow for Warner Bros., Republic and several independents. It was also said that Berkeley asked Carole to marry him.

Following the role of the ingenue in a Shubert musical on Broadway, Carole's only commercial venture on the stage, Hal Roach signed her for *One Million B.C.* * with Victor Mature and wrapped her in a loincloth. This was followed by a featured role in *Topper Returns*, also for Roach.

Then came a big break for Carole. She signed a contract with 20th Century-Fox through the auspices of famed studio head, Darryl F. Zanuck.

It was then that the rumors and accusations began in the drawing rooms, country clubs and watering holes.

Her films at Fox included *Moon Over Miami, Dance Hall, Hot Spot,* and *Cadet Girl.* There was also *Road Show, Winter Time,* one of Sonja Henie's annual ice extravaganzas, *Having Wonderful Crime, After the Thin Man* and several others well worth forgetting.

But in 1942 came *My Gal Sal, It Happened in Flatbush, Orchestra Wives* and *Manilla Calling* and her longed-for career toward stardom was on the move.

Her first marriage to Wheeler had lasted 25 days. But on July 4, 1940 Carole married again, this time to yachtsman Willis Hunt, Jr., a yacht broker and Los Angeles society figure. This marriage lasted two months and she received her divorce after informing a Los Angeles judge that Hunt had told her, "You're a fool. Just like everybody else in the moving picture business!"

Following the divorce Carole decided she needed a change and signed up with the USO for the overseas tour that was to continue for a year. It was while in London, however, that she became a bride for the third time. He was Major Tom Wallace, a former member of the Eagle Squadron of the Royal Air Force who switched to the 8th Air Force when America entered the war. They were married in London in 1942. Two years later Carole divorced Wallace in Las Vegas and the records were sealed.

> Carole Landis was to have one more
> chance at finding happiness in a marriage,
> but not to the one man she craved above
> all others . . .

---

* This was remade in 1966 in Great Britain and starred another struggling young actress, Raquel Welch, and started her on the road to stardom.

This ultimately led to her death; this and, many believe, another compelling reason: those accusations about her early days in San Francisco as well as her stardom in Hollywood and how it was attained.

Because her roles in many of her pictures were similar to those of her idol, Carole Lombard, she was pinpointed by many as the natural successor to the madcap Lombard. (The then wife of Clark Gable, Lombard was killed in a TWA plane crash in Las Vegas in 1942).

☆ ☆ ☆

Carole Landis had a style that was, many believe, imposed upon her by many of her wartime experiences. She wore casual clothes and at one dinner with us at the Duke Street Officer's Club, she wore jeans, lumberjack shirt and a Harris Tweed jacket. But because she wore the casual attire so well, and with a flair, no one objected.

Rex Harrison said in his autobiography that ". . . Carole was quite ambitious and wanted to make films, but for reasons I never got to the bottom of, she couldn't during the time I knew her, she couldn't get into any major studio; only the independents would hire her along with British producers for those awful 'Quota Quickies'."

"But," added Harrison, ". . . those were the days of the drawing rooms of Beverly Hills and Bel Air, the wealthy 'Hollywood ranchers,' and the so-called ladies none of whom considered Carole a lady."

Harrison, apparently, had not heard the rumors about Carole and the "bottom" to which he could "never get to."

Nevertheless, while Carole Landis was working her tail off in USO Camp Shows – and developing a case of malaria in the South Pacific from which she never completely recovered – those "ladies" of Hollywood were attending social events, afternoon teas at the Riviera Country Club, volunteering a few hours a week at the USO in Hollywood, all the while bemoaning the fact they couldn't find any good servants. Because of the war, Japanese domestics had all been interned.

Many of the cattier Hollywood Wives spread the rumors that Carole Landis had made it from bit player to leading lady under the "sponsorship" of various movieland males in a position to help her, including her long ago friendship with Busby Berkeley. This, in addition to "that" rumor about her early days in San Francisco, a rumor which had been depressing her for several years.

Many of those so-called "ladies" who made those statements and spread the rumors had followed the same road to stardom, or into those drawings rooms, or ranch houses as the wives of executives or actors they were accusing Carole of following. Hypocrisy at its Hollywood worst.

They were also jealous of Carole's popularity with the press, the crews and with fellow actors. They were envious that Carole could tell a good joke, often on herself.

In Hollywood, fame's door had opened and closed for Carole Landis, to all intents and purposes shutting her out of any major studio work because of nasty, ugly accusations spread by those long ago bitches of the industry. Some, incidentally, are still alive and, if they read this, will know what we are talking about.

It was these women who had used their influence with their husbands – the movers and shakers of the industry – to wind down Carole's career.

That drawing room crowd forever prevented Carole from becoming the great star she could have been under different circumstances. She was the right girl at the wrong time and was well aware of those rumors and accusations and that she could not overcome them.

To have denied them publicly would have made it worse. They were well aware of this and capitalized on it – to Carole's detriment. Hedda Hopper was one of those bitches to whom we refer and who considered herself the Morals Czar of Hollywood, along with Louella Parsons. Hopper "hinted" at them in one or even more of her columns. *

✦ This, then, was the mood, the atmosphere and the psyche under which Carole Landis was laboring while she prepared dinner for herself and Rex Harrison on that fatal Sunday night.

✦ It was to be the last dinner on this planet for Carole Landis.

---

* Hopper and Parsons were later to crucify Ingrid Bergman for her affair with Roberto Rosselini. So a hatchet job on Carole Landis would not have been out of character. "The Two Piranhas" also attacked Frank Sinatra and Ava Gardner, and Rita Hayworth's globe-trotting with Prince Aly Khan. They fully supported the "establishment," doing the bidding of the social arbiters of the "Bel Air Circuit" which is still in existence today with its "A", "B," and even "Z" lists as to who is invited to what parties and into which drawing rooms.

♦ Because of his cavalier attitude following her death, Harrison never fully recovered his stature with the British colony in Hollywood. The members all considered him a cad for not "taking his licks" and admitting his affair with Carole.

♦ And it was to be a hell of a long time before he was to ever make another film in Hollywood.

★ ★ ★

Rex Harrison considered himself on easy street and on top of the world when he and his wife, Lilli Palmer, moved from England to the Hollywoods in the late 1940s.

Little did they ever envision leaving Hollywood under a cloud less than three years later and that they would be at the center of one of Hollywood's biggest scandals – until that time.

Lilli Palmer said many years later that almost as soon as they arrived in Tinseltown where Rex had been set to star in several films for 20th Century-Fox, "All the so-called 'ladies' in Hollywood threw themselves into his arms.

"Rex was not one to resist the temptations," she added. "One woman was not enough for Rex; he just couldn't be faithful. He'd see some woman, she would flutter her eyelashes, and he'd believe that he'd fallen head over heels in love with her. It was just his personality," she remarked.

Lilli Palmer accepted Rex Harrison's occasional infidelities. She knew they were purely physical conquests which never, it seemed, altered the way that Rex felt toward her.

Then came Carole Landis.

They first met at the Racquet Club in Palm Springs introduced by one of its owners, Charlie Farrell. They were immediately attracted to each other; this was to continue unabated for months in Hollywood and in England.

At the time, Carole was married to her fourth husband, Horace Schmidlapp, a supposed New York millionaire. The marriage for Carole, however, turned out to be a Dutch treat affair. As Schmidlapp lived in New York, and Carole in California, she paid most of her own California living expenses.

Rex Harrison quickly succumbed to Carole's charms and immediately embarked on another adventure. Gossip arose very quickly about their extramarital activities as they continued their romance. Their affair was becoming more and more widely known. Harrison, who loathed the press anyway, found himself becoming increasingly challenged about the relationship.

Because there was very little work for Carole in Hollywood, in late 1947 she went to London after being offered two films by British producer Edward Dryhurst, *The Noose* and *The Brass Monkey*, two Quota Quickies for the British market. With Carole as one of the stars, these could also be released in the U.S.

Handily for both, Harrison was also assigned by 20th Century Fox to star in *Escape in England* as one of Fox's annual British productions.

The picture was filmed almost entirely on location near Dartmoor and Harrison had rented a cottage in Plymouth. Lilli Palmer remained in Hollywood with their son, Carey. Because of this, Carole and Harrison were able to spend most weekends together in Plymouth away from the prying eyes of Britain's tabloid press.

> And this was the man who denied, following Carole's death, that they had been having an affair; that they were just good "professional friends. Besides," he added, ". . . Carole is a good friend of my wife."

On returning to Hollywood, Rex would constantly visit Carole at her Capri Drive house – only a few minutes away from his and Palmer's home in Mandeville Canyon. This finally and inexorably led to a quarrel between Lilli and Harrison. She decided to visit friends in New York.

The only witness to Harrison's not-so-discreet visits was Fannie Mae Bolden. Bolden was to say later that she had no doubt that Carole was deeply in love with Rex.

"She would make me so mad because he would be eating his meal and she would just sit there watching him. And he would be eating just like a dog, like it was going out of style."

Carole Landis was obsessed with Rex Harrison but the romance was going nowhere. She took numerous photographs of him which she developed herself in the darkroom in her house. Because she developed them herself one must conjecture as to the type of photographs some of them might have been.

Rex Harrison and his then wife Lili Palmer three years after Carole's suicide. They are pictured at Columbia Studios where both were appearing in The Stanley Kramer Company production of "The Four Poster." This was to be Harrison's first picture in Hollywood in three and a half years following Carole Landis's suicide. (*Marvin Paige's Mot. Pict. & TV Research Svc.*)

Carole Landis at 8th Air Force headquarters at Bushey Park just outside London. (L to R:) Mitzi Mayfair, Martha Raye, Kay Francis, Carole and two U.S. Army Officers attached to the Special Services division in spite of their lapel insignia. These were the "Four Jills in a Jeep," the subject of a book by Carole and a 20th Century-Fox film. (*Marvin Paige's Mot. Pict. & TV Research Svc.*)

Carole with 8th Air Force Major Gus Daymand at Ciro's in Hollywood on Carole's return from the ETO following a USO tour to London. *(Marvin Paige's Mot. Pict. & TV Research Svc.)*

Director Busby Berkeley, one of Carole's early lovers at Warner Brothers and who gave her her first film "break." He is shown here on the set of the Eddie Cantor film, "Forty Little Mothers." *(Marvin Paige's Mot. Pict. & TV Research Svc.)*

Fannie Bolden recalled three or four years ago in another interview, ". . . she had pictures of him all over the wall of her bedroom."

According to Bolden, Carole fully expected Rex Harrison to divorce Lilli Palmer and marry her. Approaching 31 at the time and with a failing career because of those rumors and accusations being made by The Bitches of Bel Air, she felt it was time to settle down and have children. *

What was obvious to everyone – at least to those of her inner circle who knew of the affair – was that Rex Harrison was the wrong choice for her future happiness and security. He did not want to lose the stability that his marriage to Lilli gave to his life, and Lilli, he was sure, never regarded Carole as a threat to the marriage.

He realized that he would soon have to decide where his future lay – a fact of which Carole was equally aware that July 4th as she prepared dinner for herself and Harrison.

He made his decision clear during the evening and told Carole that he had accepted the leading role in a New York play and would be leaving California for many months. Little did he know how many.

Carole had reached the end of her rope, both financially and emotionally. She had no work in sight, she had sold her house, her car and dismissed her press agent because she couldn't afford to pay him. The bills were piling up and escrow would not close on her house for several weeks.

She had filed for divorce earlier in the year from Schmidlapp and her attorney Jerry Giesler had worked out a property settlement between them. All Carole would get was the proceeds from the Capri Drive house which would just about pay all of her debts.

☆ ☆ ☆

About nine o'clock on Sunday night July 4, Rex Harrison said he left Carole's house to visit Roland Culver, another of Hollywood's British contingent who lived nearby. Harrison wanted to talk to Culver about the play he was going to do for Leland Hayward in New York.

---

* Many years later Rex Harrison said that he was "very taken" with Carole's all-American spirit and sense of freedom. He said she was a feminist long before the launching of the women's liberation movement. That ". . . this was something else about Carole which upset the drawing room crowd"

In his autobiography, Harrison wrote: "I went to Carole's for supper and I discussed the play with her. She thought it was marvelous but upset at my leaving California.

"She seemed a little down but I'm afraid I didn't realize or notice the extent of her depression.

"I left Roland's about 1 a.m., went home and called Carole to say good night. At the back of my mind, I felt she sounded a little strange but I made nothing very much of it."

The next day, Monday, Harrison spent practically the entire morning and through lunch discussing *Anne of the Thousand Days* with playwright Maxwell Anderson in Malibu.

"When I got home. I called Carole to tell her I was back. The maid answered and said she'd knocked on Carole's door a couple of times but with no response.

"I thought (and hoped) she might have gone out, but I felt a little worried, so I drove around to the house and rang the bell. I tried the door just as Carole's maid was about to open it."

It was then that Harrison started to panic when he discovered Carole lying on the floor of her bathroom, with her head resting on a light brown jewel box. His immediate thoughts must have been, "Scandal time, old boy. Brace yourself," with no thoughts for the soul of Carole Landis.

His later lies and actions bore this out.

☆ ☆ ☆

Just what were those rumors and accusations that the establishment "ladies" had been making about Carole which were depressing her, destroying her Hollywood career?

When Carole left for San Francisco after winning a couple of beauty contests in San Bernardino, she had $16 and change and her Greyhound Bus ticket. From that moment on her life in San Francisco was clouded in mystery and rumors of a "mysterious past." This came up several times when she was asked about it by reporters but she always changed the subject. This "mysterious past" was talked about and embellished on the Bel Air circuit for years.

The stories that she had been a teenaged call girl for the owner of The Royal Hawaiian Cafe were passed around as fact. It was known that the cafe was a tourist trap and, it was said, gave her the opportunity to meet and "entertain" lonely tourists and conventioneers, which paid her far more than dancing the Hula; or so the accusations went.

These rumors snowballed into character assassination – that she had also became Busby Berkeley's mistress while working at Warner Bros., and that he had "pulled some strings" with Jack Warner to get her that stock contract.

Carole was once questioned about these and other rumors and the ones which upset her the most. "Anyone in public life," she replied, ". . . gets used to unkind rumors after a time. Though all of them are very upsetting when they are published and spoken about publicly, particularly by those in the business who are, shall I say, jealous of your success. I have learned to stand up to them by ignoring them and not dignifying them with an answer".

But it while she was at 20th Century Fox that the accusations which ended Carole's career in Hollywood, at least to all intents and purposes with the major studios, surfaced. They were not pleasant. Most of them were vicious lies.

Darryl F. Zanuck was noted for playing matinees in his back office around 3:30 every afternoon with the contract player of his choice. Darryl "signed the checks," so to speak, and decided which options were picked up every six months. Because of this power there was reticence but seldom an argument if any young lady he desired decided she had a headache or some other ailment on the day Darryl decided she should come to his office for ". . . a story conference" or to ". . . discuss future projects!"

Nearly everyone "in the know" at the studio claimed that Zanuck called on the busty, lusty Carole two or three times a week for the "traditional rite of passage" entered into by many of the female contract players at the studio.

The accusations were also made by her detractors that Carole had been having an affair with Jacqueline Susann, a press agent who later wrote *Valley of the Dolls* and two other forgettable novels; all, however, were best sellers but became so-so films at 20th Century Fox.

The accusations were also made, to put a spin on the story, that Zanuck somehow preferred women who themselves preferred, or enjoyed, women. In those days, homosexuality and lesbianism were frowned upon by the strict "moral" code of the industry and were rarely mentioned in polite circles. But the Bitches of Bel Air did not move in polite circles! Nevertheless, Carole Landis's detractors kept them going until she could no longer obtain work at any of the major studios or few independents.

No one has ever been able to understand why this was done to her. It was a known fact that many other actors and actresses had led far more dissolute lives than Carole Landis ever had. The accusations and rumors ruined a career which could have put Carole in the forefront as a popular, much-in-demand leading lady.

But Fate – and Rex Harrison – loathed by practically everyone in Hollywood for his stand offish attitude – decreed otherwise for Carole Landis on the night of July 4-5, 1948.

And it destroyed Rex Harrison's Hollywood career for many, many years.

☆ ☆ ☆

When Harrison discovered Carole lying on the bathroom floor around 3:30 p.m., he momentarily paused before calling for Fannie Mae Bolden to join him. He obviously wanted a witness to his actions from then on.

In his autobiography he wrote: "I first thought she might have fainted, and I went over and tried to pick her up. My one thought was 'How could I bring her back?'

"She was cold, she was gray and to all intents and purposes she was dead. [Nevertheless] I tried everything; holding her, moving her, shouting her name. I bent down and thought I felt her breath. I tried her pulse. I couldn't believe she was dead. I had had no experience with a dead person."

Harrison then went to the phone beside the bed and saw the note Carole had left behind – a pencil-written note on her monogrammed stationery and addressed to her mother:

Dearest Mommie:
I'm sorry, really sorry to put you through this. But there is no way to avoid it.
I love you, darling. You have been the most wonderful Mom ever.
And that applies to all our family. I love each and every one of them dearly.
Everything goes to you. Look in the files, and there is a will which decrees everything.
Goodbye my angel.
Pray for me.

With the pencil she scrawled, not her name, but . . .

Your baby . . .

Harrison claimed in *Rex* that there was no other note. But it was reported that she had left behind a separate note for him and that he pocketed it before anyone else could see it. He foresaw a scandal brewing and the studio had to be notified.

But, first, he asked Fannie Mae Bolden to help find Carole's address book to see if he could locate the name of one of her doctors. He never told anyone why he didn't just call the police or an ambulance.

After going through the book fruitlessly, or so he said, he got into his car and drove to his own home as fast as he could to get the telephone number of his own doctor. *

At this point, he claimed later, he did not realize that Carole was past resuscitation. He eventually reached his doctor's assistant who said it would take him at least a half hour to get to Carole's home.

"I rang the Culvers who lived nearby and asked if they knew a doctor in the area. They suggested I ring St. John's Hospital in Santa Monica, and the police if she had taken an overdose.

"I reported to the hospital and the police that I had found Carole, and that she needed immediate assistance."

By the time Harrison returned to the house on Capri Drive, the police had arrived and had been let in by Fannie Mae.

Harrison spoke briefly to the police of finding her body and told them that he had dinner with Carole ". . . who was just a good friend" the night before.

"I left her about 9 p.m. She had been in good spirits and I cannot understand why she did this." He then left the house hastily through the French doors, over a backyard fence and then by a circuitous route through the neighborhood, eventually reaching his car unseen.

He had spotted the reporters and radio newsmen arriving at the house while talking to the police in the living room of the Landis home. He did not wish to see them until he had discussed the situation with 20th Century-Fox. He could not afford a scandal at this stage of his career.

☆ ☆ ☆

---

* Harrison never explained, nor was he asked, why he didn't just ask "Information" for the number from Carole's telephone instead of wasting time with the 15- or 20-minute drive (at rush hour) to his Mandeville Canyon house. It is believed he took the time to not only call his doctor, but the studio and, probably, a lawyer, calls he did not want to make in front of Fannie Mae Bolden.

When the news of Carole Landis's death broke in the press on Tuesday morning July 6, Hollywood was stunned at the circumstances. Most people agreed she was a happy girl who loved life and laughter. Everyone of her close circle of friends called her a "good scout" and she was adored by the crews of the pictures on which she worked, not only in Hollywood but also in London where she had made several pictures.

What got Hollywood upset over the tragedy was that Carole had, at one time, been one of the town's most popular personalities and at the same time Rex Harrison one of its most loathed actors. He had snobbishly refused to cooperate with the press, who retaliated by sticking needles into both Harrison and his pictures.

Harrison also alienated every technician and actor on his sets at 20th.

The Hollywood Reporter wrote about Harrison:

> "We don't remember an actor, foreign or domestic, who has breached so many rules of good taste in his conduct among fellow workers.
> "The wonder of the whole thing is that he hasn't had his face smashed in before now." *

If Rex Harrison had few friends before the circumstances of the death of Carole Landis became known, he had nothing but enemies when they were learned.

True, Carole had been scandalized by the doyens of the industry, but the run of the mill employees who, themselves, could not understand why she was being ostracized and maligned, immediately condemned Harrison.

The only people who sprang to Harrison's side – and that was to protect their investment in *The Foxes of Harrow* and *Escape*, were the studio press agents under orders from Harry Brand whose wife, Sybil, was one of the leaders of the Bel Air circuit, but one of the very few, as far as could be ascertained, who kept her mouth shut about Carole's past.

---

* Coming from an "establishment" publication which relies on the industry for its very existence through advertising, those words were a good indication of the low esteem in which Rex Harrison was held then, and throughout his career insofar as Hollywood was concerned.

While the Hollywood press corps tried to dig up the facts, the press agents, through threats of advertising boycotts, tried to bury them in, at least, the local press.

Lilli Palmer was hastily summoned from New York to discount the rumors that flew thick and fast throughout Hollywood via jungle telegraph.

One top columnist, who had poured invective upon Harrison for months, Hedda Hopper, openly reported – with what truth is not known – that there was, indeed, a second note left by Carole and that Harrison had pocketed it when he fled the house in a blue funk, ostensibly to obtain the telephone number of his doctor.

In another column, Hopper wrote, obviously attempting to undo her guilty conscience of maligning Carole in earlier columns,

> "Carole had been deeply in love with a
> man who was forced to tell her that nothing
> could come of their romance."

Lilli Palmer arrived back in Hollywood via American Airlines within 12 hours after she had been so frantically summoned by Harry Brand who had taken charge of damage control for the studio.

On Wednesday, two days after he discovered the body, Rex Harrison stepped from behind the studio curtain it had thrown up for him for 24 hours.

The press was waiting on his door step as he emphasized:

"Carole Landis was NOT in love with me. This was a blatant lie as everyone was aware.

"That is all pure Hollywood gossip. You know what that is!"

He continued the lies during the entire press conference and added: "Carole never told me she loved me."

He was then asked what they discussed during their dinner together on the Sunday night.

"We talked of our plans for the future, my play and a picture Carole had been signed for in England in September."

"Is that ALL you talked about for two hours?" he was asked.

"That's all the comment I'm going to make," he said in his most imperious British accent.

With that, the butler came out and called him to the telephone. The door was closed, while the reporters milled about making and comparing notes.

Their patience was rewarded because ten minutes later Harrison

Gossip columnist Hedda Hopper who, in concert with "The Bitches of Bel-Air," took pot shots at Carole's early life but then rallied to her belated defense following her suicide. Hopper harshly criticized Harrison, who proved himself such a cad when Carole told him she was pregnant! *(Marvin Paige's Motion Picture & TV Research Service)*

came out but this time accompanied by his wife. "I am terribly upset about Miss Landis's death," said Lilli Palmer. "I met her many times in London and we went to several parties together. I never came to her house here as I am unknown in Hollywood. We shall both attend her funeral."

Everyone could sense that everything was over between Rex and Lilli Harrison, that here was a woman bravely standing by her husband to save his face and his reputation.

They were soon to be divorced.

☆ ☆ ☆

When her body was found on the bathroom floor, Carole was clutching a small brown envelope with the imprint of Carlton House, 22 East 47th Street, New York. On the envelope, scrawled in ink, were the words:

"Red – Quick – 2 hrs. Yellow, about 5. Can take 2."

This was not in her handwriting but was obviously written by a doctor. The autopsy showed they were sleeping pills. How many were in that little brown envelope of death was not known. There was one little white pill left in it when Harrison discovered her body.

Dr. Maynard Brandsma, Carole's personal physician, told the coroner that he had given her prescriptions for amoebic dysentery contracted while she was in North Africa during WWII and he knew that she suffered from recurring bouts of malaria which sometimes interfered with her work.

"I gave her no sleeping pills of any kind," he said.

- ◆ If Carole Landis had not taken her own life over an unrequited love affair with Harrison, what, then, was the reason?

- ◆ That was what both the police and the hundreds of people in Hollywood who knew and loved Carole – the little man, the technicians, the publicists – and her fan club wanted to know.

Carole's mother, Clara Landis, heartbrokenly told what she felt:

"My baby Carole had her troubles," she said in Carole's house three days after her daughter's death. "She had married a rich man but she was in deep financial trouble. She had sold this house, her car, her home. Little things in order to keep going until she got work again. Work that was being denied her because of nasty, scurrilous rumors.

"Things had been piling up for her. She told me of her financial worries despite her marriage to Horace Schmidlapp, a rich man. Why, only a short time ago, in bitterness, she said to me, 'Mother, marry a rich man and then support yourself'.

"A month ago I was staying with her when she called Mr. Schmidlapp long distance. She started talking to him at midnight and finished at 2 a.m. I heard her say, 'You know I never spent a cent of yours, except on the house and expenses'.

"I know she offered to pay him back for a fur coat."

Carole Landis, for all her outward gaiety, never found happiness. Her final try came when she married Schmidlapp in 1945 in New York. She once said she wore her heart on her sleeve. In March 1948, four months before her death, she had arrived back from filming *The Noose* and promptly filed suit for divorce against him on the grounds of cruelty.

◆ Was this because she had fallen desperately in love with Harrison and hoped eventually to marry him?

◆ Could this scenario have been discussed during their weekends together in Plymouth?

The answers to these and other questions were never answered.

On hearing of her death, Schmidlapp immediately flew to Hollywood. In his suite at the Bel Air Hotel he emphatically denied all the charges leveled at him by Carole's mother.

"Her charge that I failed to support Carole properly is absurd and ridiculous," he said. "During the two and a half years of our marriage, I paid for everything. A house that cost over $100,000; boat, train and plane fares because we were living all over the country and a lot of the time in England. I paid all her household expenses and clothing.

"There was a time in London when she did buy some clothes with her own money. Carole did not want for anything. Of course, I stopped paying as soon as she filed for divorce.

"I am completely mystified at her suicide. I cannot see why she should have taken her own life. I spoke to her last week by telephone and she was in high spirits. But, I had not seen Carole since January in London."

★ ★ ★

Rex Harrison and Lilli Palmer were among the top stars who attended the funeral at Forest Lawn cemetery. But it was the public who provided the spectacle. Hundreds arrived four hours ahead of time. They came on foot, in buses, in cars, in taxis. They saw Harrison and his wife enter the chapel just minutes before the services began – a down-to-earth trouper's funeral in the Church of the Recessional.

With the Harrisons was Rex's only close friend in Hollywood, Roland Culver, accompanied by agent Jack Bolton.

The five entered the Chapel through a side door and into a semi-private room close to the gleaming white casket. Lilli Palmer walked ahead, Harrison between Culver and Bolton.

Following the church service, all five left the cemetery before the casket was closed and borne to the grave sight on the slopes of an evergreen-shaded hill for burial. Schmidlapp was swept aside by the vulgar, gawking crowd as he tried to reach his assigned chair at graveside. Instead, he stood with bowed head on the fringe of the crowd still jostling and pushing forward as Carole Landis disappeared from view into the earth of Forest Lawn cemetery. Her final "credit" was: "Carole Landis – 1917-1948"; her grave with the simple marker is on the Forest Lawn "tour."

★ ★ ★

There was to be one final, bizarre twist to the death of Carole Landis which was only revealed by Harrison many years later in his autobiography.

In the evening following the discovery of Carole's body, the actor retreated to the Culvers on the instructions of the studio in order to "hide out." On his arrival, he was given two small suitcases. They had been found by a visitor of the Culvers just outside a little used gate in the lane alongside the house when they arrived for cocktails on Monday a few hours before Harrison showed up. Wrote Harrison:

"Carole must have left them there while
I was with the Culvers the night she took

her life, for it contained all the letters I had ever written to her, along with other personal mementos, gifts I had given her, and photographs of me and of us together.

Carole had evidently taken them out of the house to prevent my being embarassed by them. It was typical of Carole's sweet nature to act so thoughtfully when she was, obviously, in such an appalling state of mind. If the press or the Police had discovered those letters, what whooping and jubilant screams would have gone up from the Hearst press and other newspapers determined to increase their circulation at the expense of her tragedy. All were later burned."

☆ ☆ ☆

So ended the tragedy of Carole Landis, a bright, young star of the Hollywoods, a rebel and a feminist long before it became fashionable.

But questions about her suicide will always remain with us about her untimely death.

◆ Why was Carole Landis singled out by the Bitches of Bel Air for those vicious, unfounded rumors and accusations?

◆ How did Carole deliver the suitcase of Harrison's letters to the Culvers?

◆ Why did Carole never publicly denounce the accusations against her?

◆ Could there have been a spark of truth, or partial truth, to some of them and she was afraid they would further harm her career?

◆ To set one of those rumors to rest, if she had been one of Darryl Zanuck's "afternoon mistresses," then her contract would never have been allowed to lapse at Fox. She was the only one of Zanuck's many mistresses who had any talent. Or was pressure put to bear on Zanuck by "outside influences" not to renew her contract?

✦ Why did Rex Harrison continually lie about his affair with Carole Landis? It was common knowledge and he would have been held in a little higher regard if he had admitted to having had an affair with her. Instead, he was ostracized and did not work in Hollywood for many years.

✦ Or did she commit suicide because she was two months pregnant with Rex Harrison's child? In his own callous way, we have learned from someone very close to Carole, Harrison told her, "I'm a married man and you'll have to deal with it yourself!"

This was the real reason for the complete cover-up of the reason for Carole Landis's suicide as engineered by Harry Brand and the Fox publicity staff. They realized that in those days, when Ingrid Bergman had been run out of town on a rail by Hedda Hopper over her unwed pregnancy, this could kill Harrison at the box office and *The Foxes of Harrow* in which Harrison was starring.

☆ ☆ ☆

Even though Carole Landis was singled out for many unfounded accusations and rumors, she still had been a dues-paying member of the oligarchy for several years and many members rallied to her defense by ostracizing Harrison. They were well aware of the true story behind Carole's unfortunate suicide.

Rex Harrison had not only "bucked" the oligarchy in many ways, including snobbery and ignoring the tenets of the industry, but his biggest mistake was totally avoiding, and refusing to cooperate with, the Hollywood press corps and studio publicists long before the Landis affair exploded and forced him to deal with it – on their terms.

Nevertheless, regardless of the moral aspect, the big mystery is why Carole was the target for those rumors and accusations when most of them were never verified or proven.

This will always have to remain one of Hollywood's Unsolved Mysteries.

Marilyn with J.F.K. and R.F.K. at a party in 1962.

The Cover-Up
Which Won't Go Away . . .

Marilyn Monroe following her wedding to "Joltin' Joe" DiMaggio. It was the latter who arranged for Marilyn's funeral and interment at Westwood Memorial Park. He also banned most of Marilyn's friends from her funeral claiming they ". . .were responsible for her death," in a manner of speaking. This upset the Hollywood community. *(John Austin Collection)*

7... Marilyn Monroe: The Mystery Which Won't Disappear

"In the official police report a few days later, the time lag before calling the police had been cut down to one hour. I couldn't believe it. I knew the fix was in . . ."

– Sgt. Jack Clemmons
Los Angeles Police Dept.

But First . . . These Words For Our Audience!

Since the first volume of *Hollywood's Unsolved Mysteries* was published in January 1990, many more facts have come to light on the still unsolved mystery of the death of Marilyn Monroe.

Many theories, and even pertinent facts, have been imparted to us anonymously and otherwise by people who have contacted us since the book was published.

Through discussions on 150 radio shows and on such national TV shows as *Larry King Live, Inside Edition, AM-LA,* and *Inside Report* we learned how many people across the United States were aware of the massive cover-up to protect the Kennedy family over Marilyn's murder.

On many of those radio shows, it was reported that Marilyn underwent an abortion at a Los Angeles hospital on July 20, two weeks before her death. She confided in several intimates that a "top government official" made her pregnant. When the official heard this from Marilyn, he flew into a rage, marking the end of the affair, to all intents and purposes, between Marilyn Monroe and Bobby Kennedy.

It was also learned that the FBI was convinced that the late attorney general plotted her death. We now believe it was engineered by the former bootlegger, Joseph P. ("Papa Joe") Kennedy, in concert with Chicago mafia figure Sam "Mo-Mo" Giancana. Joe Kennedy had been cozy with mob figures ever since he bootlegged Scotch whiskey with the notorious mobster Frank Costello during prohibition.

Joe Kennedy had become very concerned that the affair with Marilyn could greatly harm his plans for a long-lasting "Kennedy Dynasty" in the White House and the Congress. Hence, there was a strong motive for him, a notorious womanizer himself—to "eliminate" Marilyn.

He also knew that his archenemy, J. Edgar Hoover, was knowledgeable about John and Bobby's affairs with Marilyn and could "blow the whistle" at any time. The end of his cherished "Kennedy Dynasty" would be the result.

All of the reports about the affairs were logged and filed by the late FBI director, as were further reports as they arrived from his field agents in Los Angeles and Lake Tahoe, where Marilyn spent her last complete weekend in the company of Giancana, Peter Lawford and others. It was at Lake Tahoe that weekend that Marilyn said she would soon hold a press conference to announce her involvement with Bobby and John Kennedy and that she had aborted Bobby Kennedy's fetus.

It was that ill-fated pronouncement
that sealed the fate of Marilyn Monroe.

As we wrote in Volume One of *Hollywood's Unsolved Mysteries*, Hoover was particularly interested in everything Bobby Kennedy was up to, especially focusing on his liaisons with Marilyn. Hoover was also knowledgeable of the Kennedy's plans to replace him as FBI chief with the highly regarded "lily white" Police Chief of Los Angeles, William H. Parker. This the director was determined to prevent, and did, even though Parker covered up Marilyn's murder—his promised part of the bargain. This included shredding over 80 percent of the LAPD file* on the

---

* See *Hollywood's Unsolved Mysteries*, Chapter 3, 94-101. (Shapolsky Publishers, New York, 1990.)

investigation after showing it to Bobby Kennedy in his office at the Department of Justice, following Marilyn's murder. Parker died several years later without realizing his cherished dream of becoming director of the Federal Bureau of Investigation.

★ ★ ★

MORTICIANS ALMOST BLEW APART THE COVER-UP OF MARILYN MONROE'S DEATH

Guy Hockett, one of the executives of the Westwood Memorial Park in West Los Angeles, and his son almost disclosed the carefully designed masking of Marilyn Monroe's death during the early morning hours of August 5, 1962.

★ ★ ★

When the morticians were called to Fifth Helena Drive and were told that Marilyn had died three hours previously, Guy Hockett gave his helper a knowing look.

Marilyn Monroe's body was stiff and, in order to place it on their gurney, it had to be bent, with some difficulty. A body that had been dead for only three hours would have been much easier to handle.

Hockett later estimated that Marilyn had been dead "closer to eight hours than three." This would have placed her death at about 8:00 p.m. Saturday night, August 4, 1962.

★ ★ ★

Amidst the turmoil in the house that night, which looked like Grand Central Station at rush hour, no one but an LAPD sergeant expressed any doubt as to the manner of Marilyn Monroe's death: it was suicide of course!

But, as Sgt. Jack Clemmons of the Los Angeles Police Department has said many times, "As soon as I walked into that bedroom, I knew there had been a murder committed."

To Clemmons's police instincts, it was obvious that evidence had been destroyed and a cover-up was already in place.

★ ★ ★

AS THE EVENTS OF THE NEXT FEW DAYS WERE TO REVEAL, THE AUTOPSY PERFORMED ON THE BODY OF MARILYN MONROE WAS STAGED FOR ONE PURPOSE: TO KEEP THE TRUTH FROM BEING REVEALED

★ ★ ★

"I KNEW THE FIX WAS IN" – THE SAGA CONTINUES

★ ★ ★

When Jack Clemmons, the watch commander at the West Los Angeles Division, took the call from Marilyn's house that early morning hour of August 5, 1962, he decided that it was a "high profile" case, and that he had better cover it himself until the homicide detectives could be notified.

Clemmons said that, when he first walked into the house at 4:35 a.m., August 5, 1962, he immediately felt there had been a murder. The number of people present, highly unusual for a suicide or a natural death, also "told" Clemmons, from years of experience as a policeman, that a cover-up could be in progress.

From the position of the body he knew that it was not a suicide. "She was lying stretched out, face down, cattey-corner to the bed, and the house was full, I mean full, of people. It was Grand Central at rush hour.

Marilyn with Betty Grable at a 20th Century Fox party. It was said that Marilyn "would experiment in 'love techniques' " with her girl friends. Grable did not like her. *(John Austin Collection)*

Marilyn with her long time close friend, Robert F. Slatzer. The latter has been the most vocal of those claiming that Marilyn was murdered, a view shared by many people including the author and the first Los Angeles Police Department officer on the scene. "As soon as I saw the report the next day, I knew the fix was in!" according to Sgt. Jack Clemmons. *(John Austin Collection)*

Robert F. Kennedy working in his office. *(Wide World)*

"Obviously, Marilyn had been placed in that position. I was shown the nightstand, by her doctor, with eight or ten empty pill boxes that had contained barbiturates. Her doctor said she must have swallowed them all."

Whichever doctor made that statement – Dr. Ralph Greenson, Marilyn's psychiatrist, or Dr. Hyman Engelberg, her internist – certainly couldn't have been thinking ahead. They should have known that a death of this nature would undoubtedly go through the autopsy process, and that the pills (they) claimed Marilyn *swallowed* would not be evident.

Or had they been administered in some other way?

Clemmons said, "I instinctively looked around the room, and in the bathroom for a glass used for the ingestion of what must have been a great many pills. There was none in either room."

It was discovered that the bathroom adjoining the bedroom was being remodeled, and there was no running water available in her bedroom suite.

"In my opinion," said Clemmons, "Marilyn Monroe was murdered that night in her home on Fifth Helena Drive. In fact, it was the most obvious case of murder I ever saw. Everything was staged. The body was rigid and artificially placed. It was not the sort of position in which you die."

Clemmons also told an interviewer that when he arrived on the scene, he was startled to see that Marilyn's body was a telltale shade of purple.

Lividity, the settling of blood within the body, takes place over a long period of time.

> This meant that Marilyn Monroe had been dead for quite some time.
> Blood always seeks the lowest level of the body, turning it from an ashen grey to purple depending on the length of time a person has been dead.

Milo Speriglio, who, as President of Nick Harris Detectives in Los Angeles, has spent more time investigating the Marilyn Monroe death than any other single investigator, has written the following on the case: "Sergeant Clemmons' eyewitness reports of Marilyn's body and his description of its advance state of rigor mortis, helped me to establish the time of her death as not on August 5, 1962, as reported by her handlers, but sometime between eight and nine p.m. on Saturday, August 4, 1962. That left a mysterious gap of several hours before the police were called."

This would also bear out the knowing looks of the Hockets when they picked up the body, but, as discrete morticians, they kept their mouths shut for many years.

What occurred during that extensive time lag?

For one thing, paramedics from Schaeffer Ambulance of Santa Monica came flying up the 300 yards of the Fifth Helena cul-de-sac to Marilyn's house at number 12305.

One of the ambulance attendants on duty that night said that it was never ascertained who called the ambulance from her house. The call, however, came in before midnight. As he and his partner were about to place Marilyn in the ambulance, a male individual in the house came forward and injected Marilyn directly into the heart, claiming he was a doctor. The attendant later said that whoever it was "counted down her ribs like a pre-med student in order to find the right spot!"

The paramedics had spent some time trying to revive her, and color was finally returning with their efforts. But, as soon as she was injected, the color drained from Marilyn's face.

She was taken to Santa Monica Hospital, five miles from her home. When she was wheeled into the emergency room she was comatose and in full view of everyone but not recognized because of her condition.

A little while later, she was "retrieved" by her handlers and returned to her bedroom in Brentwood by the same ambulance. The rationale was that she might still be alive, and could identify them if she was revived.

Could this be because they were in Lake Tahoe the previous weekend as "guests" of Sam Giancana?

★ ★ ★

As we wrote in volume one of *Hollywood's Unsolved Mysteries*, Marilyn had an abortion on July 20th – two weeks before her death. This particular pregnancy upset Marilyn considerably. Close friends and confidantes at 20th Century Fox revealed several years later that she confided in them that it was a "top government official" who "made" her pregnant. He responded to her claims by shutting off his private telephone line in his office. The affair was over.

It is known that Bobby Kennedy changed his unlisted number a week before Marilyn's murder. Her telephone records from General Telephone confirm the fact she had the prior number into Kennedy's office at the Department of Justice. (The records were temporarily seized by the FBI – which was under Bobby Kennedy's control – the day following Marilyn's death.)

Enter Sam "Mo-Mo" Giancana, former bootlegger, "Papa Joe" Kennedy and other players in the high stakes game of preserving the Kennedy image and their long and carefully planned dynasty in the White House and in Congress. Unfortunately, Joe Kennedy hadn't considered the libido of his sons.

After this slight by Bobby, Marilyn sat at home and brooded. Then at the invitation of the well-known pimp and procurer for the Kennedys, Peter Lawford, she decided to go to Lake Tahoe for the weekend, the weekend prior to her death.

During the week before her departure, Marilyn called several friends to say she would be holding a press conference when she came back and would name the father of the aborted fetus, and reveal other secrets she had locked in her little red diary. She told her close friend Peter Lawford that she was tired of "being passed around like a piece of meat by the Kennedy brothers."

Little did Marilyn realize, that by making those phone calls and then the same statements at Tahoe in the presence of Giancana, she had signed her own death warrant.

Mo-Mo would see to that after a few "phone calls."

☆ ☆ ☆

From FBI reports, which have filtered down through various sources over the years, the special agent in charge of the Los Angeles office sent a memo to Hoover stating: "Robert Kennedy is deeply involved emotionally with M.M. Informants report that he might have told M.M. that he would divorce his wife to marry her!"

Hoover, probably because of his alleged asexuality, was abnormally interested in the sexual exploits of his amorous boss. He was also well aware that Bobby Kennedy (in concert with John) was trying to find a successor for him, a quest Hoover was bound and determined to prevent. He would leave when he was good and ready, and that would be feet first, not on his behind.

Hoover had plenty of ammunition to keep him firmly entrenched in the FBI. After all, there were all those files in his office for the Kennedys to contend with. And many of those files held very uncomplimentary reports of the Kennedy brothers, dating as far back as the 1940s. This included J.F.K.'s wartime affair with Inga Arvad, then working as a columnist for the *Washington Times-Herald.*

Arvad was also suspected of far more devious Nazi activities which, through her many weekend assignations and dinner "dates" with J.F.K., could have jeopardized wartime security, as he was a naval officer.

For his "future use," Hoover then issued orders that all Kennedy escapades were to receive top priority. As a result, dozens of highly trained agents, especially during the "Camelot Years," were used to gather an incredible file on the Kennedys. We learned in the course of investigating Marilyn Monroe's murder that J. Edgar Hoover received several reports of what were described in FBI parlance as "Sex Parties," involving Peter Lawford, John Kennedy, Robert Kennedy, Chief Parker of Los Angeles, and several other ranking Camelot sycophants.

As it was well known, Hoover and the Kennedys had a hatred for each other without parallel in Washington. This probably started when the Victorian morality of J. Edgar Hoover objected to the womanizing of the three Kennedy brothers and Papa Joe. But, particularly, it manifested when John Kennedy was involved with Inga Arvad, because of her Nazi connections. She was a personal friend of Hitler and other Nazi leaders, and was suspected of being an active agent for the Third Reich.

This information, plus the "Marilyn Monroe Connection," kept Hoover in office, instead of him being replaced by Chief Parker. But Parker was not aware of this. With the resources of the LAPD Intelligence Unit, he was playing hard ball. Even though he was a strong Kennedy ally and participant in the "parties," he also kept taped records just in case he might have to "nudge the memories of the Kennedys and their promises."

The FBI was also well informed about Parker's transgressions, but the tapes were so well guarded in LAPD headquarters that the Feds were unable to get to them.

According to a high ranking LAPD veteran who recently passed

STATE FILE NUMBER	**CERTIFICATE OF DEATH** STATE OF CALIFORNIA—DEPARTMENT OF PUBLIC HEALTH	LOCAL REGISTRATION DISTRICT AND CERTIFICATE NUMBER
		7053 17716

DECEDENT PERSONAL DATA

1A. NAME OF DECEASED—FIRST NAME	1B. MIDDLE NAME	1C. LAST NAME	2A. DATE OF DEATH—MONTH DAY YEAR	2B. HOUR
Marilyn		Monroe	August 5, 1962	3:40 A M

3 SEX	4 COLOR OR RACE	5 BIRTHPLACE (STATE OR FOREIGN COUNTRY)	6 DATE OF BIRTH	7 AGE (LAST BIRTHDAY)	IF UNDER 1 YEAR	IF UNDER 24 HOURS
Female	Cauc.	Los Angeles, Calif.	June 1, 1926	36 YEARS		

8 NAME AND BIRTHPLACE OF FATHER	9 MAIDEN NAME AND BIRTHPLACE OF MOTHER	10 CITIZEN OF WHAT COUNTRY	11 SOCIAL SECURITY NUMBER
unk unk.	Gladys Pearl Baker —Mexico	United States	563-32-0764

12. LAST OCCUPATION	13. NUMBER OF YEARS IN THIS OCCUPATION	14 NAME OF LAST EMPLOYING COMPANY OR FIRM	15 KIND OF INDUSTRY OR BUSINESS
Actress	20	20th Century-Fox	Motion Pictures

16 IF DECEASED WAS EVER IN U.S. ARMED FORCES GIVE WAR OR DATES OF SERVICE	17 SPECIFY MARRIED, NEVER MARRIED, WIDOWED, DIVORCED	18A. NAME OF PRESENT SPOUSE	18B PRESENT OR LAST OCCUPATION OF SPOUSE
none	Divorced		

PLACE OF DEATH

19A PLACE OF DEATH—NAME OF HOSPITAL	19B STREET ADDRESS—GIVE STREET OR RURAL ADDRESS OR LOCATION DO NOT USE P.O. BOX NUMBERS
	12305 -5th Helena Drive — INSIDE CITY CORPORATE LIMITS ☐ / OUTSIDE CITY CORPORATE LIMITS ☐

19C. CITY OR TOWN	19D. COUNTY	19E LENGTH OF STAY IN COUNTY OF DEATH	19F LENGTH OF STAY IN CALIFORNIA
Los Angeles	Los Angeles	3½ YEARS	36 YEARS

LAST USUAL RESIDENCE — WHERE DID DECEASED LIVE—IF IN INSTITUTION ENTER RESIDENCE BEFORE ADMISSION

20A. LAST USUAL RESIDENCE—STREET ADDRESS	20B. IF INSIDE CITY CORPORATE LIMITS	IF OUTSIDE CITY CORPORATE LIMITS	21A. NAME OF INFORMANT (IF OTHER THAN SPOUSE)
12305 -5th Helena Drive	☒ CHECK HERE	☐ ON A FARM ☐ NOT ON A FARM	Mrs. Inez C. Melson

20C. CITY OR TOWN	20D. COUNTY	20E STATE	21B. ADDRESS OF INFORMANT
Los Angeles	Los Angeles	Calif.	9110 Sunset Blvd.

PHYSICIAN'S OR CORONER'S CERTIFICATION

22A. PHYSICIAN I HEREBY CERTIFY THAT DEATH OCCURRED AT THE HOUR DATE AND PLACE STATED ABOVE FROM THE CAUSES STATED BELOW AND THAT I ATTENDED THE DECEASED FROM ___ AND THAT I LAST SAW THE DECEASED ALIVE ON	22B PHYSICIAN OR CORONER—SIGNATURE	DEGREE OR TITLE
	By Theo. J. Curphey M.D. Coroner / Lionel Grandison Deputy	

22C CORONER I HEREBY CERTIFY THAT DEATH OCCURRED AT THE HOUR DATE AND PLACE STATED ABOVE FROM THE CAUSES STATED BELOW AND THAT I HAVE HELD ___ ON THE REMAINS OF DECEASED AS REQUIRED BY LAW	22D ADDRESS	22E DATE SIGNED
autopsy	HALL OF JUSTICE LOS ANGELES	8-28-62

FUNERAL DIRECTOR AND LOCAL REGISTRAR

23 SPECIFY BURIAL, ENTOMBMENT OR CREMATION	24 DATE	25 NAME OF CEMETERY OR CREMATORY	26 EMBALMER—SIGNATURE (IF NOT EMBALMED) LICENSE NUMBER
Entombment	Aug.8, 1962	Westwood Memorial Park	Charles Woodard 2673

27. NAME OF FUNERAL DIRECTOR (OR PERSON ACTING AS SUCH)	28. DATE ACCEPTED BY LOCAL REGISTRAR	29. LOCAL REGISTRAR—SIGNATURE
Westwood Village Mortuary	SEP 12 1962	Jeanne M. Kerl, M.D.

CAUSE OF DEATH

30. CAUSE OF DEATH — ENTER ONLY ONE CAUSE PER LINE FOR (A) (B) AND (C)	APPROXIMATE INTERVAL BETWEEN ONSET AND DEATH
PART I DEATH WAS CAUSED BY. IMMEDIATE CAUSE (A) **ACUTE BARBITURATE POISONING**	
CONDITIONS IF ANY WHICH GAVE RISE TO THE ABOVE CAUSE (A) STATING THE UNDERLYING CAUSE LAST — DUE TO (B) **INGESTION OF OVERDOSE**	
DUE TO (C)	
PART II. OTHER SIGNIFICANT CONDITIONS CONTRIBUTING TO DEATH BUT NOT RELATED TO THE TERMINAL DISEASE CONDITION GIVEN IN PART I (A)	

OPERATION AND AUTOPSY

31. OPERATION—CHECK ONE	32. DATE OF OPERATION	33. AUTOPSY—CHECK ONE
☒ NO OPERATION PERFORMED ☐ OPERATION—FINDINGS USED IN DETERMINING ABOVE STATED CAUSES OF DEATH ☐ OPERATION PERFORMED—FINDINGS NOT USED IN DETERMINING ABOVE STATED CAUSES OF DEATH		☐ NO AUTOPSY ☒ AUTOPSY PERFORMED—FINDINGS USED IN DETERMINING ABOVE STATED CAUSES OF DEATH ☐ AUTOPSY PERFORMED—GROSS FINDINGS NOT USED IN DETERMINING ABOVE STATED CAUSES OF DEATH

INJURY INFORMATION

34A. SPECIFY ACCIDENT, SUICIDE OR HOMICIDE	34B. DESCRIBE HOW INJURY OCCURRED
Probable Suicide	As Above

35A. TIME OF INJURY HOUR	MONTH DAY YEAR	35B. INJURY OCCURRED	35C. PLACE OF INJURY	35D. CITY, TOWN, OR LOCATION	COUNTY	STATE
3:40 A M	8-5-62	☐ WHILE AT WORK ☒ NOT WHILE AT WORK	Home	Los Angeles	L.A.	Calif.

Rev. 1-1-58 Form R.O-11

Certificate of death (reproduction).

76A890— Odb 3–63

"ORIGINAL COPY"   81128
File #_____

OFFICE OF COUNTY CORONER

Date Aug. 5, 1962   Time 10:30 a.m.

I performed an autopsy on the body of   MARILYN MONROE

at the Los Angeles County Coroner's Mortuary, Hall of Justice, Los Angeles,

and from the anatomic findings and pertinent history I ascribe the death to:

ACUTE BARBITURATE POISONING

DUE TO: INGESTION OF OVERDOSE

EXTERNAL EXAMINATION:

The unembalmed body is that of a 36-year-old well-developed, well-nourished Caucasian female weighing 117 pounds and measuring 65½ inches in length. The scalp is covered with bleached blond hair. The eyes are blue. The fixed lividity is noted in the face, neck, chest, upper portions of arms and the right side of the abdomen. The faint lividity which disappears upon pressure is noted in the back and posterior aspect of the arms and legs. A slight ecchymotic area is noted in the left hip and left side of lower back. The breast shows no significant lesion. There is a horizontal 3-inch long surgical scar in the right upper quadrant of the abdomen. A suprapubic surgical scar measuring 5 inches in length is noted.

DIGESTIVE SYSTEM:

The esophagus has a longitudinal folding mucosa. The stomach is almost completely empty. The contents is brownish mucoid fluid. The volume is estimated to be no more than 20 cc. No residue of the pills is noted. A smear made from the gastric contents and examined under the polarized microscope shows no refractile crystals. The mucosa shows marked congestion and submucosal petechial hemorrhage diffusely. The duodenum shows no ulcer. The contents of the duodenum is also examined under polarized microscope and shows no refractile crystals. The remainder of the small intestine shows no gross abnormality. The appendix is absent. The colon shows marked congestion and purplish discoloration. The fecal contents is light brown and formed. The mucosa shows no discoloration.

PORTIONS OF AUTOPSY REPORT

SPECIMEN:

Unembalmed blood is taken for alcohol and barbiturate examination. Liver, kidney, stomach and contents, urine and intestine are saved for further toxicological study. A vaginal smear is made.

T. NOGUCHI, M. D.
DEPUTY MEDICAL EXAMINER

TN:ag:G
8-13-62

THE FOREGOING INSTRUMENT IS A CORRECT
COPY OF THE ORIGINAL ON FILE AND/OR
OF RECORD IN THIS OFFICE.
ATTEST MAY 1 9 1964

THEODORE J. CURPHEY, M.D.
CHIEF MEDICAL EXAMINER-CORONER
COUNTY OF LOS ANGELES
BY...........................,DEPUTY

STATE OF CALIFORNIA, }
County of Los Angeles } ss.

№ 28182

On this 14th day of May in the year nineteen hundred and sixty-four before me, HAROLD J. OSTLY, County Clerk and Clerk of the Superior Court of the State of California and for the County of Los Angeles, residing therein, duly commissioned and sworn, personally appeared

R. H. Rathbun , DEPUTY CORONER known to me to be the person whose name is subscribed the within instrument, and acknowledged to me that executed the same.

IN WITNESS WHEREOF, I have hereunto set my hand and affixed the official seal of said Superior Court the and year in this certificate first above written.

HAROLD J. OSTLY, County Clerk,

By_____ Deputy

76C821—2/57

PORTION OF AUTOPSY REPORT

Autopsy report (reproduction).

away, one "Sex Party" included eight participants: Parker; the two Kennedy brothers; one other man believed to be a local official of the Democratic Party; three women; and the ubiquitous Peter Lawford—all cavorting in a Los Angeles mansion. To gild the lily, Secret Service Agents patrolled the grounds to ensure privacy. Similar parties were also held at New York's Carlyle Hotel, where John Kennedy maintained a year-round suite. He carried on a liaison with Marilyn before he became president, even during her marriage to playwright Arthur Miller.

☆ ☆ ☆

While Marilyn realized that John Kennedy regarded her as a sex toy – and that when they made love, he was making love to Marilyn Monroe, film star, not the love of his life – she believed that her relationship with Bobby was evolving into something far deeper. But, according to the top FBI official in Los Angeles, she realized at long last that Bobby had no intention of marrying her either.

To add insult to injury, while the Bobby Kennedy affair was a mess, Marilyn heard about 20th Century Fox's intentions of cancelling her contract. An FBI report revealed, "M.M. telephoned B.K. from her home in Brentwood when she heard this.* Kennedy told her not to worry about the contract, "that he would take care of everything!"

In spite of Bobby Kennedy's promise of "taking care of everything," 20th Century Fox notified her agent that because of "unauthorized absences" from *Something's Got to Give*, her contract was terminated.

> If Bobby Kennedy had the power to "take care of everything" in a positive sense, would he not have had the power to negate her contract as well?

There were dozens of calls from Marilyn which she placed person-to-person (later revealed when her telephone records were released) to Bobby at the Department of Justice. It was starting to become

---

* For several weeks before her death, Marilyn suspected that her telephones were tapped. Until her death she developed a habit of carrying around huge sacks of quarters. She once told Robert Slatzer, a former husband and long time confidante, of this fear. She felt all her calls to Kennedy and others were being monitored and so preferred to make all her important calls from call boxes on San Vicente Boulevard near the Brentwood Country Market.

impossible for the Kennedys to keep rumors of their affair from leaking all over Washington. Marilyn Monroe was becoming a serious problem for the Kennedys. When Bobby was advised by M.M. that she was pregnant with his child, his fears heightened to almost paranoiac levels.

Unfortunately for Marilyn, she made the "pregnancy" call from her house, which was "bugged." During that call ". . . Bobby Kennedy was irritated and unpleasant words were exchanged between them," according to FBI documents.

"Monroe threatened to go public and reveal her relationship with Bobby. She also mentioned that she would drag J.F.K. into the scandal," that particular report concluded.

This was the gist of the conversation played back for Sam Giancana, proving Marilyn's fears that there was not just one, but several, taps on her telephones and in her house.* This conversation also ended the affair between Marilyn Monroe and Bobby Kennedy. Upon the conclusion of this chat he changed the number of his private line and stopped this intimate relationship.

The debate of her relationship with Bobby Kennedy and the information she would subsequently reveal at her press conference was also the basis of the statements Marilyn made to her friends during her final week in Los Angeles and Lake Tahoe, the statements which finally and irrevocably sealed her fate. Sam Giancana told several people at the resort, "This is one dangerous dame."

Marilyn's close friend, Peter Lawford, became concerned about Marilyn's irrational intentions and tried to talk to her and calm her down. Lawford maintained close contact with Dr. Greenson, and had him prescribe some barbiturates for her before she left for Lake Tahoe.

☆ ☆ ☆

Sam Giancana decided to protect his powerful friends in the White House from having their careers ruined. He chose to take action "with prejudice," to put it mildly. This was a paradox because Sam Giancana and John F. Kennedy were, at the time, "sharing" a mistress, Judith Campbell Exner. Exner wrote a book about the affair wherein she said that she sometimes carried "brown envelopes" to John Kennedy from Giancana prior to her trysts with J.F.K. (The Exner book was later

---

* Some of the "tapping paraphernalia" was discovered several years after her death when a roofer accidentally put his foot through a weak spot in the tile roof and discovered a maze of wiring and bugs.

withdrawn by the publisher "because of outside pressures."(!))

Another person with whom Exner shared her favors was John Roselli, a long time "hanger-on" to the motion picture crowd. He was the one-time manager of Frank Sinatra, a close friend of Alfred Bloomingdale * and a close associate of Giancana. Roselli was found floating in a 50-gallon oil drum in Miami's Biscayne Bay in 1976. This was shortly *after* he had testified in the reopened investigation into the assassination of John F. Kennedy. Giancana had his lights put out in the kitchen of his Chicago home shortly *before* he was to testify on the same matter.

It is believed that Giancana asked Roselli to supervise the political assassination of Marilyn Monroe. We understand that three mob hit men were involved – two of them infamous figures in the world of mobsters and who have since been eliminated with "extreme prejudice." Only one of Marilyn's murderers remains free today and he is, we are told, still a "hitman" for the mob.

Investigator Speriglio with Nick Harris Detectives claims that this information came to him through someone who was with one of the killers the night Marilyn was murdered. He stated, "He talked, because soon after Marilyn's death his relative was murdered too, by one of those who liquidated Marilyn."

Speriglio claims he checked out the names of Marilyn's killers with three independent sources. "None of them knew each other personally," he said in an interview, "but they all came up with exactly the same three names."

To the hitmen and Sam Giancana, Marilyn Monroe, in her then state of mind, induced by a steady diet of prescription drugs from Greenson, was a walking time bomb who could have brought down the United States government, its then president and attorney-general. This was something the country could not afford.

☆ ☆ ☆

Chief Parker did a good job in instructing the LAPD in covering up the murder of Marilyn Monroe. The "official accounts" which are nowhere to be found in the LAPD archives were, according to police statements following the crime, a jumble of confused contradictions, none of which could be confirmed. No one was allowed to see the

* See *Hollywood's Unsolved Mysteries*, Volume 1, Chapter 2, "Who Really Killed Vicki Morgan?"

official file.

This was verified by Mayor Sam Yorty. Sam told us that he asked for the file after he became mayor and was told that it could not be located. He told *The Los Angeles Times* in a 1985 interview:

"I just remember at this late date, that after I was first elected mayor, Parker told us that Bobby Kennedy was in Los Angeles on the weekend of Marilyn's death when he was supposed to be in San Francisco for a Bar Association meeting. . ."

". . . I don't believe there is *any* file on that. Parker kept it separately. After he died, I sent for it and they didn't have it."

★★★

There are many questions concerning Marilyn's death that will never be answered because of the cover-up which was so adroitly handled by Chief Parker, public relations expert Artie Jacobs, the Kennedys, their associates, and by journalists who were not allowed access to any of the official records for many years.

◆ Did housekeeper Eunice Murray, hired by Dr. Greenson to "keep an eye on Marilyn," find Marilyn and notify Greenson at 1 a.m., as she originally claimed in her statement(s) to the police? Or did she report the body at 3:30 a.m., the time mentioned in the autopsy report?

◆ Why did the "official" report differ from the account given to Sgt. Clemmons, the first officer on the scene?

◆ Why did the coroner conclude that Marilyn died after swallowing a lethal number of barbiturates when his examination showed that her stomach was DEVOID of ANY BARBITURATES?

◆ Why did he specifically write the phrase "no needle mark" on the report, when Marilyn's own physician's records show he administered injections to her shortly before she died?

◆ Why did the coroner's report make light of the marks on Marilyn's body, bruises that could only have been made while she was alive?

According to the police "report," the "drama" began to unfold at 4:35 a.m. when Clemmons arrived at Marilyn's home. The report, filed by Detective Sergeant R.E. Byron, painted the following scenario:

> Murray noticed a light shining beneath the locked door of Marilyn's bedroom at 3 a.m. She looked through the windows from the outside and saw Marilyn lying in an "unnatural manner".
>
> Worried, she called Greenson, who arrived ten minutes later from his home on Franklin Ave, less than a mile away. He then broke the window, saw that Marilyn was dead and called Hyman Engelberg, her internist.
>
> Ten minutes later, Engelberg arrived and pronounced her dead.

☆ ☆ ☆

All this contradicts what Clemmons, the first police officer on the scene, claims Greenson, Engelberg and Murray told him during the bedlam taking place at Marilyn's house.

"At 4:25 a.m., as watch commander at the West Los Angeles Division, I received a call from Dr. Greenson who told me that Marilyn Monroe was dead," he said in an interview, when the truth started to emerge about Marilyn's murder.

"When I arrived on the scene I was shown in by Mrs. Murray, and inside were two doctors and several other people milling about. "I noticed that the room seemed 'picked up and neat.' I was shown Miss Monroe's body which was on the bed and covered with a sheet. Mrs. Murray told me she had awakened around midnight to go to the bathroom and noticed the light was on in Marilyn's room." (In an earlier interview, Clemmons said that when he arrived, Mrs. Murray was washing clothes, ". . . strange circumstances to be doing the family wash," he thought at the time!)

"I was very concerned about the lapse of time before the police were called and asked the three in turn why they had waited over four hours before notifying the police!"

Then came the statement from Greenson which illustrates the life and death power of the oligarchy:

"You can't die in Hollywood without the
studios being notified first!"

Said Clemmons, "Greenson told me he had to notify the studio
before calling the police!

"I replied, 'That's baloney'!"

At that, Byron and the homicide squad arrived and Clemmons
turned the investigation over to them. "A couple of days later, I saw
the report made by Byron and was astounded," Clemmons said. "The
times and timing were all different. The time lag before calling the
police had been cut down to an hour."

"I couldn't believe it. I knew the fix was in," said the disillusioned
officer.

★ ★ ★

Following Byron's so-called "investigation," the body of the
former film goddess, as ugly in death as she was beautiful in life, was
turned over to the Hocketts, who delivered it to the coroner at 9:00
a.m. for the autopsy.

★ ★ ★

As soon as Marilyn's body arrived at the Los Angeles County
Morgue, the controversy began – and has remained ever since. Dr.
Thomas Noguchi, not yet the controversial coroner he was destined
to become, performed the autopsy. Almost immediately, he declared
a verdict of suicide. (A copy of the report, signed by Noguchi, is
reproduced on another page.) The conclusion by Noguchi, which was
orchestrated by coroner Theodore J. Curphey, concluded that she
died of "an acute barbiturate poisoning, ingestion of overdose."

The operative word in this statement is "ingestion."

While the autopsy showed some quite high levels of barbiturates
in her body, *there was no trace of drug residue in her stomach.*

This immediately put the lie to what the doctor(s) told Clemmons
on his arrival, that she had "swallowed" many Nembutal caps –
"yellow jackets" in street parlance. If this had been the case, the
yellow dye from the caps would have lined her stomach and been
noticed (and reported on) by Noguchi in his signed report.

Several years following her death, using Noguchi's autopsy report
as a reference point, a noted New York pathologist related:

APPLICATION FOR FEDERAL EMPLOYMENT

57-10:

ATTACH SUPPLEMENTAL SHEETS OR FORMS HERE

● ANSWER ALL QUESTIONS CORRECTLY AND FULLY

1. Kind of position applied for, or name of examination	Announcement No.
F-deral Administrative and Management Examination	167

2. Options for which you wish to be considered *(if listed in examination announcement)*

Information Specialist (Motion Pictures)

3. Primary place(s) of employment applied for *(City and State)*

Washington, D.C.

4. Name *(First, middle, maiden, if any, last)*

Margot Patricia Newcomb

5. Address *(Number, Street, City, Zone, State)*

2920 P Street, N.W.
Washington, D.C.

6. Home phone	7. Office phone
452-8901	DU 3-4160

8. Legal or voting residence *(State)*

California

9. Height without shoes	10. Weight
5 feet 6 inches	114

11. Sex ☐ Male ☒ Female

12. Marital status ☐ Married ☒ Single *(Incl. widowed, divorced)*

13. Birthplace *(City and State, or foreign country)*

Washington, D.C.

14. Birth date *(Month, day, year)*	15. Social Security Number
July 9, 1930	559 45 8494

16. If you have ever been employed by the Federal Government, indicate last grade and job title:

GS-13 Information Specialist
(Motion Pictures)

Dates of service in that grade
From May 6, 1953 To Present

17. AVAILABILITY INFORMATION:

DO NOT WRITE IN THIS BLOCK
For Use of
Examining Office Only

☐ Appor. ☐ Nonappor.
Material ☐ Submitted ☐ Returned

Notations:

App. Reviewed:

App. Approved:

Option	Grade	Earned Rating	Preference	Augm. Rating

☐ 5 points (Tent.)
☐ 10 points Comp. Dis.
☐ Other 10 Point
☐ Disal.
☐ Being Investi-gated

Initials and date

20. SPECIAL QUALIFICATIONS AND SKILLS

A. Kind of License or Certificate *(For example, pilot, teacher, registered nurse, lawyer, radio operator, C.P.A., etc.)*	B. State or other licensing authority	C. Year of first license or certificate	D. Year of latest license or certificate

E. Special skills you possess and machines and equipment you can use. *(For example, short wave radio, multilith, comptometer, key punch, turret lathe, transcribing machine, scientific or professional devices.)*

F. Approximate number of words per minute:
Typing _____ Shorthand _____

G. Special qualifications not covered in application. *(For example, your most important publications (do not submit copies unless requested); your patents or inventions; public speaking and publications experience; membership in professional or scientific societies, etc.; and honors and fellowships received.)*

21. EDUCATION

A. Place "X" in column indicating highest grade completed													B. If you graduated from high school, give date	C. Name and location of last high school attended
1	2	3	4	5	6	7	8	9	10	11	12		June, 1948	Immaculate Heart Hollywood, California
											X			

D. Name and location of college, or university	Dates attended From	To	Years completed Day	Night	Credit hours Semester	Quarter	Degree received	Year received
Mills College	1948	1952	4				BA	1952

E. Chief undergraduate college subjects	Semester Hours Credit	Quarter Hours Credit	F. Chief graduate college subjects	Semester Hours Credit	Quarter Hours Credit
Psychology major					
History &					
Government					
Liberal Arts Course					

G. State major field of study at highest level of college work

Psychology

H. Other schools or training *(for example, trade, vocational, Armed Forces, or business)*. Give for each the name and location of school, dates attended, subjects studied, certificate, and any other pertinent data.

22. FOREIGN TRAVEL		23. FOREIGN LANGUAGES										
Have you lived or traveled in any foreign countries?		Enter foreign language and indicate your knowledge of each by placing "X" in proper column	Reading			Speaking			Understanding			Writing
			Exc.	Good	Fair	Exc.	Good	Fair	Exc.	Good	Fair	Exc. Good Fair
☒ Yes ☐ No		French		X			X			X		X

If "Yes," give in item 39 names of countries, dates and length of time spent there and reason or purpose *(military service, business, education, or vacation)*.

24. REFERENCES

List three persons living in the United States or territories of the United States who are NOT RELATED TO YOU AND WHO HAVE DEFINITE KNOWLEDGE of your qualifications and fitness for the position for which you are applying. Do not repeat names of supervisors listed under Item 19.

FULL NAME	PRESENT BUSINESS OR HOME ADDRESS *(Number, Street, City, Zone, and State)*	BUSINESS OR OCCUPATION
David O. Selznick	1400 Tower Grove Rd. Beverly Hi. California	Producer
Lois Weber	Allan-Weber Co. NYC	Public Relations Exec.
Mr. & Mrs. Peter Lawford	625 Ocean Front Santa Monica California	Actor
George Stevens, Jr.	1330 New Hampshire Ave. N.W.	Director, IMS

18. ACTIVE MILITARY SERVICE AND VETERAN PREFERENCE

Dates, Branch, and Serial or Service Number of All Active Service

From	To	Branch of Service

NONE

Have you ever been discharged from the armed forces under other than honorable conditions?
☐ Yes *(Give details in Item 39)* ☐ No

Do you claim 5-point preference based on wartime military service?
☐ Yes ☐ No

D. Do you claim 5-point preference based on service during peacetime campaign? ☐ Yes *(Complete and attach Standard Form 15)* ☐ No

Do you claim 10-point preference? ☐ Yes ☐ No If "Yes," check type of preference claimed and complete and attach Standard Form 15, "Veteran Preference Claim." TYPE: ☐ Compensable disability ☐ Disability ☐ Wife ☐ Widow ☐ Mother

THIS SPACE FOR USE OF APPOINTING OFFICER ONLY

The information given in answer to Question 18 has been verified with the discharge certificate and/or other proof which shows that the separation was under honorable conditions.

VETERAN PREFERENCE ALLOWED: ☐ 5-point ☐ 10-point Comp. Disab. ☐ Other 10-point ☐ None

re and title _____ Agency _____ Date _____

16-76619-1

Application of employment, Patricia Newcomb.

> "These findings, according to the au-
> topsy report, are not characteristic of a
> situation where large quantities of sleeping
> pills are alleged to have been swallowed.
>
> "Knowing the results of the toxicology
> examination and the negative findings in
> the stomach, one must seriously consider
> the possibility of an injection," the patholo-
> gist explained.
>
> "If I had handled the case, I would have
> been remiss in (my) duties if I did not refer
> it to the district attorney for, at the very
> least, an investigation."

Noguchi's report noted marks on Marilyn's right shoulder and hip, as well as bruises on her colon. The pathologist painstakingly explained that these marks could only have been made when the autopsy subject was alive. These marks, except on the colon, could have been made from Marilyn being dragged across the floor – and this is exactly what the ambulance attendant says he did in a desperate bid to keep Marilyn alive.

The biggest gap of all in Noguchi's report centers on the "injection" the ambulance attendant said he saw administered to Marilyn by "someone" who interrupted his attempts to bring some life back to his patient. Noguchi did not mention it at all. In fact, he specifically noted that *there were no needle marks on the body*. Either as an oversight or on someone's instructions, he failed to detect the marks made by injections that Engelberg said he gave Marilyn in the days before her death. Engelberg billed Marilyn's estate for injections on August 1 and August 3rd at $10 each.

The "creditor's claim" did not state what the injections were, but he did show a "residence call" on August 3rd.

☆ ☆ ☆

Marilyn Monroe's biggest mistakes in her star-crossed life were falling in love with Robert F. Kennedy and making those statements to her friends and in the presence of Sam Giancana in Lake Tahoe during that last week.

When Kennedy's feelings toward her cooled – right around the

Marilyn and her husband at the time, Arthur Miller. Close friends said it was Marilyn's on-going affair with John F. Kennedy that caused the divorce between them. They are shown here at a London night club. (*John Austin Collection*)

Eunice Murray, the housekeeper installed by Dr. Ralph Greenson to keep an eye on his prize patient. Murray disappeared for ten yers following Marilyn's death. When she was asked about it on her return, she finally admitted that she had lied on the orders of Dr. Greenson that Bobby Kennedy visited Marilyn on the afternoon of her death. (*John Austin Collection*)

time she became pregnant with his child – Marilyn, not a mentally strong person after years of brainwashing(s) by psychiatrists and ex-husband Arthur Miller, began to unravel. This was helped along by injections of tranquilizers and sleeping aids administered by Drs. Engelberg and Greenson during the last weeks of her life.

It was in this weakness of mind and spirit that a scorned Marilyn threatened to tell all about her Kennedy romance at a press conference on the Monday following her death. She also vowed to reveal government secrets Kennedy had imparted to her, such as CIA plots to assassinate Fidel Castro and Kennedy's mindset to put Jimmy Hoffa of the Teamster's Union behind bars.

In her naivete, Marilyn jotted all these things down in her red diary. She told a close confidante that she kept the notes in order to "remember" their conversations the next time they met and so could talk intelligently about them. The confidante, upon seeing the diary's contents, advised her to destroy it immediately.

She did not. After her death the red diary was believed to have been "taken" from the coroner's office – even after being inventoried – by the late Police Chief William H. Parker. *

One person who saw that diary was Lionel Grandison, the Los Angeles coroner's aide who was forced to write on line 22c of her death certificate, that it was a "probable suicide." Ten years later, in an interview with the now-defunct *Los Angeles Mirror-News*, he stated that he was forced and coerced, under threat of dismissal by coroner Curphey, to sign the death certificate. Noted Grandison,"The diary came into my office with the rest of Miss Monroe's personal effects."

The next day the diary had not only disappeared from his office, but its very existence had been struck from the inventory he had painstakingly compiled. The diary is believed to have been retrieved by Parker who took it to Washington, D.C.,where it was destroyed in Kennedy's office before Parker left – without being named director of the FBI, as he had hoped.

★ ★ ★

And here the mystery of what happened to Marilyn Monroe that

---

* Chief Parker, who took the LAPD from a graft-ridden organization to a model police department, was, as we wrote in volume one, considered to be "lily white" and "incorruptible." With the Kennedy promise, he digressed and did their bidding in maneuvering the "cover-up." This caused Sergeant Clemmons to say later, "I couldn't believe that her death was listed as a 'probable suicide' and not murder which I had told the detectives I firmly believed it was."

August night of 1962 stands today, no closer to a definitive solution than it was five, ten or even twenty years ago.

Most of the principals – *Eunice Murray, Robert* and *John Kennedy, Dr. Greenson, Arthur P. Jacobs* (who "fudged" things with the press that evening after being called away from a Hollywood Bowl concert), and *Peter Lawford* have died.

Also deceased is *Bernard Spindel*, who is just one of the many people who "bugged" Marilyn's home and telephones – the latter for *James Hoffa* in order to "get something" on the Kennedys in his ongoing battle to stay out of jail.

Dr. Greenson died a bitter and broken man. Whenever he was asked about Marilyn Monroe's death, he answered all queries with, "You'll have to ask Bobby Kennedy about that, not me!"

Dr. Hyman Engelberg has always refused to talk about the case. It is alleged that several members of a golf club in Los Angeles attacked *Engelberg* in the men's lounge and knocked him against some lockers because of involvement with Marilyn's well-being, or lack thereof. Engelberg has consistently stuck to the suicide theory in the rare instances when he has ventured an opinion about the case. He is still practicing medicine in Beverly Hills.

The coroner's report contradicts Engelberg's records in the case. Even though Noguchi said he found no needle marks, Engelberg administered an injection to Marilyn within 24 hours of her death.

Sergeant Jack Clemmons of the Los Angeles Police Department either resigned or was fired, depending on whose version you believe, his or the LAPD. With their record of cover-ups in the case, we prefer Jack Clemmons' account that he resigned because of the blatant cover up in Byron's report.

Lionel Grandison, the deputy coroner's aide on duty the Sunday morning Marilyn's body was brought in, resigned the position and has been involved in several businesses since then, including producing television documentaries in Los Angeles. He still sticks to his "no suicide" stance.

Patricia Newcomb, Marilyn's publicist at the time, was an employee of *Arthur Jacobs*. She spent that last Friday night, and most of Saturday, with Marilyn – until Bobby Kennedy arrived with Lawford. Immediately following Marilyn's murder, she left for Hyannisport and the Kennedy compound. She then left for a six month "sabbatical" in Europe, to escape the prying questions of the press. On her return she was employed by the United States Information Service – WITHOUT FILLING OUT AN APPLICATION FORM FOR EMPLOYMENT

FOR SEVERAL MONTHS!

After working with Pierre Salinger, John Kennedy's former press secretary, in his unsuccessful bid for a Senate seat representing California, Newcomb went to work for Bobby Kennedy in the Department of Justice in a private office six doors away from his office. No one ever did discover just exactly what it was she did for justice!

Eunice Murray, Marilyn's housekeeper, appointed by her socialist-leaning friend Dr. Greenson, steadfastly denied that Bobby Kennedy had visited Marilyn on that Saturday, the day of her death. Strangely, she too took an extended vacation in her native England for many months following Marilyn's death. She had never been known to be too affluent, at least not so as to afford a lengthy sojourn in Europe.

Ten years later, prior to her death, Murray finally admitted that Bobby Kennedy *had* visited Marilyn that afternoon, accompanied by Peter Lawford. She also admitted there were many acrimonious words between Marilyn and Kennedy in Marilyn's bedroom. Lawford was with Newcomb. They were not present in the bedroom, but in the living room.

We are inclined to agree with Milo Speriglio, the private investigator who has been delving into the case for many years. "I don't believe the Kennedys were *directly* involved in Marilyn's murder, but I do suspect the plotters were acting on their behalf."

This is the opinion of another authority:

> The statements made during Marilyn's visit to Lake Tahoe – whether drugged, sober or whatever – sealed her fate.
>
> Because of Joe Kennedy's prior involvement with mobsters, from business "associate" Frank Costello in bootlegging scotch whiskey during prohibition to mob finance genius Meyer Lansky, Sam Giancana was "in touch" with Papa Joe" the week before Marilyn died. It is believed that Giancana despatched "experts" to Los Angeles to take care of "the situation."
>
> Marilyn, Giancana vowed, had to be silenced. She could bring down the entire Kennedy dynasty if she went public with the statements she threatened to make.
>
> It should also be remembered that Sam

Giancana and Jack Kennedy were, at the time, "sharing" the same mistress, Judith Campbell Exner. Giancana considered himself a "personal friend" of the Kennedys and did not want to see them destroyed. He felt there was a close bond between them. In Exner, apparently, there was.

But, be that as it may, Giancana had no compunction about destroying the life of Marilyn Monroe, who probably would not have gone ahead with her plans anyway. In order to call a press conference, she would have had to work with her publicist, Pat Newcomb and Newcomb's boss, Arthur Jacobs. When they learned of the subject matter, they would have undoubtedly prevented her from doing so.

Marilyn, with the knowledge gained from pillow talk with both John and Robert Kennedy, could have been a national security risk. But, would she, in her naivete, have realized the importance of the things she had been told by them? And on the other hand, would they have been so loose lipped with national security matters to impart them to Marilyn Monroe?

We think not; her mind could have been too far gone with prescription drugs and injections administered to her by Greenson and Engelberg for her to really understand with any insight what she had heard.

★ ★ ★

The circumstances surrounding Marilyn Monroe's death – call it murder – are extremely suspicious and dangerous, and the events following her death are even more so.

They reek of intrigue, pay-offs, and a fix at the highest levels of municipal, state and the federal governments.

Have things gotten so bad in the United States that a probable murder, in the case of Marilyn Monroe, was suppressed because pressure (or "considerations") were

brought to bear, because someone important was involved? Were the Kennedys
above the law?

Is everyone really equal before the laws
of the United States, or have some people,
families, or industries, gotten so powerful
that they make their own rules?

☆ ☆ ☆

One final note about the disposition of
the Los Angeles Police Department file on
the "investigation" into the death of Marilyn Monroe.

When Lieutenant Marion Phillips, the
former senior "desk man" in the Los
Angeles Police Department Intelligence
Unit (which handled the investigation),
was asked about the case file several years
later, he said he was told in 1962 that Chief
Parker had taken the file "to show someone in Washington, D.C. That was the last
we heard of it!"

☆ ☆ ☆

We rest our case!

Nevertheless, no matter who the culprit or culprits, or the instigator
of the cover-up of Marilyn Monroe's death, it will always remain the most
controversial of all Hollywood's unsolved mysteries.

**An early studio portrait of Marilyn, at the time of her role in "The Asphalt Jungle" in
1950, and against the wishes of director John Huston.** *(John Austin Collection)*

Marilyn singing "Happy Birthday, Dear Mr. President" before a large crowd at a Madison Square Garden fundraiser. According to witnesses, she was not wearing anything underneath her dress. *(UPI)*

Spencer Tracy (who called Harlow, "A square shooter if there ever was one") and
Jean in a scene from "Riff Raff", one of several films in which they co-starred.
(*John Austin Collection*)

"You Always Hurt
The One You Love . . ."

Harlow autographing a portrait of herself by a fan. *(John Austin Collection)*

8... Jean Harlow's Infantile Husband

"She didn't want to be famous, she
wanted to be happy."
— Clark Gable, 1937

"No matter what I do, I always end up on Page One!"
— Jean Harlow, 1935

The body of Paul Bern, the husband of MGM screen goddess Jean Harlow, was found lying prone on the bathroom floor adjoining the master bedroom. It was discovered by their butler, John Carmichael, on Labor Day, September 5, 1932. Carmichael was well aware that a servant's first duty is always to his master's best interests. Even in death, John Carmicheal knew what those interests were, and whom to call first in such an emergency situation. He had worked for members of the oligarchy for many years and intended to go on doing so. He also knew the rules of the game: under such circumstances you *never* call the police first.

Instead, Carmichael called MGM. The studio police officer on duty that Labor Day holiday immediately notified MGM's Chief of Police, W.P. "Whitey" Hendry, who was at his home in Santa Monica.

Hendry knew what to do in situations such as the death of an executive under strange circumstances which could affect the "image" of the studio. Quickly he placed two phone calls. One of them was to Louis B. Mayer, the loathsome, autocratic head of MGM; the other to Irving Thalberg, Bern's immediate superior. Nobody had yet bothered to notify the police – not even Hendry, a former LAPD cop himself. He decided to go to 9820 Easton Drive first and look over the situation. There might be something that required "fixing" or "sanitizing."

Both Mayer and Thalberg, because of Bern's importance to the studio, and the fact that he was the husband of one of their biggest stars, sped in chauffeur driven limousines to Easton Drive. Louis B. Mayer was first on the scene; Thalberg and Hendry were next to arrive. It was not until two hours later that the Los Angeles Police Department was notified of the death.

Just what happened during those two hours will probably never be known definitively. But some of it can be pieced together from reports, inquest testimony and grand jury transcripts from two sessions, as well as the legendary whispers passed down over the years.

☆ ☆ ☆

Paul Bern was born Paul Levy in Wannsbeck, Germany on December 3, 1889. Bern's family emigrated to the United States in 1898 when Paul was eight.

His biographies reveal that when he was 14, Paul's formal education ended. Those who met him later in life, nevertheless, assumed Paul Bern was a highly educated individual. He *was* very well educated – but it had been a self-education.

Paul Bern had grown up in the same neighborhood as the (eventual) mob "finance director," the infamous Meyer Lansky. Both were small physically and had good minds, which probably contributed to their friendship. One summer day, Lansky rescued his friend from a gang of young Irish toughs who were engaged in the local sport of "cockalizing." They opened Bern's fly to expose his circumcision. What they found, however, amused them even more. Paul's penis had never matured at puberty.

After seeing what the youths were laughing at, Lansky felt sorry for his friend. He wanted to continue their friendship, but a shamed Bern avoided him thereafter.

Paul Bern's first job was with the Produce Exchange Company in New York at a salary of $3.50 per week. While learning shorthand in night school, he obtained a job with the New York Gas Company as a stenographer. He began to write.

Deciding to devote himself to the theatre, Paul started as an actor with a small travelling company. He ended up as a stage manager for another small travelling troupe, as vaudeville-like acts abounded in those days. All were scratching out a living performing in civic halls and small theatres on the East Coast.

After tiring of life on the road, Paul returned to New York and had a short stint as a press agent for a Broadway show. Several months later he entered the motion picture business by going to work for the Canadian Picture Company in Toronto. It was at that juncture that Paul Levy changed his surname to Bern. While working in Toronto in the then-infant industry, Bern realized that everything creative in the industry was happening in a small town called "Hollywood." He boarded a train bound for Los Angeles to seek his fame and fortune. He knew little about the town or the production end of the industry, but Paul Bern was a fast learner.

His first job was that of a film cutter; progressively he worked his way into the scenario department – as scripts were known in those days. He very soon became a script editor, directed some films and, at 37, became a supervisor at MGM.

Irving Thalberg noticed Bern's ability in a multitude of production jobs and made him his general assistant – in effect, the number three man at MGM, behind Thalberg and Mayer.

In a prophetic article in *The New York Morning Telegraph* in 1927, Herbert Cruikshank shared a great deal of insight on Bern:

> "Meet Paul Bern, and know that you
> stand in the presence of one blessed or
> cursed with the fearsome, terrible quality
> that sears souls, destroys minds it so
> brilliantly lights, that with the fierce fury of
> a flagellant, whips its slaves on to accom-
> plishment – to immortality – to death.
> I mean the tragic quality of genius."

Flowery prose, certainly, but unquestionably true to all those who knew Bern.

Cruikshank went on to further describe Paul Bern.

> "A slight man, insignificant in stature,
> slender of shoulder, only as tall as a girl. He
> has a deal [sic] of forehead, topped with a
> mop of hair, soft and fine spun – beautiful,
> perhaps, in a woman, in a man quite
> probably presaging premature baldness.

The eyes are slightly bulging and deeply
ringed with a sooty rim that seems to make
them smolder and then flash fire much in
the fashion of live coals lying in the smoky
gray and burned out black of ashes."

Bern's intellect was, certainly, brilliant, but it was accompanied by a temperament far more compassionate than most. Many people in Hollywood called him "Hollywood's Father Confessor." Many people, not only on the MGM lot, but most of his acquaintances, took their troubles to Paul Bern for advice, help, and sometimes, sympathy.

But there was also a noted peculiarity about Paul Bern the producer. He thought that every movie he was associated with ought to have a happy ending. Sad endings, he told many of his co-workers, left an audience depressed. Paul Bern hated unhappy endings to anything in life.

This attitude was to haunt him during his lifetime.

☆ ☆ ☆

Paul Bern took little part in Hollywood's party life and was considered something of a mystery man inside the enigma that was Hollywood. In fact, Bern lived in such an out-of-the-way location that he was forced to put a sign beside the dirt lane that led to home which read, "This Way To Bern's House."

He spent many secluded hours reading scripts and novels to recommend to Thalberg, all the while improving his mind. Occasionally he was seen at the more exclusive parties – never the wild ones where cocaine was available for the asking. From time to time he could be seen in such well know night spots as the Trocadero and the Coconut Grove.

Despite his clandestine habits, when Paul Bern began to appear in public with Jean Harlow, nobody attached much significance to his sudden sociability. It took everyone by surprise when they showed up at the Marriage License Bureau in Los Angeles to get a license to marry.

Harlow told the hovering court house/city hall beat reporters, "We were surprised ourselves. Mr. Bern did not propose until last Sunday, and I accepted. We had spoken of marriage casually before then, but not until Sunday was the subject seriously considered."

On July 2, 1932, the actress and the genius with "death in his eyes" were married in the home of Jean's mother and stepfather. Among the guests were Irving Thalberg and his wife, as well as another major MGM star, Norma Shearer.

Jean Harlow was to rue the day she agreed to marry Paul Bern. What happened on their short marriage would eventually cause her death at a very young age, at the height of her stardom.

The Jean Harlow of MGM had come a long way from Kansas City from a short marriage which took place in Chicago and ended in Los Angeles a year later . . .

★ ★ ★

Harlean Jean Carpentier – she was later to drop the Harlean and Carpentier, her father's name, and adopt her mother's parents' surname – grew up in Kansas City, Missouri. She spent the humid, Midwest summers with her grandparents, Mr. and Mrs. S.D. Harlow, in Bonner Springs, Kansas, a rural farming community.

Jean enjoyed the farm life and the animals but hated returning every fall to the Barstow School, a private establishment for young ladies.

In 1921 her parents divorced, and her mother took Jean to Los Angeles where she was enrolled in the Hollywood School for Girls. Her mother dated various men on the fringes of the film business: extras, occasional actors, and production people. Jean enjoyed visiting the movie studios of Mack Sennett and Hal Roach, the comedy kings of the film world of the 1920s. Harold Lloyd, Laurel and Hardy, and Buster Keaton were just getting started when she made her early visits.

In 1924, disappointed over a love affair, her mother removed Jean from school rather abruptly and moved the pair back to her home town of Highland Park, Illinois.

Now that she was blossoming into maturity, the boys began to notice Jean Carpentier's slender young body, her pert, firm breasts and pretty face. She refused to wear a bra, a libral statement she maintained throughout her life. The boys loved it, as would movie audiences a few years later.

At 16, Jean met and fell in love with Charles Fremont McGrew II, a wealthy young man and several years her senior. Against her mother's wishes – and lying about her age – they were married in Chicago. Her mother, also, had recently married a lounge lizard by

Harlow and Clark Gable in a scene from "Red Dust." It was well known that Harlow and Gable had an affair during the filming of "China Seas." Gable always called her "a good scout." *(John Austin Collection)*

Powell and Harlow two months before she died in 1937. *(Marvin Paige's Motion Picture & TV Research Service)*

⭐ ⭐ ⭐

It was in Philadelphia while making four-a-day stage appearances with *Hell's Angels* to standing room only crowds that life was to change dramatically for Harlow. She became a star.

In the audience one matinee was Abner "Longie" Zwillman who introduced himself to Jean. She fell for him. She did not learn until later that he was a well known mob figure. "Longie" followed her around the country tour as often as he could and told her he would see her in Hollywood "very soon."

Zwillman became Jean Harlow's boyfriend whenever he was in town. Jean was sitting on top of the world. But Zwillman, now feeling that Harlow should be making more money and with a major studio, not an independent like Howard Hughes, began to ask for some long overdue favors from high ranking members of the oligarchy.

The first was Harry Cohn. The uncouth producer needed $500,000 to buy out one of his partners and form Columbia Pictures. Zwillman came up with the cash, literally, in a suitcase.

He also learned that Hughes needed immediate cash. He used the tactic that Billie Dove was now more jealous than ever of Jean Harlow and suggested Hughes loan her out to other studios where she could be more active. Hughes took the advice and loaned Harlow out at $3,500 per week to major studios. He was paying Jean $250. In rapid succession her pictures included *The Iron Man* for Universal and *The Public Enemy* with James Cagney at Warner Brothers. This was followed by *The Secret Six* at MGM, *Goldie* at 20th Century Fox, and *Platinum Blonde* at Columbia (for Zwillman's old friend, Harry Cohn).

It was then that Zwillman made his major move for the career of Jean Harlow, a move he eventually came to regret. He suggested to Howard Hughes that, since he was awaiting the cash for *Hell's Angels* to come in, he release Jean from her contract so she could become a major star for another studio.

Hughes, who was averse to dealing with mobsters, agreed to release her contract to rid himself of Zwillman's presence around his offices. Hughes sold the contract to MGM where Jean was immediately signed for $1,250 per week, a tremendous salary in those days, even by Hollywood standards. But with several major films behind her (such as *The Public Enemy* and *Hell's Angels* doing tremendous box office business), Louis B. Mayer felt she was a bargain and insisted on a long term contract with raises every six months.

Howard Strickling and his top flight publicity staff were ordered

a wealthy young man and several years her senior. Against her mother's wishes – and lying about her age – they were married in Chicago. Her mother, also, had recently married a lounge lizard by the name of Marino Bello. After a few weeks of Chicago, Jean talked her bridegroom into buying a house in Beverly Hills, so she could get away from her mother and stepfather. Jean was young and quite immature, but her husband overlooked this. He showed her off at Hollywood parties, and made a lot of contacts for her.

Weekends were spent at Agua Caliente, just below the Mexican border, and their afternoons were enjoyed at the race track. Jean loved to bet and mingle with the movie crowd at the Turf Club, then owned by Joseph Schenck.

Because she hated to be away from her daughter, it wasn't too long afterward that her mother and Bello moved to Los Angeles. Bello felt it would be a mecca for his various "get-rich-quick" schemes by using the contacts of Jean and her husband.

Meanwhile, through those contacts, and through contacts she had picked up around Agua Caliente, Jean started working in various films, including Hal Roach's Laurel and Hardy comedies. Her husband objected to this, particularly because she was an extra, but he came to find out he had no control over his wife's ambition to act in movies.

Jean Harlow's first big job was at Paramount Pictures in Clara Bow's *The Saturday Night Kid*. As she became known amongst the movie crowd, Jean made friends with the veteran actress, the much-loved Marie Dressler. It was Dressler who recommended to Roach that Jean be given larger parts.

Roach was not aware of Harlow appearing as an extra in some of his earlier films, and gave her a few lines in a series of comedies. Her first major appearance with her name below the title as a supporting player was in a Laurel and Hardy comedy, *Double Whoopee*, in 1928.

In 1929, because of the continuing objections of McGrew to her career, Jean filed suit for divorce. Soon after, her husband had arranged for a photographer at a Hollywood party to take some nude shots of his wife, drunk in a bedroom. The fate of their marriage was sealed. Jean recovered the negatives and prints and she received a divorce just a few weeks following her 20th birthday.

⭐ ⭐ ⭐

Because there was no time for a honeymoon, Jean and Paul's wedding night was spent in the house on Easton Drive. Following the departure of the last of the guests, Bern and his bride continued celebrating until both were happily drunk.

They retired to the all-white master bedroom, Jean in a revealing nightgown. She waited, impatiently, for Bern to come to bed and consummate the marriage. Finally, he appeared in a bathrobe but seemed preoccupied and distracted. The closer Jean tried to get to him, the further he retreated.

It was then that Bern revealed his terrible secret. He told her he would not be able to consummate their marriage. His organ, Jean then discovered, was the size of a child's and it rendered him impotent. Drunk, Bern threw himself at her feet, begging for her understanding. He hoped Harlow could work her "screen magic" on him. He claimed she was a "sex goddess" and could help him get an erection, something he'd never had before. Jean, furious, told him she was no goddess and that she thought she had married a man who loved her for herself, not her glamorous image. She was furious at Bern's betrayal, and that he had not at least warned her before their wedding. If ever there was a reason for premarital sex, this unholy union of Paul Bern and Jean Harlow was a textbook example.

In an alcoholic rage, they ranted and flailed at each other. Jean's taunts pushed a proud, humiliated Bern over the edge. He threw her to the floor and, while trying to perform fellatio, bit her thighs so savagely he drew blood. With uncontrollable fury, she was to tell her agent Arthur Landau that Bern then beat her unmercifully with his walking stick until he passed out.

Jean immediately called Landau and asked him to come and get her. He arrived in less than twenty minutes. Harlow jumped in his car crying, and obviously in great pain.

Once inside the safety of the Landaus' home, Jean lowered the blouse she had quickly donned before leaving. As Landau related in his biography of Jean Harlow, she whimpered, "Look at my back!"

She showed the Landaus five long welts stretching from her hips to her shoulders, and there were even more marks across her buttocks. They gasped when she revealed the bloody teeth marks on her inner thighs.

She told the Landaus she never wanted to see him again.

Landau was on the telephone with MGM executives until dawn, deciding what must be done. A scandal had to be avoided at any cost. Once again, the oligarchy "decided" what a well-known married

couple would "have to do" in order to protect its image and box office stability . . .

It was "agreed" that Harlow and Bern would remain together in the house on Easton Drive until after "a suitable length of time." Six months was agreed upon. They would then quietly divorce.

The charade began immediately with their "formal" wedding reception and obligatory publicity pictures for the fan magazines the next afternoon at Easton Drive, which had been hurriedly catered by the MGM commisary crew. Most of Jean's friends were dressed to the hilt, but Jean's known casual manner allowed her to get away with loose fitting green pyjamas. She carefully maneuvered her way out of painful embraces of congratulations.

Jean Harlow gave the performance of her life . . . the happy blushing bride – Mrs. Paul Bern.

The beating she took from Bern the night before was to be the ruin of Jean Harlow. She would never totally recover from the internal damage she unexpectedly suffered that night. It was only when she later started to urinate constantly that she knew something was wrong.

☆ ☆ ☆

Following her appearance in *Double Whoopee* with Laurel and Hardy, a young Texas millionaire, Howard Hughes, was producing silent films and had just completed the biggest budget film ever, *Hell's Angels*. The film had cost Hughes more than $2 million.

Hell's Angels was a story of World War I pilots and starred a famous Norwegian actress, Greta Nissen. Unfortunately for Nissen, and for Hughes, "talkies" had arrived and the film in its current state had to be scrapped. Following tests, Hughes realized that Nissen's broken English could not make the transition to sound and be understood.

Jean Harlow was on the same studio lot working regularly in the Roach comedies. She had suffered what she felt was an unfortunate accident. An inexperienced hair dresser accidentally "overcooked" Jean's hair in a peroxide mixture, and as a result was now "platinum blonde." Jean's luck turned abruptly, however, when Hughes spotted her walking across the studio lot. He immediately tested her for the remake of *Hell's Angels*.

As a platinum blonde, Jean turned out to be exactly what Hughes was looking for. He signed her to a long term contract. This did not sit too well with Hughes's current love, a very jealous actress, Billie Dove. She was later to be a catalyst for another break in Harlow's career.

by Mayer to set about "creating" Jean Harlow into a major star – the biggest star in Hollywood was their goal.

It was not very long after signing her contract at MGM that she first met Paul Bern. She was told by her handlers at the studio, and her agent, Arthur Landau, that Bern had the reputation of being kind and helpful "to young actresses" and was known in studio circles as a "ladies man." Jean took an instant liking to the thin, balding little man.

★ ★ ★

Jean Harlow's marriage did not sit too well with "Longie" Zwillman who, because of "business," was spending most of his time on the East Coast. He set his minion, Johnny Roselli, to work to find out all they could ". . . about this guy Paul Bern!"

★ ★ ★

What Zwillman found out about Paul Bern was to turn his life upside down. He eventually imparted to Jean that Paul Bern already had a wife, Dorothy Millette, whom he had married secretly. They had lived openly as man and wife at the Algonquin Hotel in New York. Bern, he added, was still supporting Dorothy Millette with regular checks of around $300 per month. Johnny Roselli had done his research carefully for his mentor, Zwillman, on both coasts. *

Zwillman also revealed that Bern had paid the cost of Millette's expenses at a nursing home for the mentally ill for several months. After returning to the Algonquin Hotel apparently cured, Millette, hearing about Bern's marriage, was now on the west coast living at the Palace Hotel in San Francisco. Bern was aware of this and wrote her at the Palace as evidenced by a letter uncovered following his death.

All this just added to the fire of hatred that Jean felt for her "husband." Nevertheless, the studio "insisted" she stick it out in the house on Easton Drive, the house Bern had given her for a wedding "present," mortgage and all!

---

* Johnny Roselli's name keeps turning up in these Unsolved Mysteries: in the Vicki Morgan case as a friend of Frank Sinatra and Alfred Bloomingdale (Vol. One); in the Marilyn Monroe case as a henchman of Sam (Mo-Mo) Giancana. Roselli was also a public relations "consultant" at The Last Frontier Hotel in Las Vegas in 1954 when a deal for Ronald Reagan to appear as MC for the stage show at the El Rancho fell through when he needed the work. As soon as Roselli got word, Reagan was signed to appear at The Last Frontier. He then segued into The General Electric Theatre on television sponsored by General Electric and MCA, Inc.

She went into a state of depression – self-destructive depression. Feeling sorry for herself, she donned a red wig many nights on leaving the studio and frequented places such as the Clover Club which had gambling condoned by the Los Angeles Vice Squad, The Trocadero and even some small, tacky saloons in downtown Los Angeles' Main Street.

She had one night stands with taxi drivers, and other men she met in the bars. She was promiscuous, carefree and drank excessively. MGM was so powerful in those days that it kept most, if not all, of Jean's escapades from the press. Not even Jean's relatives around the country knew of her peccadilloes. *

☆ ☆ ☆

Upon arriving at MGM on Saturday morning, September 4th, to continue working on *Red Dust*, in which she was starring with Clark Gable, Jean received a call from Zwillman. His manner was casual, as Jean knew it on their many trysts in a cottage at the Garden of Allah in Hollywood. Nevertheless, Zwillman's meaning was clear. She was not to go home that evening, but to spend the night with her mother.

Jean told Zwillman that she and Bern had already planned to have dinner with her mother on Sunday night. Zwillman told her that was fine, but that he also wanted her out of the house on Saturday night as well.

Bern was not aware that Jean would not be home that evening when Dorothy Millette called to demand that he meet with her and her "attorney." Bern said he would reserve a bungalow at the Ambassador Hotel and privacy would be assured.

Harold Garrison, who served MGM executives as handyman and chauffeur – and lived at the Bern-Harlow home – drove Bern to the Ambassador Hotel about 7 p.m. Garrison was told by Bern to have dinner, then come back and wait in the street behind the hotel.

At Zwillman's insistence, Dorothy was disguised in a black wig and dark glasses. She was waiting when Bern arrived. She introduced the man with her as "Abe Long," a name he often used.

---

*To show the lack of knowledge of Jean Harlow's relatives, following a brief message in our previous book, *Hollywood's Unsolved Mysteries*, we received several letters from people who claimed to be relatives denying she even KNEW or had any knowledge of Zwillman, or her promiscuity! Neither were they aware that Harlow was the godmother to Benjamin "Bugsy" Siegel's daughter, the mobster assassinated in 1947. This is how effective Howard Strickling was in "controlling" the Hollywood press about Harlow's extra-curricular activity.

Bern appeared to be more puzzled than alarmed that she would bring along an attorney after he had been supporting her for years without benefit of counsel. Nevertheless, he tried to keep everything on a high plane and civilized.

After they had finished a room service meal which Bern insisted upon, Dorothy cut short Bern's incessant chatter about affairs of the day.

How, she asked him, could he do to another woman what he had done to her. If he had any explanation or excuse, she wanted to hear it. Bern went into his "sobbing act," as Jean Harlow described it to her mother, when he was at a loss for words of an emotional nature.

But then by his own will power and an attempt to turn the proceedings around, Paul regained control of himself. He told them he knew all too well what he had done to Jean but he had no choice. He had been asked by the studio heads to marry her. The studio ". . . wanted to protect Jean from an 'Eastern gangster' who had been demanding that she marry him." Zwillman liked the way things were going.

★ ★ ★

Jean Harlow was never told, prior to her marriage, that Paul Bern was "requested" by Thalberg and Mayer to woo and marry her.

Paul Bern realized he would be doing the same to Jean as he had done to Millette prior to their marriage: hide from her the size of his penis and his impotence.

Following a briefing from Howard Strickling and Thalberg, Bern was told the studio "had to protect itself – and Jean – from the 'clutches' of an 'Eastern gangster' who could cause problems for MGM, possibly the industry, if it was learned that one of its top stars was screwing a New York mobster at the Garden of Allah."

★ ★ ★

Following this revelation by Bern, Zwillman casually asked him if he knew the name of "this gangster!"

"No," admitted Bern, ". . . but I can find out. Joe Schenck knows." *

Zwillman remained impassive but asked no more questions. Dorothy Millette, who knew Bern well, took charge. Her insight into her husband's "problems" soon had him wiggling.

He finally acknowledged that it was a marriage in name only and since the marriage was of that nature, he did not worry about bigamy. His only motive in agreeing to it was to improve his standing with Thalberg and Mayer, so that he could continue to care for Dorothy in the years to come.

He then changed his story and said he had "volunteered" for the job of "protecting Jean from this gangster!"

Dorothy Millette was about to call him a liar, but wanted to talk to Jean Harlow first. Zwillman terminated the meeting by telling Bern he had 24 hours to find proof of his story. Tomorrow night they would come to his home for the showdown. If Mrs. Dorothy Bern remained unsatisfied, legal action would be taken.

Bern was pensive when he entered his limousine. Not a word was said as Garrison drove him to Easton Drive.

☆ ☆ ☆

If there was anything that Louis B. Mayer hated as head of MGM, it was paying employees for not working on federally mandated holidays such as Labor Day. But, to Mayer's fiendish mind, there was no law to say he could not make people work on Sundays. There were no strong unions or guilds in those days to force a five-day week on the studios.†

---

*Like Johnny Roselli, a friend and "associate," Joe Schenck, was also involved in many iniquitous dealings in Hollywood. He forced Louis B. Mayer to "contribute" $350,000 in order for he and Darryl Zanuck to gain control of Fox Films to form 20th Century Fox. The other $350,000 of the capital came from the President of Loew's Inc., the parent company of MGM, and his brother, Nick Schenck! Joe demanded this, stating that he was "responsible" for providing MGM with its top star, Jean Harlow. Schenck told Mayer that he forced Howard Hughes to sell her contract to MGM after being "softened up" by Zwillman. Mayer, however, insisted on a high paying job for his son-in-law, William Goetz, another example of the incestuousness of the oligarchy.

†As director Victor Fleming told Mayer when he insisted that Fleming shoot on Sunday to make up for Labor Day, "You can insist that actors work on a Sunday but not that they have to do their best." Mayer told Fleming, in his unctuous manner born of selling scrap iron in Canada before entering the film business, "A good director can get the best out of his actors any day of the week!"

Two of the top MGM stars, Robert Taylor and Jean Harlow, in a pensive mood on the set. *(John Austin Collection)*

At the studio on Sunday, Jean spent the day in a rain barrel for a scene in *Red Dust* but nothing went right.

Watching Clark Gable get hot and bothered for her body simply was not as much fun as it had been. Gable told Harlow that he was going fishing the next day, Labor Day, in hopes that it would relax him.

Jean's stepfather, Marino Bello, was never very far from Jean's paycheck. He had come to the studio to pick her up and volunteered to go to show Gable how an Italian tied flies. Jean was happy that the hyperactive Bello would be out of town. It gave her an excuse to spend another night with mama. A night which would be forever etched in the memory of Jean Harlow, the oligarchy and Hollywood historians.

✩ ✩ ✩

After Jean Harlow had learned of Paul Bern's marriage to Dorothy Millette, Zwillman "suggested" that Jean take a few days off and go to San Francisco to meet with the "other" Mrs. Paul Bern. Zwillman would meet her there.

The meeting took place at the Plaza Hotel where Dorothy Bern was then living – still on those monthly checks from "her husband." She turned out to be ten years older than Jean, ten years younger than Paul. They talked of the "little man" who had done so much to mix up their lives. Dorothy had been a struggling young actress in one of the theatrical troupes for whom Paul Bern worked on the East Coast. They had fallen in love, married secretly, and lived as man and wife at the Algonquin Hotel.

Like Jean, Dorothy had not learned the truth about her husband until their wedding night. The shock had been a lasting one, but she agreed to stick it out and give Paul a sense of virility.

After a year, she admitted, she had cracked up under the strain and Bern placed her in an expensive sanatorium in Connecticut. She was still there when he went West on a "quest of sexual stimulation," as he had put it to her before leaving.

It was only after she learned he had remarried without benefit of a divorce that Dorothy agreed to meet with Jean at the "suggestion" of Zwillman. Having met Jean, she liked her, but there was still the question of what to do about Paul Bern.

"Things have to be handled properly," Zwillman observed.

The way he said it caused a chill to come over Jean Harlow. Perhaps, she thought to herself, she had read something into those statements that wasn't meant to be there.

Little did she know how wrong she was. It was only a matter of time.

Zwillman was silent during the ride back to the Mark Hopkins where Jean, her mother and Marino Bello were registered. A block from the hotel, Zwillman stopped the Pierce Arrow and told Jean to walk the rest of the way. He did not want them to be seen together any more than necessary. He told Jean he would see her in Los Angeles in a few days.

☆ ☆ ☆

The household help of Carmichael, the cook, Garrison, and the gardener said that Bern spent all of Sunday alone, eating and drinking a lot more than usual. They said later that Bern received two telephone calls he said were "anonymous." Carmichael, who answered one of the calls, said it was a man's voice.

Bern took the receiver off the hook; Jean was unable to reach him when she tried. He was very depressed and very apprehensive about the second meeting that night with Dorothy Millette and her "attorney"!

Zwillman deliberately delayed Dorothy's trip to Easton Drive. He wanted Jean to come along, and needed to be sure the help was in bed and there weren't too many people around when they arrived. The Pierce Arrow with Zwillman at the wheel and the two Mrs. Berns in the rear seat drove up the rise to the house.

Zwillman rang the door bell while Jean and Dorothy stood behind him. When Bern opened the door he was naked. Zwillman forced his way in, Millette close behind. Harlow stayed on the steps. Bern retreated to the bathroom to get a robe. Millette followed him. She pulled out a revolver and shot Bern in the head. He fell to the bathroom floor. Zwillman placed a note on the dresser that Bern had written to Harlow weeks before – the note was to look like it had been written that night as a suicide note. (It is believed that Bern had contemplated suicide soon after their wedding night because of the harm he had done Jean with his cane.) At one of their meetings soon afterward at the Garden of Allah, Harlow showed the note of atonement to Zwillman who took it from her.

The note read:

Dearest Dear:

Unfortunately, this is the only way to make good the frightful wrong I have done you and wipe out my abject humility.

> *I love you,*
> *Paul*

A postscript read:

You understand that last night was only a comedy.

Zwillman matter-of-factly wiped the .38 free of any of Millette's fingerprints and pressed it into the still warm, but lifeless, hand of Bern in order to obtain his fingerprints on the weapon. He then removed it and placed it near the body. A typical "mob touch!"

Millette and Zwillman then joined Harlow in the powerful touring car. Jean was dropped off near her home and Zwillman headed up the coast highway to return Millette to her hotel in San Francisco, eight hours north. He did not want Dorothy Millette seen on a train or in a taxi. He knew the studio would be called first and that Mayer and his minions were "experts" in making a murder a suicide for the sake "of the industry!"

★ ★ ★

When the police were finally called by Carmichael and arrived on the scene at Easton Drive, Mayer left. But as he drove down the winding driveway, he spotted Howard Strickling. They spoke briefly.

"Paul left a note," Mayer told him. "I decided it shouldn't be seen by anyone outside the studio, Howard, so I took it."

At that, Mayer handed the note to a shocked and dismayed Strickling. He was horror struck that Mayer would interfere and try to destroy what appeared to be evidence.

"You can't do that," he told him – and very few men in Hollywood were ever able to say that to "LB." "This could be a homicide investigation regardless of what the note says. If anyone ever finds out you took that, there'll be a god-awful stink. You've got to go back and give it to the cops."

Mayer had his chauffeur turn the limousine around in the narrow space and meekly gave the note to the officer in charge. The officers read the note, and tried for a moment to figure out its hidden meaning. Then they went back to their examination of the scene.

The investigation revealed that Bern had been shot while standing, nude, before a full length mirror in the dressing room off the bathroom adjoining the master bedroom. A .38 calibre bullet had entered his right temple – Bern was right-handed – passed through his brain, and emerged at the back of the head to bury itself in the opposite wall. A forensic official was in the process of digging out the bullet from the wall as Mayer handed the note over to the chief of the detective team.

The body, when found by Carmichael, was lying face down, the head turned with the right cheek against the tile floor. The death weapon lay a few feet from the body where Zwillman had "placed it." On the dresser in Bern's room was another pistol, also a .38, according to police records.

The detectives investigating the death said it ". . . was obviously a case of suicide." However, chief of detectives Chet Taylor said he felt there were too many discrepancies in this theory, and it ought to be investigated. One of the more pertinent questions he wanted answered was:

"Why did it take over two hours to
notify the police?"

A good question, but one which was never answered by Mayer, Hendry, Strickling, Carmichael or his wife, the cook.

The homicide team made the usual investigation of the house and grounds, and they questioned the gardener and Garrison, the chauffeur. Other teams fanned out to the Bello home to question Jean Harlow. However, a monkey wrench was thrown into this aspect of the investigation because "Jean's physicians" – *called in by the studio - - decided she "was too hysterical to be questioned at this time."* The police did not find out until a year later that Jean and her family were practicing Christian Scientists, and they did not even know a physician.

The "investigation" at the Bern household brought out that Jean and Paul Bern "had gotten along very well together" while they were in the house and *within earshot of the staff of four.*

This point, however, was to be violently disputed during later stages of the investigation.

✯ ✯ ✯

The ubiquitous Joseph Schenck (shown here following his marriage to Norma Talmadge) was involved in MGM and purchased Jean's contract from Howard Hughes. Schenck later exacted a price from L.B. Mayer for enabling MGM to obtain the contract at a bargain basement price. Zwillman was also involved in the deal and in getting his part-time mistress involved with Dorothy Millette. *(Marvin Paige's Motion Picture & TV Research Service)*

The power of MGM was apparent at the inquest into Bern's death. Jean Harlow was NOT called as a witness, a very unusual omission when you consider previous inquests in Los Angeles had never failed to call the widow or widower in any homicide investigation.

According to those who were there, the questions asked of other witnesses were not nearly as pointed as they should have been.

Howard Strickling and the oligarchy had seen to that.

★ ★ ★

From the inquest emerged a concocted story:

> Bern had "created" an argument on the night of his death so that Jean would be sure to spend the night at her mother's. [She would have done so, anyway.]
>
> Early on Sunday evening she returned to Easton Drive for a peace making session with Bern. She left soon afterward to spend the evening wth her mother. Bello had "gone fishing" with Clark Gable and was not expected back until sometime Monday and Mrs. Bello did not like to be alone.
>
> The inquest, however, could determine no motive for the suicide. The note was too ambiguous to fathom a reason for suicide and no one knew what it meant. Jean Harlow could not explain it when she was asked about it following the inquest.

The top writers in Hollywood couldn't have concocted a better screenplay than the one created over Paul Bern's body that Labor Day morning at Easton Drive.

★ ★ ★

The official version of the inquest released to the press was that Bern had been suffering from a physical infirmity making any marriage he entered into highly embarrassing.

The strange part about the Bern-Harlow marriage to the unknowing press and the public was:

Why did a man suffering from such an infirmity marry such a person as the highly-sexed Jean Harlow? This question, of course, could only be answered by Thalberg, Mayer or Strickling, and they were not about to comment, and probably were not aware of Bern's problem.

☆ ☆ ☆

On their mid-morning arrival in San Francisco at the Plaza Hotel, Zwillman told Millette to be seen around the lobby before she went to her room and went to sleep. She purchased a paper and spoke with the desk clerk.

Two weeks later an item about her received scant attention in the local press:

"The body of a woman identified as Dorothy Millette of New York was found in the Sacramento River. Her shoes, coat and purse were found on the deck of the Delta Queen 14 days ago and linked to the victim. Her death has been ruled a suicide."

During a background investigation by the police, it was learned that Dorothy Millette had left the hotel with a small bag Tuesday afternoon and boarded a cruise liner that plied the Delta between San Francisco and the California capital, Sacramento. Two weeks later two fishermen had found the badly decomposed body of Millette and called the police.

The official verdict of her death was suicide.

From a broken heart?

From a guilty conscience in shooting her husband, Paul Bern?

Or general emotional instability following a stay in a mental institution? Had she suddenly realized during the drive back to San Francisco that she would not be supported any longer by the man she had killed and that she had no prospects for work?

Did Zwillman have the "suicide" "taken care of" to rid himself of the only witness who might ever talk?

☆ ☆ ☆

Suicide victims seldom take time to remove shoes and other items of clothing before killing themselves. These could have been removed for her to make it look like a suicide by whomever Zwillman had "hired." When the San Francisco police gained access to her room at the Plaza Hotel following discovery of her body, they found a memo pad beside the telephone on a nightstand. There was nothing written on the pad but the impressions from a previous sheet of paper could still be discerned. Only one word, however, could be raised with the existing chemical tests of the day.

That word was "justification."

Two letters were also discovered among her effects; one was from Paul Bern, one from his secretary, Irene Harrison.

The letter from Bern read:

Dear Dorothy:

I was very happy to receive your letter.

I have been desperately trying to get away from here for both vacation and change of scene for the last year, but so far it has been quite impossible.

I read with great interest that you are contemplating a trip to San Francisco. Of course I cannot give you any advice because you yourself can be the only person to know what is best. If you do go, I hope that it will be a happy change.

I understand that the Plaza Hotel is a fairly reasonable and attractive one.

If you do change to any other place we will find some way of supplying you with funds in a manner convenient for you.

My love and best wishes always,

Paul

Sometime in June, Bern's secretary sent a letter to Dorothy Millette at the Plaza Hotel.

Dear Miss Millette:

According to the arrangements agreed upon I am enclosing a money order for $160, now due. Mr. Bern has already left on his vacation, but I am at the office in the meantime, and if I can help you in any way, please don't hesitate to ask me. I hope you are comfortably settled in your new home.

Sincerely yours,

Irene Harrison
Secretary to Paul Bern

★ ★ ★

A year following Bern's death, a new grand jury was appointed and its first order of business was to investigate the investigator – district attorney, Buron J. Fitts. *

In order to do this, the jury foreman obtained the records of the previous grand jury which had looked into Bern's death. The foreman claimed, "We are only interested in Fitts's expenditures for the grand jury."

But Buron J. Fitts, who had been "on the take" for years, took the "offense is the best defense" posture, releasing some of the testimony before the grand jury in the previous hearing to remove the focus from himself.

It turned out that the most unusual revelations were in the testimony of Davis, the gardener and Irene Harrison, Bern's secretary.

Davis's testimony was startling, to say the least.

"I think it was murder. I thought so from the very beginning," Davis related. He told the panel that Carmichael had "lied" about the tragedy. He said Jean Harlow and Paul Bern did not have a fight the evening before Bern's death. He said they always had gotten along well as far as he could tell. "He (Carmichael) said that Harlow and Bern were always embracing and kissing each other, and Bern was talking of committing suicide; when they really didn't do much

---

* Like Johnny Roselli and Joe Schenck, the name of Buron J. Fitts also recurs in many of Hollywood's unsolved mysteries through the 1930s and even into the 1940s. Fitts was a great "help" to the industry, and vice versa, through the years starting with the continuing cover-up in the William Desmond Taylor murder. With the help of the oligarchy, he was eventually appointed a Superior Court Judge! He eventually committed suicide with the same Smith & Wesson revolver used to slay Taylor. He had agreed to destroy it years earlier.

hugging and kissing, and Bern never did say anything about taking his own life!"

Then Davis claimed the suicide note was not in Bern's handwriting. [Whether the handwriting was ever checked by an expert was never discovered.]

Irene Harrison claimed that Jean Harlow had been the pursuer – not Bern – during the courtship period. Harrison also noted that she had obviously been "coached" by the studio in her testimony. "Mr. Bern didn't look particularly happy at the reception following the ceremony," she observed.

Then came a question that led to all kinds of speculation asked of Garrison, the Berns' chauffeur:

"Did you hear about the time Mr. Bern found his wife in the hotel in Los Angeles with another man?"

Garrison swore under oath that he had not. He also replied "No" when asked if he had ever seen Jean Harlow out with anyone other than Bern.

★ ★ ★

The transcript released by Fitts also contained the information that after Davis was questioned by the police, he was summoned by telephone to the Bello home where Jean had taken refuge from enquiring reporters – and the police. Once at the Bello home, the stormy Bello told Davis:

"It looks like you're talking too much. Move your wife and family to the garage apartment and keep your damned mouth shut about all this."

According to Davis, Bern had loathed Bello and Bello certainly had never liked Bern. Perhaps, as some friends said later, by Jean getting married, it shut off a lot of Bello's income. Once Jean married, he had to earn a living.

After this new inquisition, the Bern death was still *officially* a suicide.

A suicide it has remained ever since. Today, the only people debating the verdict are journalists, such as Ben Hecht who reported in the November 1960 issue of *Playboy:*

> "Paul Bern, remembered for having committed suicide as the impotent bridegroom of Jean Harlow, the great cinema sexpot, did no such thing. His suicide note,

hinting that he was sexually impotent and had therefore 'ended the comedy' was a forgery.

"MGM studio officials decided, sitting in conference around Bern's body, that it was better to have Paul dead as a suicide than as the murder victim of another woman.

"It would be less a black eye for the biggest movie making heroine, La Belle Harlow. It might crimp her box office allure to have her blazoned as a wife who couldn't hold her husband."

☆ ☆ ☆

Although Paul Bern was out of Jean Harlow's life, his impact was everlasting. To begin with, it took Jean several weeks to recuperate from his death and return to work on *Red Dust*. When she did, she looked haggard and tired but she managed to finish the film.

After a proper period of mourning for the sake of appearances, Harlow, free at last, ended the sham with gusto! The sex symbol without a man made up for lost time with several drunken sexual binges in Northern California where she was not as likely to be recognized. She again donned the red wig on most days. All of these binges Strickling and MGM managed to keep out of the papers.

One year and two weeks following Bern's death, Jean earned herself another stall in Louis B. Mayer's dog kennel. First, she told him to go to hell when the loathsome man went on the make and asked her to screw him on his infamous office couch.

Then, she earned Mayer's everlasting enmity. She eloped with her *Red Dust* cameraman Hal Rosson, 16 years her senior.

Mayer was furious! He believed that a married "sex symbol" was box office "poison." It didn't last long. They divorced after seven months of a sexless marriage. Rosson moved to London and worked in the British film industry for several years.

Jean, however, was a workhorse for MGM. She made a hit with Clark Gable in Anita Loos' *Hold Your Man*.

She played a star surrounded by a freeloading family in *Bombshell*, her favorite film. And her scenes opposite the surly Wallace Beery in *Dinner at Eight* were considered to be some of her best work. In 1935,

Louis B. Mayer, one of the most loathed men in Hollywood.

MGM starred her in a musical, *Reckless*, and used doubles for her singing and dancing. It was while making this film that she met the one great love of her life, the urbane William Powell.

Shortly after the two met they fell in love. Their first public exhibition of this attraction, a passionate kiss, was captured by a photographer. Their fans thrilled to the news. This put to lie the "theory" of Louis B. Mayer that the public would not accept a married "sex symbol." "Harlow & Powell Kiss" was on the cover of *Time* magazine.

Jean Harlow was maintaining a grueling six-day-a-week schedule of filming. Up at 5:30 a.m. and at the studio by 7 a.m., she was making film after film to pay off her debts, and those incurred by Bern, during their brief marriage, as well as the bills her stepfather had run up in her name before he ran away from Mama Bello.

At a party on the set of *Riff Raff*, which she was making with Spencer Tracy, Harlow and Powell announced their engagement. They said they were to be married in a few months.

This was not to be. In December 1935, while making *Wife vs. Secretary* with Gable and Myrna Loy, Jean collapsed. Mama nursed Jean at home with with a Christian Science practitioner at her side, but her bladder condition was far more serious than either would admit. Her film crews were so accustomed to Jean's frequent breaks to go to the bathroom, that Mayer ordered a portable john to be installed on the sound stage for her. But now bladder problems had made her too ill to work. All of Jean's problems resulted from that terrible beating the horrible little man, Paul Bern, had given her with his cane on their wedding night.

Jean had never gone to a doctor, and therefore had no knowledge of the internal injuries Bern had inflicted. She did not know that the beating had severely damaged her kidneys. Because she and her family were practicing Christian Scientists, no effort was made to obtain treatment or even a diagnosis of her problems from a physician. No amount of cajoling by MGM officials or Powell could get her to change her mind. Not wanting to stir up any commotion, she kept her problems to herself. Jean never told anyone about the pains in her lower back; not even her fiancee, Powell, because "the doctor thing" would come up again. Unaware of how serious her condition was becoming, she put off even considering seeing a physician. After a few days rest, she was back at work as diligently as before. Harlow filmed *Personal Property* with Robert Taylor. In January 1937, she left for a publicity tour with Robert Taylor to promote the film.

Paul Bern, a studio picture when he first became employed by Irving Thalberg.
(Marvin Paige's Mot. Pict. & TV Research Svc.)

Wedding Reception of Paul Bern and Jean Harlow insisted upon by the studio even though Bern had done irreparable damage to Jean's kidneys on their wedding night. Jean wore loose-fitting green lounging pyjamas to cover up the marks on her back and give her less pain than with tight clothes. (L to R) Irving Thalberg, Harlow (with her mother hidden behind her), Norma Shearer (Thalberg's wife), Jean's step-father, Marino Bello, con man and seldom far from Jean's pay check, and Bern. *(John Austin Collection)*

Four months later, Harlow became seriously ill with an inflamed gall bladder. Powell urged her to take a rest and for God's sake to see a "real doctor." But, *Life* magazine's recent cover girl was in the middle of shooting yet another film, *Saratoga*, with her old friend Clark Gable, and would not be bothered.

At 26, with all her debts erased, and an impending marriage to another great star of the thirties, Jean Harlow's hard work was finally paying off. She thought she was headed for a very fruitful and stable period in her young life.

Then on Saturday, May 29, 1937, almost five years since that beating by the fiendish Bern, Jean Harlow collapsed in Gable's arms during a scene in *Saratoga*.

She was exhausted and assumed she just needed another rest over the weekend. She went to Mama Bello's despite the protest from her fellow workers that she be taken to a hospital.

Her already damaged kidneys, severely weakend by the gall bladder attack, were beginning to fail.

But no one, not even Jean, knew what was happening. The studio should have exercised contractual control over Jean Harlow and insisted she see the studio medical doctor who was always on call. This was a fatal error.

Mama Bello saw this as a chance to put everyone in her debt by some inverse sense of reckoning. She and a practitioner tried to "heal" Jean through "simple" prayer. She assured all of Jean's friends who telephoned over the next few days that Jean was "recovering very quickly."

When Jean Harlow did not return to the set by Tuesday morning, her friends decided to see what was happening.

Arthur Landau, Gable, Frank Morgan, Powell, director Jack Conway, and producer Bernie Hyman literally had to force their way into the Bello home. Reluctantly, she led the sextet into Jean's bedroom and pointed triumphantly toward her daughter. "Doesn't she look better now?" Mama Bello asked them.

The six men stared in horror at the sight. Jean Harlow lay semiconscious, moaning and belching, nauseated, and burning with fever. Her back, chest and shoulders were racked in pain, her pulse erratic.

Mama Bello's idea of "better" was killing her daughter.

She had been devoutly adhering to Christian Science principles and adamantly refused to let a doctor see Jean.

Landau and Hyman tried frantically to reach Bello and Jean's real father for permission for surgery, but neither one could be located.

With time running out, they searched for another way around the stubborn Mrs. Bello, who was adhering strictly to the tenets of her family religion.

At last they discovered a paragraph in the Christian Science doctrine, or whatever, which stated that "nurses" could be present in extreme cases. Mama finally yielded to their pleas but frustrated the nurses' every effort in caring for her. She remained in the room constantly and even slept there as Jean lay dying.

By Sunday, June 6, the situation was desperate. Jean's closest friends stood by helplessly, watching her life slip away. She now needed massive sedation for her pain as her kidneys were literally being ripped apart by her diseased gall bladder, which should have been removed many months before. One of the nurses said she could smell urine on Jean's breath, a sure sign of uremic poisoning.

With nothing left to do, Hyman and Landau went to see L.B. Mayer in his beachfront home. Mayer was no fan of Jean Harlow even though she was one of his studio's major box office draws. Immediately he called Jean's mother and ordered her to allow Jean to go to the hospital. Mayer was the one person Mama Bello feared most, and consented.

The ambulance screamed its way through the streets to the Good Samaritan Hospital. Jean was diagnosed as being too weak to undergo surgery, so emergency blood transfusions were to be administered during the night.

By morning she was comatose; her breathing weak and shallow. Doctors called in the Los Angeles Fire Department Inhalator Squad but even that was useless. William Powell maintained a 24-hour vigil at her bedside.

At 4:37 a.m., Jean Harlow was dead, the residual effect of a beating administered to her by Paul Bern. The same man two members of the oligarchy had "ordered" to woo and marry Jean Harlow to protect MGM's image. By doing so, they contributed to Jean Harlow's death, even though it occured five years later. In essence, she was "murdered" by Paul Bern on her wedding night by that beating with his cane.

While the studio never gave a reason, the powers that be at MGM must have had somewhat of a guilty conscience. Several months after Jean's death, her estate was probated to be worth less than $50,000 with some debts still to be paid. MGM agreed to pay her mother (who had divorced Bello in 1935) a lifetime pension of $500 per month. This was paid until her death in 1958.

The murder of Paul Bern and the very tragic, unnecessary death of Jean Harlow certainly have to be ranked very high on any list of *Hollywood's Unsolved Mysteries.*

Jean and her mother on the set of "China Seas" at MGM. *(Marvin Paige's Mot. Pict. & TV Research Svc.)*

"The Mexican Spitfire." *(John Austin Collection)*

An RKO-Radio Studios portrait of Lupe. *(Marvin Paige's Mot. Pict. & TV Research Svc.)*

9... "The Mexican Spitfire" Laughed No More

"Wild no! Eef I feel gay, I act gay. Eef I feel
like a happy puppy, I wiggle like a happy puppy.
When I am mad, I scream. When I'm in love, I seeng.
When I make love, I scream in ecstasy. Ees
this being wild? No! It ees being Lupe!"

–Lupe Velez
from a 1939 interview

When the maid went to the second floor bedroom of Lupe Velez at 9 a.m., on the morning of December 5, 1944, there was no Lupe in sight. The eight-foot-square bed was empty.

The aroma of scented candles could not erase the stench; it reminded one of the odor left behind by Skid Row derelicts after a bout with Muscatel and homemade gin.

Juanita, her chambermaid, followed the trail of vomit she saw on the nap of the white carpet to an adjoining bathroom quarters of the Spanish style house on Rodeo Drive in Beverly Hills. There she found Lupe Velez, with her head down the toilet bowl – drowned, or so the coroner ruled.

A huge dose of Seconal sleeping pills downed by the fiery actress had not been fatal. Instead, they joined company with a spicy Mexican dinner and apparently revived the dazed Lupe. Being the fastidiously neat person she was, Lupe, to the trained eyes of the police investigating her death, had attempted to reach the bathroom in order not to throw up on the huge bed.

From the marks on the orchid tiled bathroom floor, it was apparent that Lupe had slipped in her vomit. In an attempt to throw up in the toilet, she had fallen head first into the bowl of the Hush Flusher deluxe model onyx toilet, and did not have the strength – or the will power – to pull her head out of the huge, water-filled bowl. The large dose of Seconal she had ingested had totally dulled her senses, but not killed her.

This was how Louella Parsons described the "scoop" on the farewell scene in a page one, black bordered "exclusive" of the death of Guadalupe Velez de Villalobas, aka Lupe Velez, aka "The Mexican Spitfire."

★ ★ ★

The wind was howling in the small village of San Luis Potosi, Mexico, and the rain was so fierce it was penetrating the windows of Colonel Jacob Villalobas's casa. It was a wild night – and the worst storm to hit the village in years. In a bedroom of the casa, a woman writhed and moaned as her labor pains worsened. The local midwife clocked the time between pains on an ancient clock in a room lit by the flickering light of candles. This was on July 20, 1909; electricity had not yet arrived in San Luis, Potosi.

The troubled prayers of the midwife amidst the storm were an insightful prediction of the stormy life which the newly born Guadalupe Velez de Villalobas was to live for the next thirty-four years.

On her birth, the midwife, peering at the red-faced, squalling infant wrapped in a blanket, uttered some prophetic words, "She is stormy, this one. I pray to the good God for her soul!"

★ ★ ★

In the free-wheeling playground of Hollywood in the 1920s, Lupe was perhaps the most free-wheeling of all; one of the least inhibited in an era of few inhibitions. It was the days of bootleg whiskey and nouveau riche moguls who arrived in Never Never Land on the back of produce trucks as junk dealers, glove salesmen and fish mongers, junk peddlers and brothel keepers; graduates from the tough sidewalks of New York and points east.

Many habitues of Hollywood parties of those days repeated tales about how Lupe climaxed the boasts about her charms by lifting her dress up around her neck. As Lupe refused to wear any lingerie underneath, this was a fairly effective way of demonstrating those charms and dispel any doubts about them.

Lupe was a tiny woman, five feet one-and-a-half inches and her weight never varied more than a pound or two from her normal 108 pounds. They say that until her death, she looked like a teenager.

Lupe achieved Hollywood stardom at the age of eighteen, and many people have said that may have been her downfall. For the rest of her life she was well known for childish appetites, whims and the gaiety and rage which appeared to everyone to be so shallow. But none of these foibles made Lupe unattractive. All Hollywood loved Lupe Velez, the Mexican Spitfire, the girl from San Luis. She was warm-hearted, generous to a fault, fun, loving, and completely without malice toward anyone or anything.

☆ ☆ ☆

Lupe's Catholic schooling ended at the age of fourteen and she went to work as a shop girl in Mexico City.

During one of the constant revolutions that disrupted Mexico in the early 1920s, Colonel Villalobas was away with the army chasing banditos, who in turn were chasing the federales. The Villalobas family was destitute.

Ever since she appeared as the lead in a musical comedy at a child dancing school (when the family was between revolutions), Lupe knew she wanted to make acting her career. She went to a theatre in Mexico City and applied for a job. As she was to relate in an interview years later, the manager of the theatre asked to see her act, but she didn't have one. He told her he needed someone who could dance like Gilda Gray * and sing an American song. Lupe spent the entire afternoon at a Gray movie absorbing the elements of the shimmy. She then stood in front of a phonograph record store listening to customers try out American recordings. The next morning she presented the theater manager a "Lupe version" of the shimmy, while she sang "Charlie, My Boy" in broken English. The song was the current rage in Mexico City, and that was all Lupe had heard in that record store the day before. She got the job.

Chorus boys, wealthy stage door johnnies, and the neighborhood

---

* Marianna Michalski, a Polish dancer, who changed her name to Gilda Gray, was a star of silent films, and is credited with inventing the "shimmy." Her first film was *Aloma of the South Seas*. She died in obscurity in 1959.

boys were quick to realize that the early-ripening madcap was physically ready for a roll in the hay, even if Lupe was unconscious of it herself. Impatiently, Lupe brushed away their advances. She preferred to sit in what consisted of her dressing room, a closet next to the stage, practicing "face making " in a mirror, to mooning in the moonlight with horny men.

"All the time I study," she said. "Hour and hour I change the hair to find how Lupe looks best. I study pretty ladies. I follow them in the street. I watch every move. I learn from it all," she related.

Lupe became locally famous for the wild abandon of her dancing act. Then a visitor took word of it back to Hollywood where director Richard Bennett was casting *The Dove* and needed a girl to fill a role. He sent Lupe an offer.

In later years, Lupe claimed she had been a headliner in Mexico and was earning $350 per week. Actually, her salary was $50 a week and it went through her fingers as fast as she got it. On the night she left for Hollywood, she drew her last pay envelope. She blew the equivalent of $29 on a new dress and boarded the train with $21.

What happened next is typical Lupe folk lore. "On the train is thees beautiful man," she related later. "I flirt with heem, of course. And he, goddamn, steals from me $20! Always men hurt Lupe. Always I must fight weeth them. Always! Always! Never have I met a man I did not have to fight, and fight, and fight."

She arrived in Los Angeles with a single dollar bill in her purse – and the telegram from Bennett.

She eventually found a hotel clerk who would give her a room even though she had no money. He accepted the telegram as a guarantee that the room would be paid for. Unfortunately, Lupe had been delayed in leaving Mexico due to problems in obtaining a passport and visa so Bennett had already filled the role.

He did, however, recommend her to Fanchon and Marco, who organized girlie shows which toured the sticks and stocked some of the better vaudeville houses in the bigger towns. They put Lupe in *Music Box Revue*, one of their better units put together for the Los Angeles trade. Fannie Brice saw Lupe in it and sent Flo Ziegfeld an enthusiastic telegram. He asked Lupe to come to New York for a tryout.

If Lupe had accepted the showman's offer, things might have turned out far better for her in the long run. Instead, after turning her down repeatedly, MGM suddenly decided that it wanted Lupe Velez! However, she refused a screen test and got on a train bound

Gary Cooper, a true love of Lupe's and vice versa. But Coop, as he was known, had to give up the romance. Lupe's sexual demands were too much for him to take, including one episode crossing the intersection of Wilshire & Westwood Boulevards at rush hour with the top down on his convertible. This was an episode related to a Hollywood columnist by Coop who related it to the author over four or five very strong martinis at Stefanino's restaurant. (*Marvin Paige's Mot. Pict. & TV Research Svc.*)

Lupe and Leon Erroll, her foil in several "Mexican Spitfire" films at RKO. *(Marvin Paige's Mot. Pict. & TV Research Svc.)*

Lupe in a pensive scene from a "Mexican Spitfire" film at RKO in 1943. *(Marvin Paige's Mot. Pict. & TV Research Svc.)*

for New York. Unable to comprehend why anyone, let alone a young Mexican performer, would refuse an MGM screen test, Irving Thalberg sent Harry Rapf rushing across town to intercept Lupe. Apparently, he was so breathlessly persuasive that he and Lupe jumped off the Santa Fe Chief just as it started to move out of the Pasadena station.

☆ ☆ ☆

Once it had her under contract, MGM was at a loss to know what to do with her. There was no Zorro, or films about one of the numerous Mexican revolutions being made at the time; not even a Pancho Villa epic. For lack of something better to do, they cast her in a two-reel Laurel and Hardy comedy, in which her face was the recipient of custard pies.

Her uninhibited actions on and off the screen made her well known all over town, long before her first week as an MGM player was over. This proved to be very fortunate, for Douglas Fairbanks Sr. was looking for a girl to fill a role his screenplay described ". . . as willing to fight a man as love him!" It was a tailor-made role for Lupe.

"That's Lupe," Fairbanks was told by at least a dozen people who had seen her around the Culver City studio. "When she puckers up her lips, it is impossible to tell if she is going to kiss you, bite you, or spit on you!" Intrigued by the description, Fairbanks went to see her, and then borrowed Lupe from MGM – to its considerable profit – for *The Gaucho*, his independently-produced swashbuckling tale of an Argentine cowboy. Lupe was required only to be herself, and her fiery, sexy performance was a smash hit with audiences and producers.

Fairbanks, who was part owner of the recently formed United Artists, bought seventeen-year-old Lupe's contract. She then found herself playing Chinese, Eskimo, Japanese, Hindu, Swedish (a Swedish Mexican?!), Malayan, Javanese and French roles. Her popularity climbed at the box office with each picture, and by the time she was nineteen, Lupe Velez was a top Hollywood star.

☆ ☆ ☆

In a town so famous for its unconventional people, Lupe exceeded even the antics of Clara Bow and John Barrymore. In the beginning, she pretended to understand less English than she really did.

Hollywood wits thought it a great joke to teach her blistering curses, telling her these were sophisticated Hollywood idiom.

Mischeviously, Lupe went along with the gag. She pretended to believe them. With that innocent air she could assume so skillfully, she would interlace her casual talk with very unladylike purple phrases.

Interviewers from fan magazines, newspapers and studio publicists fell for the gag. Almost every story written about Guadalupe Velez de Villalobas in the twenties relates how Hollywood humorists took advantage "... of poor little Lupe!" What they didn't realize was that Lupe Velez had used all those words and more when she blistered the hides off American immigration authorities, when they would not let her enter the United States without a passport and visa, an oversight which cost Velez her role in *The Dove*.

This is the way Lupe Velez was described in various noteworthy sources in the late 1920s:

> *"Lupe Velez – to put it mildly – is a nut."*
> – *Saturday Evening Post*

> *"She is perpetual motion, a description with which her worn out boyfriends agree."*
> –*Vanity Fair*

> *"Lupe acts, in general, as if she'd just downed several bottles of Tequila."*
> –Florenz Ziegfeld

In typical fashion, Lupe shrugged it off. "People come to my movies to have a good time If I don't have a good time, they don't either."

Lupe's first big, widely publicized love affair, was with the discarded lover of Greta Garbo, John Gilbert. (Garbo preferred her lady friends.) In her book, *From Under My Hat*, Hedda Hopper recalled an incident about Lupe and the time The Mexican Spitfire asked her whether or not she should marry Gilbert. "After all," said Lupe, "I'm no lady!"

Hopper, in her own inimitable way, replied, "Lupe, what's the advantage of getting married? Tell me now, honestly!"

According to Hopper, that was the answer Lupe had been waiting for. Beaming, she rushed over to Gilbert and yelled, "Hey, Jack! We don't have to get married!"

When the romance with Gilbert soured because of his difficulty in making the transition from silent to sound, Lupe met the first great love of her life – Gary Cooper. She was an incurable flirt, but this was the real thing.

She met Cooper when she was loaned to Paramount Studios to star opposite him in *The Wolf Song* as the Spanish love interest. She became his love interest off screen as well.

Cooper's romance with Clara Bow had just ended when Lupe reported for work on *The Wolf Song* set. According to those who were there, and the Hollywood press corps, it was love at first sight for both, and most definitely an attraction of opposites. Cooper was quiet; Lupe was loud. He was even-tempered; she was volcanic. He used a minimum of words. She talked constantly.

It was a hectic romance, spent mostly horizontal when they were away from the studio. Quite often they were horizontal in each other's dressing rooms between takes. But what was obvious was that it was a genuine love on both sides. By Hollywood standards it lasted a long time. Three years after they met, a reporter cornered Cooper with the question, "What is the biggest thrill you've gotten from motion pictures?"

Cooper, always a man of few words, replied, simply, "Lupe," and changed the subject. However, when he was placed in a position in the late forties, even though he was reluctant to discuss it, Cooper did make a statement, "Well, I guess I was in love with her!"

About her romance with Cooper, the madcap Lupe was not so closed-mouthed. One of her joys was to telephone some of her reporter friends and give them blow-by-blow descriptions of her love affairs, particularly Cooper. Frequently, "blow-by-blow" was an apt description.

Among the gifts Cooper bought Lupe during their romance was a male eagle for a pet. She was so enthusiastic about her adroitness in the bedroom to think that any creature should be deprived of such fun and games. Because of Lupe's insistence, Coop, as he was known, went out and either trapped or purchased another eagle – no one ever discovered how he acquired such a bird. Unfortunately for the libido of both, the second one also turned out to be male.

Eventually, Cooper had to give up the ghost he was rapidly beginning to look like. He found Lupe too demanding, sometimes three and four times a day no matter where they were. She was just too exhausting in her female demands, and would unbutton Cooper's fly anywhere she could and play it like a piccolo, or acquire the use of any horizontal surface near at hand.

Coop once described one such event to a close friend, Harrison Carroll, a columnist for the *Los Angeles Herald – Express*:

> "Coop once described for me how Lupe unbuttoned his pants and went down on him while they were driving down Wilshire, crossing Westwood Boulevard at rush hour. The light changed to red at a most inopportune time, the crucial moment of oral gratification. A delivery truck stopped in the right hand lane. Coop . . . turned beet red and lowered his 6' 4" frame as low in the seat as possible. Lupe proceeded to replace the lipstick recently deposited on his now very limp organ while they waited for the light to change. He said that was the last time he ever had the top down on his convertible with Lupe in the car!"

★ ★ ★

The breakup came in 1930. Lupe was at the peak of her fame and beauty. Slightly over five feet tall and still 108 pounds, her hair was a glossy black which set off her olive Latino complexion. Her figure was one of the most beautiful in Hollywood. No less an authority than Erroll Flynn claimed in print that she had the most beautiful breasts he had ever seen. Flynn also told a curious tale about Lupe's ability to rotate her breasts in opposite directions. He claimed he had seen her do it at a party. Another of Lupe's stunts was to be interviewed in bed, preferably by male reporters from fan magazines or newspapers. She would jump up from under the sheets in a very revealing, transparent nightgown to act out something she was describing. It wasn't always polite and it was usually very suggestive.

★ ★ ★

As a child in Mexico, Lupe was a handful. Her mother, a very devout Catholic, was constantly horrified at her daughter's actions. As a child, she was forbidden to use lipstick or face powder, so she improvised her own from strawberries and flour pilfered from the meager supplies in the pantry of the Villalobas cocina. The effect was grotesque on the nine-year-old, but Lupe was so entranced she kissed her reflection in the mirror.

Years later John Barrymore, starring with her in *Playmates*, expressed surprise at her acting ability.

"I teach me!" Lupe cried, delighted with Barrymore's flattery. "When I am a leetle girl. I put on my brother's pants and I walk and talk just like him. And I do the same with my mother, my father, and everyone I meet!

"My mamacita she says, 'Lupe, thees ees not polite.' But poof! Who wants to be polite when she can be an actress!"

As she grew older, the stage-struck little Mexican girl wanted to spend every minute in a theatre. Then she would come home and practice the dancing and emoting she had seen that day. She continued her self teaching even in the unlikely atmosphere of a convent school. One of the girls in the school knew how to strum a ukelele and taught Lupe some chords.

It was not long after that Lupe Velez made her "debut" at that Mexico City theatre dancing Gilda Gray's shimmy and singing "Charlie, My Boy."

☆ ☆ ☆

Because of her success, Lupe built a mansion in Laurel Canyon. Her bedroom was stocked with seventy-five canaries. One of her delights was to dance around the room and sing with them. She claimed to know each bird personally, and flew into a cursing rage if anyone doubted her word.

It was said that Lupe Velez never just entered a room. She burst into it. Often she would announce her presence with a loud song – in Spanish and English. After numerous lectures from studio publicists and well meaning friends, she was finally convinced that this was undignified.

She went to several parties as the "new Lupe," and moped around for half an hour. Then, unable to stand "dignity" any further, she left without a word to anyone. As she put her white convertible in gear, startled guests heard her shout, "Now, goddam, I can be happy!" Then she would wheel down a driveway singing at the top of her voice.

Those who tried to change Lupe Velez
gave up after this. Lupe was – as she tried
to tell them – Lupe – and they might as
well accept her as such!

★ ★ ★

In 1933 she up and married Johnny Weismuller, the 1932 Olympic
swimming champion, who was swinging from tree to tree as Tarzan,
and from bed to bed of as many Hollywood starlets as he could. The
marriage lasted for five stormy years, through three official separa-
tions and numerous public brawls.

As usual, Lupe was not reluctant to discuss her romance. On one
occasion she told Harrison Carroll how she would awaken in the night
and stare at Weismuller, because ". . . he ees so beautiful!

"Then for no reason I punch him right in the nose. He jumps up
and says, 'Mama, you hit me!' And I say, 'Darling, I am sorree. Heet
me back!' and he says, 'Never mind, honey, you couldn't help
yourself!'"

Once she stormed out of the house in the middle of the night,
caught a train to New York and took a Cunard liner for Europe.
Another time, she physically threw a girl out of a party for
". . . making eyes at my Johnee!"

When the marriage broke up – finally – in 1938, Lupe gave her
honest opinion of wedded bliss to *Photoplay*:

> "Marriage – eet stinks. I don't like these
> husbands saying, 'Where you been?' If you
> love a man should you seet home sad all the
> time? No! No! Lupe does not believe in
> loving just one man!"

Warming to her subject, she went on:

> "So you go weeth another man to have
> a good time. Thees husband (Weismuller)
> he gets mad! Lupe will not sit home for any
> man!"

In the next six years she had a succession of men friends. Her career reached its peak and declined, but her spectacular and colorful life had no equal and she made "good copy"for print columnists like Parsons and Hopper, as well as fodder for radio gossip hosts George Fisher and Jimmy Fiddler.

☆ ☆ ☆

In 1944 Lupe met a man who was to be her downfall, who stirred her more than anyone since Gary Cooper. He was Harald Raymond, a handsome European of doubtful parentage, as the gossips were to say later. He arrived in Hollywood in 1944 "from somewhere," as Louella Parsons wrote, ". . . and claimed to be a Freedom Fighter in Europe. *

He also claimed to have fought the Nazis in his "native" Vienna, and in Prague where he had been captured and sentenced to Dachau. He intimated that he managed an unreported escape from that infamous stalag and went to France where he fought for a time with the French underground.

Friends warned Lupe that the handsome European was using her to further his career as a so-called actor, or to at least sell his story as an adventurer for a film plot. At these suggestions, Lupe blistered the air.

> "Thees man is not like other men! I love
> heem and he love Lupe!"

Little did Lupe realize how right her friends would turn out to be about Harald Raymond, the son of an Austrian mother and an itinerant Yugoslav.

Lupe took him everywhere and introduced him to everyone. Doors suddenly swung open for him where he couldn't get past the secretaries before. But, like all of Lupe's romances, it was a typically tempestuous affair. After a while, even she began to have mixed emotions about her intimate relationship with the actor who, by now, had moved into Lupe's home on Rodeo Drive.

---

* How Raymond managed to get out of Europe and obtain air transport to the United States at the height of WWII was never explained by him or by anyone else. Sometimes, such people were brought to the United States by the government as a propaganda move to lecture on the bestiality of the Nazis, to exhort workers to push war production as hard as possible.

None of this was documented in Raymond's case.

In September 1944, Mary Morris of *PM*, the New York newspaper (a bold experiment gone awry), interviewed Lupe. It yielded a very significant bit of news. During the course of the interview – as was usual – the question of marriage arose. Lupe's reaction surprised Morris:

"I don't believe in marriage, darling. If there's children, o.k. But a woman who has a career means we're here today and somewhere else tomorrow. We travel, and in our work we have a lot of men friends. I'm just being practical when I say husband and career don't mix."

That statement ended Lupe's relationship with Harald Raymond.

In early November 1944, a few days following the *PM* interview, Lupe went to her doctor's office. When she left, she was biting her lip to keep back tears. She went directly to her home where a birthday party was being held for her brother-in-law. She immediately drew her beloved younger sister into her bedroom and closed the door. What she told Josie startled her to say the least.

> After all of Lupe's tempestuous affairs, most of them in reckless abandon anywhere, anytime, and one very active marriage, she told Josie she was three months pregnant with Harald Raymond's baby.

She told Josie she desperately needed help because she did not want the baby. "We made plans," Josie said later. "Lupe begged me to go with her to Mexico. She told me that I was married and could adopt the baby when it was born. I told her I would be back in a month and that we could talk then."

That is as far as it got. Josie had to return to San Antonio, Texas, with her husband because of a house they were building which needed their supervision.

Lupe never saw Josie again.

Following the party, Lupe called her business manager/agent, Bo Roos, and told him of her plight.

"I immediately called Raymond and asked him point blank what he intended to do about the situation," said Roos. "He told me he would have to have a little time to think it over. He called me back later and proposed a mock marriage ceremony. Then he called back again, and said he would agree to marry Lupe only if she would sign a document saying that she knew he was marrying *her* to give her baby

Johnny ("Tarzan") Weismuller, Lupe's husband for several years ". . . and a beautiful man," according to Lupe. But being Lupe Velez, she cheated during the marriage because she did not like Weismuller ignoring her by being gone so often. (*Marvin Paige's Mot. Pict. & TV Research Svc.*)

a name.

Lupe's reactions to Raymond's demands were very strong. She immediately telephoned Louella Parsons who had publicly announced a Velez-Raymond engagement the previous July. The breakup had not been announced in any column or feature. Lupe decided to take care of this oversight through Lolly Parsons and make sure that Raymond was finished in Hollywood; he would be when Parsons broke the story.

"Lupe told me," wrote Parsons, in her traditional first person style, "that she and Raymond had one big fight and she told him to get out of her house. And when I asked her how the runt spelled his name, she told me, 'I don't know. I never did know. Who cares?'

"As an afterthought," continued Parsons, "Lupe added 'I like my dogs Chips and Chops better.'"

Lupe had probably never made a truer statement in her life. When word got out to the oligarchy, he was forced to leave town. Every door was closed to him, doors which he could walk through with impunity just a few days before. A contract he was discussing for his life story as a major motion picture was torn up and abandoned.

Lupe managed to keep her pregnancy secret from Louella and Hedda Hopper and, as a result, the world. But as she was three months along it was a fact that had to be dealt with . . . and quickly.

Lupe called Roos and told him it looked like a six or seven month trip to Mexico very quietly, or to a doctor known for "accomodating" Hollywood in matters of "appendectomies!" As far as Roos could tell, at this stage no decision had been made by Lupe as to the immediate future.

That same night Lupe attended the Hollywood premiere of her latest film which was made in Mexico, *Zaza*. It co-starred Estelle Taylor, the former wife of heavyweight champ Jack Dempsey, and Benita Oakie, the wife of Jack Oakie.

After the screening, they all returned to Lupe's.

It was then that Roos called her. During one of their conversations earlier in the day, Lupe had mentioned suicide as one way out and it had worried Roos for the rest of the day. He pleaded with her not to take such a drastic step.

"Her last words to me were a promise that she would do nothing until we talked the next day," said Roos.

After the conversation, Lupe returned to the living room and talked to her two friends about the problem she was facing. "I'm tired of life," said the usually ebullient Lupe. "I have to fight for everything. I'm so tired of it all. Ever since I was a baby in Mexico, I've been fighting. I never met a man I didn't have to fight to exist."

★ ★ ★

It was obvious to Taylor and Benita Oakie, following the screening, that Lupe had thought long and hard about that possibility but neither of them thought she would go through with it. Underneath it all, Lupe Velez loved life and she loved Hollywood. She wouldn't do anything to tarnish its image.

At 3:15 a.m. Estelle Taylor left and asked Lupe to walk her down the long driveway to her car. Taylor's large sedan went down Rodeo Drive toward Sunset Boulevard, as Lupe stared after her friend before returning to the warmth of her home on this chilly December morning.

It appears by this time that Lupe had made up her mind and went to her bedroom and lay on the bed. About dawn, according to the coroner estimating the time of death, she wrote two notes in her Mexican English scrawl.

To Harald.

May God forgive you and forgive me, too, but I prefer to take my life away and our baby's before I bring him with shame or killin' [sic] him."

Lupe

On the back of the note, almost as an afterthought, she had written:

How could you, Harald, fake such great love for me and our baby when all the time you didn't want us? I see no other way out for me so goodbye and good luck to you.

Love,

Lupe.

There was another note addressed to her secretary.

You and you alone know the facts and why I am taking my own life.

Forgive me and don't think bad of me. I love you, Mammy, so take care of my mother. And so goodbye and try to forgive me. Say also goodbye to all my friends and to the American press that always was so nice to me."

★ ★ ★

The next day's headlines told the story:

FILM STAR LUPE VELEZ FOUND DEAD IN MYSTERY

The Los Angeles Herald-Express wrote:

"Lupe Velez, dynamic Mexican – American film star, was found dead from an overdose of sleeping pills in her home at 732 North Rodeo Drive, Beverly Hills.

"When found, she had her head in the toilet bowl in the bathroom adjoining her bedroom.

"A police investigator found a note beside the body after being called to the house by Miss Velez's Mexican maid.

"Velez was 33 and was known for her tempestuousness both on and off the screen."

★ ★ ★

Following the discovery of Lupe's lifeless body by Juanita, the coroner decided to hold an inquiry, as required by state law. While it was known Lupe had taken Seconal from the empty pill box beside the bed, without an autopsy he could not tell whether or not it had been a lethal dose or whether death was due to drowning, or a combination of both.

Estelle Taylor said at the inquest that Lupe talked constantly the night before her death of "My baby!"She said she had plenty of time to get rid of it, but again she said, 'It's my baby. I couldn't commit murder and still live myself. I would rather kill myself first.'"

★ ★ ★

It was a tragic end to a stormy life and even stormier career in Hollywood which started fifteen years earlier when she had arrived with $1 in her purse. At the time of her death, Lupe Velez had left her mark on the industry and Hollywood.

Despite the verdict of suicide, there are still some unanswered questions about the death of Lupe Velez:

◆ Why, after all her long affairs and one night stands spanning fifteen years, did Lupe suddenly become pregnant?

◆ She was known never to use any kind of birth control and did not like her men to do likewise. Fate?

◆ Why did she decide not to go to Mexico to have the baby and put it up for adoption?

◆ What was the REAL reason for Harald Raymond's reluctance to marry Lupe? He was told it would do him more harm than good if he walked away from her. Did he have another wife somewhere in Europe? Or in the United States?

◆ Why would Raymond pass up the chance at a lucrative career just when it looked promising – thanks to Lupe?

◆ Why did he tell everyone, immediately after Lupe's death, that he was not sure Lupe was pregnant? Why did he claim that "sometimes she said she was, sometimes that she was not."

◆ Was it because she knew her career was fading fast – there was no work in the offing and she wanted to get married for some sort of security?

◆ Did Lupe suddenly decide she did not want to die and tried to bring up the pills and save herself, and then didn't have the strength to pull her head from the bowl?

☆ ☆ ☆

In an interview following her death, Raymond said he told her on that day, December 14, he would marry her. He used the lame excuse that his English was bad and that she misunderstood him when he talked of a "fake" marriage. He said he *did not want to enter into a fake marriage*.

This statement lent credence to the possibility of a wife somewhere else.

Newsweek magazine said Raymond first admitted, and then denied, that he asked Lupe to sign a statement that he would agree to the marriage only to give the baby a name. In another statement he said, "I suggested that we announce we had married three months before to protect the child, and to really be married *as soon as my own affairs were settled.*"

Another wife?

Harrison Carroll, who had written about Lupe's career in Hollywood in his column in *The Los Angeles Herald – Express* for several years, wrote:

> "After knowing Lupe for many years, I
> am confident she was never able to give the
> other men in her life the same attention she
> bestowed upon Gary Cooper in the days
> when both were struggling for recognition
> in Hollywood."

Lupe Velez, like so many other Hollywood personalities before her, and after her, died a very lonely death; a death she did not deserve.

Harald Raymond was photographed visiting Lupe's body lying in repose in a Los Angeles funeral home. Then he quietly vanished from the Hollywood scene.

He was never heard from again even though several reporters from the Hearst papers, including Louella Parsons, tried to locate him. Whatever happened to him is another of *Hollywood's Unsolved Mysteries* for which there is no answer.

☆ ☆ ☆

> At the end, Hollywood trooped past
> Lupe's coffin to pay final respects to the
> tragic woman in whom good and bad were
> so curiously mixed.
> Among the mourners was a tiny, bowed,
> Mexican woman in dark clothing. She
> stopped to weep beside the body. Those
> close by heard her whisper in a sob-
> wracked voice: "Adios, adios, ninita mia."

("Good-bye, good-bye, my little girl.")
⭐ ⭐ ⭐

"The first time you buy a house you think how pretty it is and sign the check. The second time you look for the termites or dry rot. It's the same with men!"
– Lupe Velez

Lupe with her pet monkey. *(John Austin Collection)*

Nick Adams, Jenny Maxwell, and Joey Bishop in a bucolic TV variety show, 1962. *(John Austin Collection)*

The Rebel's
Dream Ends . . .

Nick Adams as Johnny Yuma, "The Rebel," in the TV series which ran for three years on ABC. *(John Austin Collection)*

10... The Lonely Death of "Johnny Yuma" – Nick Adams

"Absolutely it wasn't suicide. We were so close that
if he'd intended that, I'd have known about it. Murder?
I don't know. It could be foul play!"
– Actor Robert Conrad

*H*e came from the relentless poverty of Appalachia, a washed-up
coal miner's son who Americanized his name from Adamshock
to Adams. He idolized James Dean. He worshipped Natalie Wood.
He venerated Robert Wagner. He taught Natalie the facts of life, and
went along as a chaperone on her first honeymoon with Wagner.

He was Hollywood's quintessential outsider, a fighter both on and
off the screen. The cryptic police report on his death shocked and
astonished all of Hollywood:

> "Motion picture and television actor
> Nick Adams was found dead in the upstairs
> bedroom of his Beverly Hills home. The
> cause of death was not immediately deter-
> mined.
>
> "The body was discovered by Ervin
> Roeder, attorney and personal friend of the
> actor, who told police he went to Adams'

home when Adams failed to meet him for
a dinner date.''

It was late on Wednesday night, February 7, 1968, when Roeder decided to find out why Nick had failed to keep a dinner date with him the night before. ''Tip'' Roeder had been Nick Adams' attorney and close friend for several years. He said it was very unlike Nick not to show up for a scheduled appointment.

Roeder said Adams' phone had remained unanswered despite his persistent calling. This was in the days before electronic wizardry had fully developed the telephone answering machine to confirm or refute such claims. Adams did not have one.

Roeder arrived at Nick's home on 2126 El Roble Lane in the exclusive Trousdale Estates section of Beverly Hills. Nick had leased the home for several months. Roeder tried to enter Nick's home, but the front and back doors were secure – according to Roeder's account to the police. There were no witnesses to bear out his statements. *

Police reports make no mention as to why there was no car in the garage, except the car driven by Roeder. It was muddy from fresh rains. The registration was never checked. If it had been, it would have shown to be in the name of a car rental company, which rented the car to Nick's production company a few days before.

Roeder told the police he could not see or hear any signs of life, not even a light in the house. As an attorney, Roeder knew something was wrong. He forced open a rear window to gain access to the two-story house on the side of a hill.

After finding nothing remiss on the first floor, the attorney of dubious reputation walked up the stairs, cautiously, and pushed open the door to Nick's bedroom. He found what he was looking for as soon as he switched on the light.

''The Rebel,'' fully clothed in denims and shirt and with a blank stare, was propped against the wall in a sitting position. A telephone was within several inches of his left hand, next to the bed. The room was in order. But one look told Roeder his troubled friend would be troubled never more.

---

* Following his death, it was discovered that most of Adams' memorabilia was missing from the house. These items included his Johnny Yuma hat, an old coal miner's cap of his father's, and several other items his family has not been able to locate since his death. These items all disappeared during the first hour or two of Roeder discovering Adams's body.

★ ★ ★

According to Roeder's "story" of Nick's death, he told the detectives that he "immediately" placed a call to the West Los Angeles Police Station from the bedside telephone less than two feet away from Nick's body. The potentially lifesaving instrument was in its cradle, untouched by Nick.

When the police arrived, to their puzzlement they found no syringes, pill bottles or medicine glasses; nothing to indicate that Nick's death was anything but "natural causes." If it was foul play, his death was "arranged" very carefully.

The coroner was called and Nick's body, his dream ended, was removed to a cold marble slab in the Los Angeles County Morgue. This was a far cry from the limelight Nick Adams had been used to, and only two blocks away from the Los Angeles Superior Court building where Nick had waged a long and bitter divorce and custody battle with his ex-wife, Carol Nugent.

★ ★ ★

If they had handed out an Emmy each year for grit, resourcefulness and unflagging good spirits in the face of impossible odds, the winner hands down would have to have gone to an extraordinary young man christened Nicholas Adamshock in the coal mining town of Nanticoke, Pennsylvania. Aka Nick Adams, he starred for two years as ABC-TV's Johnny Yuma, aka *The Rebel*.

He also received an Oscar nomination for his role of an accused murderer in *Twilight of Honor*, and costarred with Andy Griffith in *No Time For Sergeants*.

Nick Adams came into show business from the pool halls of Jersey City. The very fact that he, a coal miner's son, imagined he could "act" seemed rather presumptuous. This becomes increasingly clear when you consider the many years of study put in by most established actors and actresses. Very few have had their own television series within a few years of arriving in Hollywood, without paying their dues.

Adams was totally ignorant of even the most rudimentary aspects of show business. He had even been tossed out of a high school play for ineptitude. Moreover, he was slight of build (just 5'8"), not handsome enough to be a leading man – a "nobody."

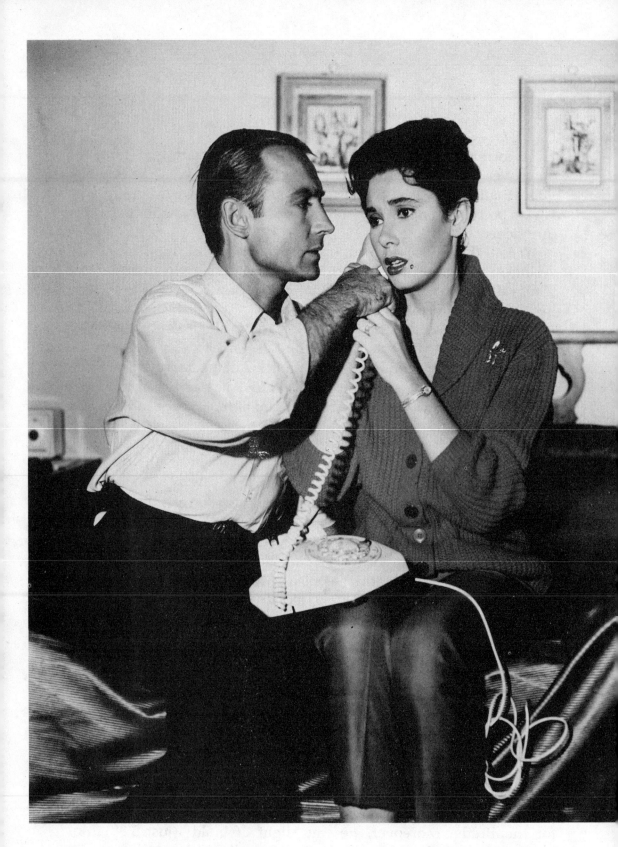

Nick Adams and Elinor Donohue in a scene from General Electric Theater's "A Voice on the Phone." *(John Austin Collection)*

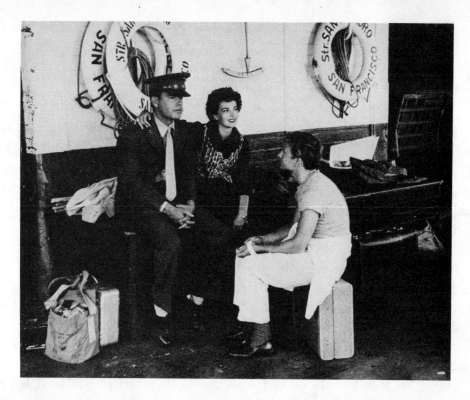

Nick Adams talking to his closest friends, Robert Wagner and Natalie Wood, on the set of "In Love and War." Adams was not in the film, but he was so close to Wagner and Wood that he accompanied them on their honeymoon, and was Natalie's first lover when she was 14 – at the request of Natalie's mother. *(John Austin Collection)*

Nick Adams and Andy Griffith in "No Time for Sergeants," 1958. *(John Austin Collection)*

☆ ☆ ☆

Were it not for his stubborn refusal to recognize anything as impossible, he probably would have remained a "nobody." His presumption paid off very nicely for the then 29-year-old Nick Adams: he was cast for *The Rebel* and was paid $5,000 every three shooting days. A tidy sum in the late 1950s and early 1960s. *

This is Adams' tale of how it all happened for him:

One day between trips to the pool hall in Jersey City, where his family had moved to get away from "the mines," he read a story in *The New York Daily News* about how Guy Madison had hitchhiked to Hollywood, was "discovered" and became a star.

Adams admitted, "I was nothin'. I wanted to be somethin'. But I didn't know how."

What Nick Adamshock did was take a bus across the East River to Manhattan, found the theatrical district and a marquee which read *"HENRY FONDA in 'MR. ROBERTS'."* He told the stage doorman, who did his best to conceal his mirth, that he wanted to be in the play.

He was told that the play was already cast and that it took a great deal of training to become an actor; Nick admitted he was downcast, but not beaten. After all, he was raised in Appalachia, one of the toughest areas in the country; hardship was nothing new to Nick.

He went around the corner from the theatre to a bookstore in pursuit of a book which would tell him how to act. Believe it! As it turned out, the store had a salesman who happened to know about some auditions being held that day at Carnegie Hall for Sean O'Casey's *The Silver Tassle*.

"What he was really doing was trying to sell me a book of O'Casey's plays," noted Nick.

He hurried over to Carnegie Hall, where he ran into an actor named Jack Palance. By mere chance, the two discovered that Palance hailed from the same coal-mining area around Nanticoke where Nick was born. Palance liked him and fixed it so he could indeed have an audition.

It was typical of Nick Adams to blithely tell everyone, including his studio biographers, that he played with Palance in *The Silver Tassle*.

---

*By comparison, a 30-minute series star in the 1930s could "earn" $40,000 every five days, and as much as $150,000 per five days for a 60-minute series.

The fact is he never got a part in the play at all. What really happened was that Palance, realizing his inexperience, sent him upstairs to the recital hall where the junior theatre was holding tryouts for *Tom Sawyer*.

Here he got a part – as Muff Potter! Subsequently he got others, gaining more and more confidence in himself, as the parts grew in size. Still, Nick Adams was nowhere. He had yet to be paid for appearing in a show. He had never played a major part, and made his meager living as a pool hustler in Jersey City.

Undaunted, 10 months later he withdrew $300 from his savings account, all he had in the world. He scribbled "Hollywood Here I Come" across the passbook and – in the great tradition of unknown stars – hitchhiked across the country to Hollywood in 1950.

☆ ☆ ☆

Hollywood obviously was not ready for Nick Adams. The Beverly Hills police picked him up and gave him a free ride to the city limits with very emphatic instructions not to return. Unfazed, Nick returned, made the rounds of the casting offices, found a place to live in a boiler room (in exchange for mowing the lawn), and somehow got himself an agent – a major feat in itself.

"I gave him *'The Silver Tassle'* bit," said Adams, ". . . and how great I was with Palance. Then I'd go into my impersonations. Then I'd just talk, figuring somebody'd just have to discover me!"

It took a while, so Nick did what he could to get by. The only problem was, he kept losing regular jobs. When his employers discovered he was an actor, they'd fire him! He was a fry cook, a delivery-truck driver and gas station jockey. He lost his service station job across the street from NBC because he delivered his Cagney impersonations along with the gas.

Adams finally landed a cushy job as usher, relief doorman and general maintenance man at a theatre in Beverly Hills. But he managed to blow that one too, in typical Adams fashion. Part of his job was to change the marquee, and one night he couldn't resist the temptation to put his name up in lights. It looked fine to everyone but the manager.

☆ ☆ ☆

There was a great deal of irony in that caper. Some eight years later his name was on that same marquee – this time for real. Nick kept a large photograph in his home showing himself standing in front of the real thing. This time, however, the marquee read:

"Andy Griffith and Nick Adams in *"No Time For Sergeants"*.

☆ ☆ ☆

In 1952 the draft got him, and the Coast Guard decided to make Nick a featured player on a frigate on the California coast. One day in June 1954, shortly after his destroyer escort pulled into Long Beach harbor, Nick was sitting in the radio shack reading the newspapers. He read that director John Ford was casting, of all things, *Mr. Roberts* at Warner Brothers studio. Recalled Nick, ". . . I figured who could play a sailor better than a sailor? Besides, Cagney was in the picture. Boy, maybe I could even imitate him in it."

To Nick's mind the part was practically fait accompli. He put on his dress whites, boarded a bus, rode to Burbank, and boldly walked through the front gate. He managed to find the casting office. Everyone was out to lunch except one man sitting with his feet up on the desk fiddling with a fishing reel. "Know anything about fishing rods, kid?" the man asked. Naturally, being Nick Adams, he said "Yes!" Adams' luck was still holding. "The man" turned out to Warner Brothers' veteran casting director Solly Biano.

"He liked me, and first thing you know we were up in Ford's office," Adams related. "Well, I started to talk. I gave 'em the old 'Silver Tassle' bit. Then I did my impersonations – Grant, Brando, Cagney. I guess Ford was pretty taken aback. He looked at me and asked, 'Where did you come from?'

"I explained I was a Coast Guard radio man with enough leave coming to me to make a picture. He said, 'Do you imitate the radio, too?' Sure, and I did – Morse code.

" 'What does that spell?' Ford asked.

" 'Give the kid a break,' I answered." The next thing Adams knew, he was on a plane to Hawaii with Fonda, Cagney and the rest of the *Mr. Roberts* cast and crew. "It was the greatest thing that ever happened to me," Nick related. "I knew every line in the script, and I was riding so high, I thought if Jack Lemmon got sick I could even play Ensign Pulver."

Biano liked Nick as did Mervyn LeRoy, who took over *Mr. Roberts* when John Ford became ill. Thus Nick Adams went on to make half a dozen movies for Warner Brothers. These pictures included a small scene with his idol, James Dean, and another tragic actor and actress from the same film, Sal Mineo and Natalie Wood – this classic bit of cinema is, of course, *Rebel Without a Cause.* During filming, Nick became oh-so-friendly with Natalie and her family. It was Adams who eventually taught Natalie "the facts of life," at the request of her mother. He even accompanied R.J. Wagner and Natalie on their first honeymoon.

James Dean and Adams also became inseparable. When Dean was killed it was an enormous shock to Nick. He began to emulate Dean's wild ways, picking up nine tickets for speeding in the course of one year. *

"I became a highway delinquent myself," he declared. "I was placed on probation but I kept on racing – nowhere."

Then, suddenly, the trail to nowhere ended.

☆ ☆ ☆

The fast lane to no place found a temporary destination when Nick met actress Carol Nugent. That is when he came up with a screen character, Johnny Yuma, and told successful television producer Andrew Fenady about it at a Hollywood party. Now in continual re-runs around the world, the credits still read, *"Created by Andrew J. Fenady and Nick Adams."*

The series, *The Rebel,* was the saga of an erroneously cashiered Confederate cavalry commander. With fists, knives, six shooters, a sawed-off shotgun and compassion, he went around solving other people's problems in the wild, wild west of the 1890s.

For two years, Nick Adams of Nanticoke, Pennsylvania, and Jersey City, New Jersey was a very hot property, as the saying goes in Never Never Land. Considering her to be a good influence, Nick married Carol and they started a family: Allyson Lee Adams was born in 1960, and Jeb Stuart Adams – now an actor – two years later.

Then the series was abruptly cancelled. The weekly paychecks stopped and Adams struggled to find parts. He did bit rolls, and an occasional foreign feature film. He made one in England, and another

---

* Of seven members of the cast and crew of *Rebel Without A Cause*, six died at an early age of tragic, mostly unsolved mysteries: James Dean, Sal Mineo (solved), Natalie Wood and Nick Adams. Jim Backus died of Parkinson's Disease in 1988. Director Nicholas Ray died of lung cancer, and producer David Weisbart of an unannounced illness at the age of 46. These deaths are recounted in *Hollywood's Unsolved Mysteries*, Volume One.

in Rome. The marriage unraveled: first a separation, then a divorce. A bitter battle for custody of the children erupted.

Luckily, the case was heard by a judge recently appointed by then governor Ronald Reagan. The judge had toiled for Reagan during his California gubernatorial campaign and was appointed early in Reagan's first term. Nick Adams had friends close to Reagan, who "made the call" to procure the judge for the trial.

Nick won the custody battle, but all was not paradise. During Carol Nugent's visitation times, her new boyfriend, Paul Rapp, was practicing parental privilege by disciplining his children. Nick got another "friendly" court commissioner to issue an order: henceforth, Carol could visit with her children but "not in the presence of non-related male adults."

About this time, Nick Adams' career started to turn the corner and pick up. He found himself once more in demand. Producers began to realize that Nick Adams could play most any type of role: a deranged killer, the boy next door, a southern rake, a deputy sheriff of the old West, or a cop on the beat. He could do them all, and be believable.

Returning from a location in Mexico, Nick had a few days at home before leaving for Rome to start work on yet another film, which would pay him $50,000, plus first class travel and all his expenses. The Italian producers wanted a recognizable name in order to release the film in the United States.

Adams called Roeder on his return and they made a date to discuss the picture, investments for the future and some other deals for pictures which were pending.

"The Rebel" never made that dinner date.

★ ★ ★

Fred Warren, Nick's next door neighbor on El Roble Lane, said Nick had the children with him the weekend before his body was discovered. They were still in Nick's custody, but while he was out of the country, they had been living with their mother. Warren told police that Nick appeared in excellent spirits as he romped in the garden behind the house with his beloved children. They adored their father and they were aware of the fight – an expensive one – which Nick had waged over their custody. To win them, Nick alleged that Carol was an unfit mother because of an ongoing affair with Rapp while the children were in the house.

That happy weekend was the last time Nick was ever to see Allyson Lee, 8; and Jeb Stuart Adams, 6.

★ ★ ★

Following the discovery of Nick's body, a lot of strange things came to light from friends and relative. First of all, the day of Nick's death, February 5, obviously prior to the time of his dinner date with Roeder, Nick's family received a lot of "hang up" telephone calls. When the receiver was picked up, the caller hung up.

Nick Adams was a prolific diary keeper. When he was on location, he carried a portable tape recorder. On returning to his home, these entries which were made on on a portable reel to reel machine (no cassette machines were then available) were transcribed by a secretary in Roeder's office – if they weren't too personal. If they were, Nick typed them up himself on an old portable in his house.

After his death, no trace could be found of Nick's journals. All, including the battery-operated recorder, were missing from his effects. Further, Nick's brother, a doctor, said much of Nick's memorabilia was also missing. This included an old miner's hat which used to belong to their father. Nick always kept it as a reminder of those days in Appalachia. "They mean something to me," he declared when it was noticed hanging on a door of his dressing room while shooting *The Rebel*, ". . . so I don't get a big head!"

Someone who knew Roeder and Adams squealed that a lot of the memorabilia from Nick's house was seen in Roeder's home which he shared with his girlfriend. *

None of it was "willed" to Roeder.

Even though it is now believed that Roeder knew exactly what had happened to Nick Adams, the police immediately assumed that his sudden death was due to "natural causes." Roeder said Nick, skilled in karate and judo, had been in excellent health.

When Carol Nugent Adams was reached at her home by reporters, she broke down when told of the tragedy. "Oh, my God! It's terrible.

---

*Ten years following Nick Adams' death, Roeder was shot in the driveway of his home after returning from a business dinner. It was believed to be a contract killing. Two days later, Roeder's girlfriend, "Jenny," was also gunned down. This was one day after advising what must be a non-attributable source that she would call and tell "them" what really happened to Nick Adams!"

I can't talk now," she gasped.

☆ ☆ ☆

What puzzled the police during their investigation following the "discovery" of Nick Adams' body by Roeder, was that no means of ingestion – as in the Monroe case – were found near the body. Furthermore, no container holding the substance was found anywhere in the house, according to the police.

Coroner Noguchi said that the dose of paraldehyde found in Nick's body following an autopsy would cause almost instantaneous death.

♦ How, then, did Nick Adams ingest the deadly substance? When he was originally given a prescription for the drug because of hypertension due to his divorce, he was warned by his doctor that it was dangerous and to be careful of his dosage.

♦ Why did Ervin "Tip" Roeder not tell the police that he was driving the car in the garage, and that it was the car Nick had rented on his return from Mexico?

These questions were never answered by the police or the coroner and have puzzled people close to Nick since February 7th, 1968, the day his body was "discovered" by Roeder.

☆ ☆ ☆

Prior to the official autopsy hearing, the coroner shed some light on the case. Thomas Noguchi – who turns up in so many of *Hollywood's Unsolved Mysteries* – said he found .037% of paraldehyde in the blood which, in itself, would not be enough of the foul smelling liquid to cause death. *

It was equivalent to .30 ccs taken orally – a normal dose. But what did cause Nick's death, either accidentally or on purpose, was mixing the paraldehyde with "sedatives and other drugs, the remains of

---

* Paraldehyde is a colorless liquid produced by the polymerization of formaldehyde, having a strong, nauseating smell and used in medicine as a hypnotic and sedative. It is sometimes used to treat cases of deliriums tremens (the "DTs") brought on by severe alcohol use or, in Adams' case we were told, severe nervous disorders or problems.

which I found in the organs," said Noguchi's report.

A telling statement was made by an investigating officer of the police department homicide division, "We know Nick had been in the habit of taking paraldehyde for a severe nervous condition brought about, chiefly, by his divorce and domestic problems. But Nick knew how and when to take it. *I am sure he would not take an overdose, or mix it with anything else.*"

Nick Adams seldom drank. "In fact," said one of his close friends, "I'd been to many parties with Nick and he was less than a social drinker. And I'm sure he would not commit suicide. He was a Catholic, and a good one, in spite of his divorce from Carol.

"I would feel remiss as an old friend if I didn't say I'm sure Nick wasn't taking paraldehyde for any kind of alcoholism. In fact a group of us were saying just the other night we'd never seen Nick even slightly intoxicated. He just did not like it."

It was known that Adams was trying to curtail his usage of paraldehyde ever since he gained custody of the children, and his life was coming back together again with acting offers. In fact, when it was prescribed for him, it was in very small quantities, no more than one or two doses at a time. This could have been the reason that the police found none of the substance in the house following Adams' death, nor any empty container anywhere in the house or in the trash cans. It was known that Adams had not renewed his dosage prescription since before he left for Mexico.

◆ Could it be that Nick Adams was forced to drink paraldehyde laced with sedatives? Or that it was given to him in some other substance to disguise the odor?

◆ The police found no trace of the substance ANYWHERE in the house, yet it was in his body. There were no empty prescription bottles, no sedatives, nothing which might have once contained paraldehyde.

◆ Could this, or all other containers, have been removed from the house by Nick's murderer?

◆ If so, why? It should have been a dead giveaway that Adams was murdered. Could this have been done the night before Roeder "discovered" the body?

☆ ☆ ☆

It was a well known fact that Nick Adams had paid Roeder's law firm a great deal of money during his divorce and that Roeder had a lot of say in the handling of Nick's finances and fees for his acting assignments.

◆ Could Nick Adams have found some major discrepancies in his accounts on his return from Mexico?

◆ Did he advise Roeder and his partner that this was the case, and that he wanted a complete accounting of his funds?

◆ Could this possibly be the reason that Nick Adams never kept his dinner date with "Tip" Roeder of February 5, 1968, and that reference to these monies and their disposition were noted in Nick's journals, hence their disappearance?

Nick Adams put his brother through medical school and sent most of his Coast Guard paycheck home to his parents to help them out with their very limited income as "supers" of a Jersey City apartment house. Because of his background of near poverty while growing up, Nick usually knew where every cent he earned was going and to whom and how.

It is a fact that he discovered that more of his funds had been going somewhere other than where they should have been going. Hence, the reason for his murder.

When one considers murder and not suicide in the demise of Nick Adams, one has to consider a glaring fact:

> There were no syringes in or near the bedroom, none in either bathroom. None near the body of Nick Adams. Coroner Noguchi stated that the mixture found in Adams' body would have caused instantaneous death. There was no time for Adams to rid the scene of any paraphernalia such as syringes or containers.

Therefore, it had to be murder!

There are only two ways that Adams could have died: murder or suicide. We can rule out suicide because there were none of the tell-tale traces usually found at scenes of bizarre deaths, such as this one.

◆ Why was there no note to his beloved children?

◆ Why was there no trace whatsoever of the means by which drugs were introduced into his body?

◆ And having won custody of his children on his terms, having finally gotten a second chance at a film career, why would a devout Catholic take his own life under those upbeat circumstances?

Who killed Nick Adams?

Why did the Los Angeles Police Department not delve deeper into the death of Nick Adams? Could pressure have been brought to bear by one or more members of the oligarchy, possibly friends of his killer, to "keep it quiet and keep it tidy?"

Probably. Conceivably.

Because of this possible scenario, only the killer – who is now (probably) dead – and "The Rebel" – know for sure. The death of Johnny Yuma will always go down as another of *Hollywood's Unsolved Mysteries*.

Fade Out . . .

EPILOGUE

... And There Are Still More Unsolved Mysteries ... Coercion Is Also a Hollywood Way of Life ...

The list of *Hollywood's Unsolved Mysteries* goes on and on. It dates as far back as 1922, with the bizarre, still unsolved murder of famed British-born director William Desmond Taylor. There have been three books on the Taylor case, and we have yet another angle to the murder for volume three.

Then there is the mysterious, unsolved death of movie tough guy Steve Cochran, who was found dead in his yacht off the Guatemala coast; his all-girl crew of eight were attempting to bring the vessel into port on their own... And the unsolved murder of actress Karyn Kupcinet still baffles the Los Angeles County Sheriff's Department. Karyn, the daughter of "Mr. Chicago," columnist Irv Kupcinet, was found dead on Thanksgiving weekend in 1963. Actor Andrew Prine's promising career was ruined over her death, as he was questioned many times by the sheriff's department.

Elizabeth Short – "The Black Dahlia" – was mysteriously mutilated ... Marina Habe, the daughter of famed German writer Hans Habe, was murdered on her way home from a date ... Barbara (Mrs. Mickey) Rooney was slain by her Yugoslav lover for reasons no one has yet to fathom. Her killer had strange connections to French star Alain Delon's bodyguard and the French underworld.

Albert Dekker ... John Belushi ... The mentally unbalanced Robert Bardo, besotted with a virginal image of *My Sister Sam* actress Rebecca Schaeffer ... and the lesbian love of a misguided woman for Sharon

Gless. The woman was intent on killing the *Cagney and Lacy* star, then killing herself.

Why? What is the fascination with Hollywood stars by the sick minds that conceive plans to kill them? Jean Spangler was a well-known extra and party girl in many films who vanished one night without a trace after leaving for a date. Was it mobster Frankie Ogul who killed her and dispersed her body in the Southern California desert, where it would never be found?

Hollywood's Unsolved Mysteries volume three will also explore the killing of Dag Drollet by Marlon Brando's son, Christian. Tahitian-born Drollet was the lover of Marlon Brando's daughter, Cheyenne. She was eight months pregnant with Drollet's baby when he was killed.

Perhaps by then there will also be a solution to yet another unsolved mystery: the double slaying of the high-powered Cuban film and video executive, Jose Menendez and his wife Kitty in the den of their luxurious Beverly Hills home. Was it because Jose Menendez, with all the outward appearances of a happily married man, had been keeping a mistress in New Jersey for years? Did their two grown sons really kill their parents as charged?

And there is still more to get into, including further updates on Marilyn Monroe and Elvis Presley.

Before ending this volume, the reader should be made aware of what has been going on and continues to thrive in Hollywood: *Coercion against the press.*

★ ★ ★

Coercion against the Hollywood press corps of the 1930s, which we went into at length in chapter 1, again came into focus in 1990 with Disney and its Touchstone Films division. In June of 1990, Disney/Touchstone pressured two magazines, *Los Angeles* in California and the *London Sunday Express*, to soften or drop articles that Disney/Touchstone believed – *without reading them* – might be unfavorable to its film *Dick Tracy*, and the film's star, Warren Beatty.

An editor of the *Sunday Express* said she was told by an official in the London office of Warner Bros. (Disney's European distributor) that two respected journalists based in Hollywood were blacklisted by Disney/Touchstone, and that no color photographs would be supplied from the production to illustrate the story if the magazine published it *"without approval and modification by Disney."* *

Hilary Clark, the officious vice president for Disney's international publicity, said, in rebuttal to the charges:

> "We would never use the term 'black-listing.' A 'representative' thousands of miles away might have said it inadvertently. It was, perhaps, an unfortunate use of words. It is by no means a mandate from the studio!"

That is not exactly the truth. A Warner Bros./Disney spokesperson in London *had* used the term "blacklisting" in this situation, and in another case previously.

Disney, and Warren Beatty, an actor known for his efforts to CONTROL JOURNALISTS, were displeased by the same *London Sunday Express* journalist's article reporting on the making of *Dick Tracy*.

In the United States, the story appeared in the June 1990 edition of *Movieline* magazine, a slick, informative journal that is definitely NOT a "fan" magazine.

A revised version – as demanded by Disney/Touchstone – was to have appeared in the London newspaper's magazine section. Disney/Touchstone/Warner Bros. got their way once again, muzzling the freedom of the Press by pressure and threats. An article by a features editor of the newspaper on another film was substituted.

As an example of how vicious the studios can be when they can't get their way, the editor said, *"The pictures were what we wanted."* She added that the newspaper AGREED IN WRITING not to use the piece in question.

> "Our lawyers were afraid that Disney/Touchstone/Warner Bros. might try to get an injunction to stop the publication of the newspaper if any of the story was used."

---

* In Hollywood language this means a piece written by a studio publicist and lauding the stars, the picture and everything about it. In other words, "boilerplate" material.

Is it any surprise, then, that so many of *Hollywood's Unsolved Mysteries* have been covered up when the studios use such raw power as a threat to stop publication of a London Sunday newspaper with circulation of 3 million issues weekly?

Dick Tracy did badly at the box office. Disney/Touchstone could have used the publicity.

At *Los Angeles* magazine, the same two journalists tried to obtain an interview with the reclusive Beatty * for a story in which his co-star, Madonna, would be featured on the cover. The editor of *Los Angeles* said that Disney publicist Frank Lomento promised, and even showed a color slide of Madonna to him. The editor agreed to the photo, but it was never delivered. Lomento called the editor after hearing about the content on the piece and insisted that:

> *pig* "... it be softened or no cover photo of (Madonna) would be supplied by Disney."
> *BAD Need's help*

The editor of *Los Angeles* said in an interview following the acrimonious dealings that Lomento added, ominously:

> "The future relationship between your
> magazine and Disney would be dependent
> on the extent of the softening."

"Freedom of the press? In Hollywood? No Way!

Hilary Clark said later, *"We don't need to cooperate with anyone we don't wish to. It's standard publicity business, no intrigue. Let's get on to other business..."*

★ ★ ★

Mickey Mouse was up to no good again following the *Los Angeles* and London newspaper contretemps, this time with the venerable Bob Thomas, the veteran Hollywood reporter for The Associated Press.

Disney refused to grant Thomas an interview with Warren Beatty

---

* It was only when Beatty, the aging, egotistical, leading man, realized his picture was not doing as well as expected, in spite of many millions of dollars spent on promotion, that he agreed to appear on television talk shows and do some selected interviews. One was with Barbara Walters on ABC-TV which, admittedly, was the worst interview ever seen on television. It was not Walters's fault, but the very dull, unimaginative, uncooperative Beatty himself who was guilty.

because Thomas wrote a review of the film for publication, before its official June 15th opening. "Warren doesn't want to talk to Thomas," a source familiar with the matter, quoted a Disney official as saying. "I will confirm that the interview was pulled from Bob Thomas because of the review."

Disney told the Associated Press they would give an interview to John Horn, also of the AP, but the wire service stood by Thomas. Ironically, Thomas wrote a positive review of the film.

Steve Loeper, a Los Angeles executive with AP, told Frank Swertlow, a *Los Angeles Daily News* columnist, "This is the first time in seventeen years working in Los Angeles that a studio has gone to such lengths to control what will be written about a film and when. I can't think of another time."

A spokeswoman for Disney also told Swertlow, "We have no comment on the matter. This is private between us and the AP."

☆ ☆ ☆

But the press control over *Dick Tracy* wasn't the only form of censorship to take place in 1990. Another blacklisting, this time by 20th Century Fox, was yet to come.

☆ ☆ ☆

In March 1990, 20th Century Fox banned famed TV critics Gene Siskel and Roger Ebert from all advance screenings of its movies over remarks they made during a TV interview about the company's film, *Nuns on the Run.*

"From now on they can catch up with our films in a theatre," said Bob Harper, the studio's director of marketing, in an interview in the toadying *Hollywood Reporter.*

Ebert (and Siskel), who use a "thumbs up" or "thumbs down" rating for reviewed films, remarked upon hearing the news, "I guess you could call it thumbs on the run!"

The producers of the *Siskel & Ebert* show declared, ". . . things got blown out of proportion" after the duo said they didn't like the film, during an appearance on a New York television show to tout their upcoming Oscar picks. Both had given the film a "thumbs down" rating and had panned it in their respective columns.

Fox contended that the pair overstepped their bounds because they attacked not only the film but also the marketing campaign and reviewers who liked it. In other words, they made a direct slap at Harper and his ego. During the television show, and to illustrate how Hollywood hypes itself and its films, Ebert held up a newspaper ad for *Nuns on the Run* with a prominent quote from New York's *Village Voice* newspaper calling it ". . . the funniest anticlerical, transvestite movie of the decade."

He then exchanged quips with Siskel about the typical Hollywood fallacy of the ad. "Yeah, this is 1990," said Ebert. "How many other transvestite, anticlerical comedies have there been so far in this decade?"

But Fox officials were not amused.

"We have no problem with them not liking the film," said Harper. "But they were on a show promoting their pre-Academy Awards show and, to our thinking, were acting in the capacity of entertainers – not critics."

When 20th Century Fox realized the ban would not hurt them, Fox, because of Siskel and Ebert's 8 million weekly viewers, rescinded the mandate several days later. But it does serve to illustrate how far the oligarchy will go to muzzle its critics.

These are just three well publicized examples of how the oligarchy still manages to manipulate the press, hard-working journalists trying to make a living. It illustrates just how the press has been exploited in many of the unsolved mysteries in this, and our previous, volume on the subject.

It has been doing this for more than sixty years, and unless someone finally blows the whistle on the Left Leaning Liberal Establishment * of the oligarchy, who dictate who works when and where and for whom, it will continue to suppress facts, and there will be many more *Hollywood's Unsolved Mysteries* in the future. This is the control the LLLE has over Hollywood and its denizens who work in, and for, the oligarchy. We sympathize with those HONEST journalists who still have to put up with subjective reporting, rather than objective writing, for fear of losing their jobs and/or careers to the egos of Hollywood.

---

* In its September 1990 issue, *New Dimensions* magazine, which supports conservative causes, did expose the Left Wing Liberals in Hollywood. Among other accusations, the series of articles stated that unless actors, producers, writers and directors support all Left Wing Liberal Causes openly and financially, they will find work offers few and far between, if any.

End Notes . . .

John Roselli. His "career" involved him with some of the nation's best-known figures. Roselli was known as "Don Giovanni" to his Mafia buddies and ran numbers and broke legs for the mob in Chicago and Los Angeles. He was the "muscleman" in the extortion schemes against Hollywood in the 1940s and is believed to have been responsible for at least two of Hollywood's unsolved mysteries.

JOHN ("DON GIOVANNI")
ROSELLI

A little background of Johnny Roselli should help readers understand some of the machinations of Hollywood and those who attach themselves to it like leeches. Roselli fell into this category. Prior to his death, Roselli figured prominently in Hollywood history from the 1930s, and in several of Hollywood's Unsolved Mysteries. These include those of Thelma Todd, Jean Harlow and Paul Bern in this edition; Vicki Morgan & Alfred Bloomingdale in the first and Marilyn Monroe in both.

★ ★ ★

Roselli, whose real name was Filipo Sacco, was known as Don Giovanni to his mobster cohorts and friends. He was born in Esteria, Italy, on June 4, 1905, and came to the Boston area at the age of six. Moving west as a teenager, Roselli settled in Chicago and became a bootlegger and gambler, working for the Capone gang in various capacities. There he was known as a muscleman who would break a few legs for anyone who paid the price.

Roselli was sent to Los Angeles about 1930 and worked in the illegal gambling wire service operated by Moses Annenberg, a former circulation manager for Hearst newspapers who had also supplied information to bookmakers across the country. Annenberg owned several publications such as *The Philadelphia Inquirer*, *The Daily Racing Form*, and two raunchy publications, *Baltimore Brevities* and *Click*. Annenberg's son is Walter Annenberg, host to presidents in Palm Springs, a close friend of Ronald and Nancy Reagan, and founder and former publisher of *TV Guide*.

Roselli, graduated into a muscleman in the Hollywood extortion schemes of the 1940s, had a stormy marriage with actress June Lang. He was eventually proposed for membership in the elite Friar's Club of Beverly Hills by his countrymen, Dean Martin and Frank Sinatra.

Roselli was later caught and convicted of drilling holes in the ceiling of The Friars in Beverly Hills which permitted excellent views of cards held by gin rummy enthusiasts such as Phil Silvers and Debbie Reynolds's husband, Harry Karl. The caper bankrupt Karl, heir to the Karls shoe fortune. Roselli spent five years of a six-year sentence in McNeil Island penitentiary.

★ ★ ★

On an even shadier side, Roselli's "business" cohorts included over the decades such mobsters as Benjamin "Bugsy" Siegel, Frank Costello – Joseph P. Kennedy's bootlegging partner – Al Capone, Meyer Lansky, Charles "Lucky" Luciano, Santos Trafficante, and Chicago crime boss, the late Sam Giancana. It was with Giancana and Roselli that John F. Kennedy shared a mistress, Judith Campbell Exner, who later stated in interviews that she often carried "little brown envelopes" between Chicago and the White House during "The Camelot Years."

★ ★ ★

Following his earlier release from yet another penitentiary, Roselli was appointed a "producer" by Bryan Foy, executive producer at the old Eagle-Lion Studios, then run by Arthur Krim, who later bought out United Artists!

Roselli had been released from the Atlanta Penitentiary after serving less than three years of a six-year sentence for his conviction in the Willie Bioff-George Brown-Joe Schenck scandal of "shaking down" the studios for labor peace, aided and abetted by Joe Schenck.

★ ★ ★

In 1975 Roselli testified before the Senate Select Committee on Intelligence Activities that he and Giancana had been recruited by Robert A. Maheu – the right-hand man of Howard Hughes and a former FBI Agent – on behalf of the CIA and others to come up with a plan to assassinate Fidel Castro. Richard Helms, the former CIA director, is quoted as saying of Roselli: "If you needed somebody to carry out a murder, I guess you had a man there who would be well prepared to carry it out." The contract price was $150,000 plus expenses. Roselli and Giancana refused the "fee" but accepted an unlimited expense account. He, Giancana, and Sam Trafficante came up with several exotic plans to put out the lights of Castro, including poisoned cigars and pills laced with botulism, but to no avail. Nevertheless, the expense account was put to good use with villas abroad, high powered boats and luxurious hotel suites.

Giancana, subpoenaed to testify before the Senate Committee with Roselli about the "contract," was shot point blank in the head by an "unknown assailant" with a .22 Duramatic automatic pistol with a silencer in his Chicago home a few days before he could comply. Whoever got that close to Giancana – the kitchen of his home – to shoot him had to have been very close to The Godfather.

Roselli was believed to have been in or near Chicago at the time of Giancana's "demise!"

According to former Senator Frank Church, Chairman of the Senate Committee, before whom he testified: "Roselli gave us a good deal of detail!"

☆ ☆ ☆

When Howard Hughes started to move in on Las Vegas and in spite of his "Mr. Clean" image before the Gaming Commission, Hughes was encouraged and helped by members of organized crime, particularly Johnny Roselli. Hughes's right-hand man who recommended "the marriage" of Roselli and organized crime to his boss was Robert Maheu. Roselli was sure that Hughes's presence in owning two or three casinos would "take the heat off" those casinos still operating illegally. Hughes and Abner "Longie" Zwillman dealt with Hughes in the Jean Harlow-MGM-Joe Schenck contract caper. Though it was not common knowledge, Howard Hughes had been dealing with organized crime for years starting with Zwillman, and then Roselli.

So much for the "watchdog" Nevada Gaming Commission.

☆ ☆ ☆

August 8, 1976, fifteen months following his testimony before the Select Committee, Roselli's body was found stuffed into a fifty gallon, chain-weighted oil drum floating in Biscayne Bay in direct line of sight of Roselli's "retirement home" in Miami.

★ ★ ★

Many have ventured the opinion that Roselli was involved in more than one of Hollywood's Unsolved Mysteries.

We believe we know which ones.

But that is yet another book . . . !

End Papers . . .

BIBLIOGRAPHY

Daily News, Los Angeles

Goodman, Ezra, *The Fifty Year Decline & Fall of Hollywood* (Simon & Shuster, 1961)

Griffith, Dr. H.W., *Complete Guide to Prescription and Non-Prescription Drugs* (Body Press, 1988)

Los Angeles Times

Noguchi, Dr. Thomas, *Coroner at Large* (Pocket Books, 1985)

Speriglio, Milo, *The Marilyn Conspiracy* (Pocket Books, 1986)

*"Things are rarely what they seem and
even more rarely what they're said to be . . ."*
– Quincy Howe
U.S. journalist
(date unknown)

★ ★ ★

*"The danger to this country is the private
seizure of power by a west coast oligarchy. It is
subject to no checks and balances; it is subject to no
elections every four years; it is subject to no criticism
and no attacks because it muzzles the press and no
one even knows about it."*

– Thurman Arnold
U.S. Justice Department
Antitrust Specialist, 1941